Pelican Books

The Third World To...

Paul Harrison is a freelance writer and journalist based
in London. He has travelled widely in Asia, Africa and
Latin America, visiting twenty-eight developing
countries. He has contributed frequently to the
Guardian, *New Society* and *New Scientist*, and to
publications of major UN agencies such as the World
Health Organization, the Food and Agriculture
Organization, UNICEF and the International Labour
Office. He is a contributor to *Encyclopaedia Britannica*.
Harrison attended Manchester Grammar School and
took masters degrees at Cambridge and the London
School of Economics. His interest in the Third World
began in 1968 when he was lecturing in French at the
University of Ife, Nigeria. He is married with two
children.

Penguin also publish his books *Inside the Third World*
(1979, second edition 1981) and *Inside the Inner City*.

Paul Harrison

The Third World Tomorrow

A report from the battlefront
in the war against poverty

SECOND EDITION

Penguin Books
in association with Harvester Press

PENGUIN BOOKS

Published by the Penguin Group
27 Wrights Lane, London W8 5TZ, England
Viking Penguin Inc., 40 West 23rd Street, New York, New York 10010, USA
Penguin Books Australia Ltd, Ringwood, Victoria, Australia
Penguin Books Canada Ltd, 2801 John Street, Markham, Ontario, Canada L3R 1B4
Penguin Books (NZ) Ltd, 182–190 Wairau Road, Auckland 10, New Zealand

Penguin Books Ltd, Registered Offices: Harmondsworth, Middlesex, England

First published 1980
Second edition 1983
10 9 8 7 6 5 4 3

Set, printed and bound in Great Britain by
Cox & Wyman Ltd, Reading
Set in Intertype Plantin

Contents

Preface

In the first decade or two of independence, national governments and international agencies alike were learners. Most of them started off pursuing false leads and committed many blunders, some of which greatly aggravated the problems they were intended to solve. The United Nations' First Development Decade (1961–70) was not a success.

Fortunately, people learn from their mistakes. In the course of the 1970s, the Second Development Decade, a new strategy of development began to emerge, based not on Western models, but on egalitarian and participatory approaches which seemed to offer a quicker way of eradicating poverty. These approaches are being developed and applied in virtually every field, from agriculture to industry, from housing to health, and from family planning to education. They have much in common, and together they add up to a coherent strategy which has much to teach Western countries.

This book is intended as a survey of the new approaches in each major field, a field report on the war against poverty for the Third Development Decade. It is illustrated by those projects which I have visited in the course of six years' research and travel in thirteen countries between 1974 and 1980: India (three visits, July/August 1974, March 1976 and June 1978), Sri Lanka (April/May 1975), Upper Volta and Ivory Coast (February/March 1976), Colombia and Peru (November/December 1976), Brazil (May 1977), Indonesia and Singapore (September/October 1977), Bangladesh (September 1978), Costa Rica and Cuba (November/December 1979) and Kenya (May 1980). My aim has been to provide a wide-ranging survey for the general reader interested in current affairs, as well as for young and old students of development and specialists in particular fields who may be interested to find out a little about what is happening in other fields. The wide scope has forced me to be selective rather than exhaustive.

I have attempted to give, in each chapter, a very brief summary of the major problems which the programmes and projects described are intended to solve. The reader will find a more extended treatment of all these problems in my book *Inside the Third World* (Penguin, 1979).

Many individuals and institutions have helped to make this book possible. My wife Alvina has patiently tolerated prolonged absences.

The travel involved would not have been possible without financial assistance from the World Bank, Population Services International, the International Labour Office, the International Planned Parenthood Federation and UNICEF. I am grateful, too, for personal encouragement and liberal provision of documents to Alun Morris and Mark Cherniavsky of the World Bank, Jan Vitek of the International Labour Office, Tim Black of Population Services International, Donald Allan of UNICEF, and the information offices of the World Health Organization, the Food and Agriculture Organization and the Organization for Economic Cooperation and Development. I should point out that the views expressed are my own and not necessarily shared by these organizations.

I should like to thank Professor Hans Singer, Dr David Morley, Professor Mark Blaug, Janice Jiggins, John Rowley, Penny Kane and Vince Cable for comments on the draft which helped to improve the final version of this book.

I am indebted, too, to the editors of *Human Behaviour, New Scientist, New Society, People* and *World Health* for permission to incorporate material from articles of mine which they published. Finally, I should like to thank all the many people, too numerous to mention, from agencies, government departments and project staffs who transported, guided and translated for me; as well as the ordinary people I met, who were kind enough to answer my questions, and some of whom figure in the following pages.

A note on quantities

Currencies quoted here in the context of first-hand reports are generally translated into pounds sterling and US dollars at rates prevailing at the time of my visit. In other cases, where dollar and sterling amounts are given, I have ignored the daily fluctuations of the currency market and converted at the rate of £1 to $2.

Areas are given in the unit used in my sources. For guidance, one hectare equals 2·47 acres.

All statements in the dramatic present relate to the time of my visits (see page 7) or the time of writing.

NOTE TO THE SECOND EDITION

The major change is the addition of two new chapters to fill important gaps in the first edition: Chapter 16 describes efforts to improve women's lot, Chapter 17 examines seminal aspects of the Cuban experience and considers whether socialism is essential to the meeting of basic needs. There is also a postscript in which I have covered some of the more promising new approaches to conservation and development. These are located at the end of the book to avoid resetting.

For Sam and Lou
in a better tomorrow

1 Back to the roots: traditional values

The village of Tampaksiring lies on the green middle slopes of Bali's mountainous spine. The large compounds hide behind long walls of ochre mud, above which peer the multiple, pinnacled shrines of family temples to gods and ancestors. A man in sarong and headband strolls down the well-kept high street, clambers up the tall stone plinth by the village entrance gate, takes up a stick and rhythmically beats the village warning bell, the *kulkul*, made of an ancient hollowed log. The Balinese month of thirty-five days has come round again and it is time for the meeting of the *banjar* or community association.

Most of the members are down at Terta Empul temple. It is said that its hallowed spring was created by the god Indra, who pierced the earth to tap a source of the elixir of immortality to help him defeat the demon king Maya Denawa. Men and women come from all over Bali to take a purifying bath in the crystal-clear waters. An important ceremony is to be held in two days' time. Four *banjars* are sharing the work of preparing for it. The men are practising the celestial tones of the *gamelan* orchestra on bells, gongs and xylophones, while the women are weaving little trays of palm leaves and moulding cakes and sweetmeats out of rice and coconut. As the *kulkul* echoes round the valley the men collect their instruments and set off up the road, playing them as they go. At the open porch of the *banjar* hall they shuffle off their sandals and spit out their plugs of betel leaves, making purple stains on the concrete floor.

Bali's *banjars* have for centuries zealously managed village affairs and administered traditional law. As the Dutch finally conquered Bali only in the first decade of this century, the island's grassroots institutions have remained surprisingly intact, a prime example of the kind of participatory, democratic and relatively egalitarian community which used to flourish in the Third World before the era of empires. The *banjar*, focus of a complex web of mutual aid and community self-help, can symbolize the authentic, indigenous roots to which development strategies are now returning after the trauma of colonialism and the mistakes of mimicking Western models.

The *banjar* owns and allocates all residential land, and organizes people into rotas to do unpaid labour on community tasks like preparing ceremonies, cleaning streets or repairing the village's three main temples. When families have to cremate dead relatives, and face bankruptcy with the cost of mountainous offerings of rice, coconut and meats and elaborate, decorated cremation towers, the *banjar* helps to meet the expenses. It acts as a court of law, witnessing marriages and divorces and deciding in disputes over land or inheritance. It is a remarkably democratic organization. Every family head is automatically a member, and can elect the *kelian* (headman) and other officials.

The *kelian* of Manukaya Anyar *banjar* in Tampaksiring is Putu Pulih Ngakan, a thirty-six-year-old farmer who also owns a souvenir shop selling batik clothes and ivory carvings outside the temple. Ngakan squats lotus-style on the central mat, calls the meeting to order and starts on the long agenda. A new market hall is being built by communal labour, but has overrun its cost estimates. Ngakan proposes that each of them should pay an extra 150 rupiahs, and they nod the motion through without dissent. Putu Pulih's brother, Madé, a resourceful, boisterous fifty-year-old who is the *kelian adat* or keeper of customs, raises the matter of inflation in the cost of funerals. He suggests that the *banjar*'s assistance to bereaved families should be raised from twenty-five rupiahs and a glass of rice per member to fifty rupiahs and two glasses of rice. There are protests from the more ragged participants at the back of the hall: 'Don't include the alcoholic drinks in the cost. No one is obliged to provide them. Just count the offerings that people have to make.' They agree to contribute twenty-five rupiahs and two glasses of rice in future. The main item on the agenda is to finalize the new *banjar* constitution, which includes a codification of the *awig-awig* or traditional laws and the punishments for their infringement. These will later be written out in Balinese script by a scribe, on a book made of thin strips of palm leaves. What should be the punishment for coconut thieves? What fine should a man have to pay if he cuts grass from the roadside to feed his cow? (The grass is divided up with scrupulous fairness.) What should be the fine for divorce? They decide that they would like to discourage people from divorcing their wives too lightheartedly, and fix a fine of 5,000 rupiahs (about £6 or $11). Yet, contrarily, they decide that if the man changes his mind and takes her back, he must pay a fine of 25,000 rupiahs for wasting the *banjar*'s time and making a mockery of *awig-awig*.

The meeting continues through dusk and evening, occasionally growing heated, but never ceasing to be amicable. An elderly member nods off, arms folded, while his neighbour absent-mindedly strokes the breast of a white fighting cock, and children play quietly in the street, and in the village temple a mother gives thanks for the safe delivery of a baby.

The *banjar* deals only with the social and residential aspects of life. Each family also has its fields, scattered in parcels among the verdant terraces that climb Bali's steep valley sides, where water trickles down through a thousand channels and rivulets, feeding the rice paddies as it goes. All the men whose land is watered from the same primary canal belong to a single *subak* – the agricultural parallel to the *banjar*. The *subak* too has its democratic council which allocates communal work such as repairing the canals and cutting the grass of the dividing paths. Although there are almost no large landowners and very few landless on Bali, land is not divided equally. But every *subak* has elaborate regulations to ensure that everything else is unimpeachably fair. Men who own more land have to contribute more communal labour – or pay someone else to do it for them. Water – as precious as land in irrigated areas – is rationed meticulously. For every measure of land he owns, a man has the right to one *tektek* of water, that is, the amount that will pass through a slot four fingers wide carved in a coconut trunk, no more and no less. Anyone who tries to divert more than this on to his land is guilty of stealing water and can be heavily fined. In the complex terrace systems, what one farmer does intimately affects his neighbour's crop. The *subak* regulates individual behaviour according to community needs. When water is short, the *subak* even plans who shall plant what and when.

Beyond the formal associations of *banjar* and *subak*, individual families are involved in a network of informal mutual help. Any man will help his neighbour build a house, repair a wall, plant paddy seedlings or plough land, in exchange for nothing more than a snack and the implicit assurance of equal help in return whenever it is needed. I met one group of twenty men, stripped to the waist, digging out and flattening land for one of them to build a house. They were working far more vigorously, cheerfully and purposefully than any paid construction workers I have ever seen.

Thus everyone in the village and the valley, in their family, social and economic life, is enveloped in and supported by a community of a richness and strength beyond all Western experience. This community extends, through religion, to the order of nature, from the sky and the fiery volcanic peak of Gunung Agung to the sea to which the ashes of the dead are committed in tiny boats of woven palm. And it reaches along the generations, linking the living with the venerated dead, who will be reincarnated in the not yet born.

On Bali the caring, egalitarian community of self-help and mutual help is found in what may be its most perfect expression. But it lies, sometimes buried or fragmented, at the roots of village life in all three developing continents. The African village was – and still is, in many parts – fundamentally communistic, with no private ownership in land. Each family was given land to cultivate according to its needs. Certainly, a man who worked hard or had more than his share of strong sons could command more land and accumulate greater wealth: but he could not pass the land on, and the wealth would be broken up among a larger number of heirs.

In India each caste has its democratic *panchayat* or council, to which every family head belongs. It deliberates on matters such as the caste trade or caste rules and customs. The caste system divided the population into groups largely based on economic specialization – priests, cobblers, sweepers, barbers, washers, landowners, labourers. They were, of course, far from equal, but each group would receive a customary share of the produce of the land in return for its services. Everyone had his niche. Everyone was guaranteed a livelihood.

Latin America had its own communalistic villages such as the Andean *ayllu*, a pre-Inca institution on which the Incas built their socialistic empire. Within the *ayllu* land was owned collectively. When a man married he was given a standard plot of land for himself and his wife, with extra measures for each son and half-measures for each daughter. Every year the land was divided up again. Woods and pastures were worked communally. Land surplus to the needs of survival belonged to the ruling Incas and to the priests and temples of the sun. This land was worked by collective labour – on a given day the men would line up with their *tacllas* or foot ploughs and dig their way across the field to the rhythm of chants, the women following behind to break up the clods. Andean peasants in remote villages work in exactly the same way to this day. Men would also contribute free labour to communal tasks such as construction of roads, canals or terraces.

The tradition of self-help and mutual support in the Third

World reaches into the household. In the extended family of three or four generations, grandparents babysit or educate children, adults look after the old, everyone supports the widowed and the sick, usually as of right and without question.

In productive life, in agriculture or industry, self-help in the form of self-employment predominates in traditional societies. Ownership of the means of production is widely spread and enterprises are overwhelmingly small-scale. And so in work, as in family life, the alienation and isolation of Western society is unknown until the process of Westernization itself spreads over all.

One should not, of course, over-idealize traditional village life. A communal lifestyle has its costs, in the limitation of individuality and privacy. Most village societies have within them, like all human institutions, elements of conflict, competition and inequality. India's caste system has its evil side, the arrogant superiority of the higher castes; even the Balinese have a mild form of this. Africa's polygamous chiefs command higher status than the ordinary monogamous man. These elements of inequality were first reinforced, long before the Europeans came, by indigenous empires which set up parasitic bureaucracies overlying the egalitarian institutions of the village. European conquest, followed by the rule of Westernized élites and the insidious spread of commercialization and urbanization, has done its bit. Almost everywhere Western values of individual self-advancement regardless of collective welfare have spread. Development has meant massive increases in inequality, the replacement of cooperation by competition, of mutual help by exploitation. The worm is in the bud, and has almost eaten right through it.

But those earlier ideals, which represent the rural roots and distinctive character of Third World societies, are not completely dead. In some places they are still a living reality. In others they are in the minds and memories of most adults.

Third World thinkers

These ideals have helped to inspire seminal models of development which have emerged from within the Third World and which, in their turn, have provided much of the inspiration and practical experience for the new approaches of the development agencies, outlined in the next chapter. They include African socialism as expounded and practised, for example, in Nyerere's Tanzania, or the distinctive cooperative model of socialism pursued by the Peruvian revolution of 1968. Of these indigenous Third World models, two stand out for their comprehensiveness and impact: those of Gandhi and of Mao.

Gandhi saw, as early as the 1920s, the pitfalls of Western-style development based on cities and large-scale industry. He hated modern machinery and mass production, not just because they were noisy, polluting and alienating, but because they generated massive unemployment among traditional sector workers: 'How can a country with *crores* [tens of millions] of living machines afford to have a machine which will displace the labour of *crores* of living machines?' Modern machinery, Gandhi realized, enriched the few at the expense of the many, and led to the concentration and centralization of wealth and power. Gandhi also saw the dangers, now apparent, of developing the cities and neglecting the villages where the mass of the population lived: 'We have to make a choice between India of the villages that are as ancient as herself, and India of the cities which are a creation of foreign domination. Today the cities dominate and drain the villages so that they are crumbling into ruin.'

At times Gandhi appeared to be waging what a friend called a 'quixotic war against modern civilization', and that made it easier for the Indian élite to dismiss his views as retrograde, romantic, nostalgic for a mythical past. But today his answer has a prophetic ring. It was to put the emphasis on development of the villages, where massive additional employment could be generated by reintroducing and improving the old traditional technologies. The symbolic focus of Gandhi's efforts was the *charkha* – the spinning wheel, which used to provide work and income to millions in the villages in the dead season when there was no work to be had in the fields. Gandhi also wanted to develop other village industries, and to return to the hand-husking of rice. The boom in rice mills had destroyed jobs, too, and by polishing the nutritious bran off the rice had led to serious nutritional deficiencies into the bargain.

But Gandhi was not simply in favour of resurrecting the old technology: he was well aware that this had failed because it could not compete with modern methods, and had to be improved. 'I would have all young men with a scientific training utilize their skills in making the spinning wheel, if it is possible, a more efficient instrument of production,' he wrote. He wanted to improve the workmanship of village craftsmen, to organize and supervise production to make it more competitive and improve quality. He suggested the use of locally available materials wherever possible.

Gandhi, all in all, was the true father of intermediate or appropriate technology. Every village was to become a self-governing, self-sustained unit, run on democratic, participatory lines by a village council or *panchayat*. Some might feel that Gandhi went too far with his concept of *swadeshi* or local self-sufficiency. He wanted each settlement to produce as much as it could for its own needs, exchanging with other villages only what it could not produce for itself. But the spirit behind the idea – that development should be as even as possible across the country and highly decentralized – is relevant today.

The villages would not fester in the old ways. Volunteers, such as students from neighbouring colleges, would come in as 'uplift workers'. They would teach a basic education focused around practical activity. They would act as health promoters, persuading villagers to improve their sanitation. Gandhi anticipated the idea of barefoot doctors: his village workers kept a small stock of basic medicines – castor oil, quinine and sulphur ointment. 'The prevailing ailments were few and amenable to simple treatment, by no means requiring expert help,' he wrote, anticipating by half a century the revolution in primary health care.

The Gandhian concept of development rejected the idea that it should aim primarily at the creation of material wealth or the satisfaction of insatiable, endlessly multiplied needs. 'In so far as we have made the modern materialistic craze our goal,' he wrote, 'so far are we going downhill in the path of progress.'

Gandhi's practice in the model communities he created and the volunteer work he and his followers did in villages was less successful than his theorizing. His 'uplift workers', often middle-class outsiders, lacked the influence over local people that one of their own number would have had. Moreover, he placed too much confidence in voluntary action. He did not want to use the apparatus of the state, which he considered a form of compulsion and institutionalized violence, to change people's way of life. He tried, for example, to persuade rich landlords to give up their excess land voluntarily in the *bhoodan* (land gift) movement. While a surprising number did comply, the vast majority did not and agrarian relations remained unchanged. Gandhi's practical failures demonstrate that government has to be committed to change, and people have to participate in it. But his influence on Indian development patterns – and through them, on efforts elsewhere – was powerful.

The model of Mao Tse-tung's China has had an even greater impact on development thinking. Pre-revolutionary China was a typical developing country, polarized into rich and poor, landed, landless and hyper-fragmented smallholders, with overblown cities, irrelevant, academic education, non-existent health services and a stagnant economy. Within a generation hunger had been abolished, and a process of widespread and balanced industrialization had got under way on a sound agricultural base. The Communist politics, fortunately, did not blind observers to the achievement. Here was a successful model for rapid development benefiting everyone, one of the most successful models for egalitarian, poverty-oriented development in the whole of the Third World.

The effort was based not on developing industry by force, on Soviet lines, but on raising agricultural production to provide a surplus that could sustain industrial development. The principal method was not miracle seeds, tractors or oil-based fertilizers, but the harnessing of the Third World's most plentiful resource: human energy. Mao's first step was a land reform that gave everyone enough land to feed themselves. But this created a mass of uneconomical smallholdings, too small for rational use of labour and better technology. So mutual aid teams were set up which would share draught animals, ploughs and manpower in the busiest seasons. In the mid-fifties cooperatives were introduced, in which all land and labour was pooled and everyone was paid according to the work they did. This created economically sized holdings without polarizing wealth or displacing large numbers of peasants. It also allowed the surplus of underemployed rural labour to be mobilized in improving the land, building small-scale irrigation works and new terraces. The next step was to fuse several cooperatives into larger communes able to tackle larger-scale improvements like dams, roads and schools. The communes became responsible for organizing and financing health and education, hence learning to develop their own potential instead of passively accepting what government provided. And as improved productivity in agriculture freed additional quantities of surplus labour, every commune could develop its own small-scale industries, repairing tools and bicycles, making building materials and agricultural tools and machinery, and processing food. This small-scale, commune-based industry was decentralized and evenly spread. It prevented surplus rural labour from flooding into the cities. From 1955 small- and medium-scale industry was encouraged in the policy of 'walking on two legs' – that is, using both modern methods and improved traditional techniques. The cutting off of Soviet aid in 1960 forced China into greater self-reliance: she had to invent much of her own technology and develop her own research and development capacities instead of depending on other people's.

In health care, Mao's reforms after the Cultural Revolution of 1965 provided the model for the primary health care systems that spread in the seventies (for details, see Chapter 10). Education, too, had been a central feature of Mao's approach from the very earliest days.

In the sixties Chinese education was thoroughly remodelled so as to eradicate the old academic and middle-class bias. Schooling was to be combined with productive labour. Schools stressed the values of cooperation instead of the Western idea of individual excellence aimed at self-advancement (see Chapter 11).

All these elements of the Chinese approach to development have been influential, although after Mao's death China herself began to move away from them. They all, in one way and another, derive much of their strength from the participatory idea of the 'mass line' – the idea that ordinary people have great wisdom and strength and can accomplish miracles when their initiative is given its head. But their energies require guidance and education, and there is no ignoring that one of the keystones of the Chinese success has been the role of the party. With its communication structure and its cadres in every block of houses or workshop, the party is a superb instrument for mobilizing the masses across a wide range of issues, and for transmitting education, information and motivation on any particular campaign.

Thus village roots, elaborated into modern theory and practice by the Third World's own leaders, can provide the foundations for a new style of development, capable of expanding material wealth without sacrificing social and spiritual welfare, a development that can be less centralized, less isolating and less aimless than that which the West has suffered and still suffers from. Such an alternative to Westernization has now been developed in its essentials and is being applied widely in the Third World, though still on far too modest a scale. This book is about that new model, and about the progress and problems in putting it into effect.

2 Basic concepts: the new development models

"The purpose of development should not be to develop things, but to develop Man." – Cocoyoc declaration

In the early years of independence in the Third World, right up to the end of the First Development Decade in 1970, a single model dominated the thinking and efforts of developing countries, development agencies and aid donors alike. Development, all but a few radical spirits agreed, involved following the yellow brick road painted by Western societies towards an Oz of industrialization and consumerism. All countries should be striving for a society of skyscrapers, with televisions in every home, cars in every garage and combine harvesters in the fields, with everyone working in humming factories and carpeted offices.

Civilization, in this ethnocentric model, meant Westernization. Received wisdom had it that all societies followed a fixed path of evolution, from hunting and gathering, through agriculture, to industry and finally to a high-technology, leisure-centred post-industrial society. Every economy had to pass through a fixed sequence of stages until it reached the point of 'take-off into sustained growth', to use US economist Walt Rostow's term. Naturally it was accepted that this evolution was a movement from primitive to advanced, that is, from worse to better, and that the changes involved were for the common good.

And so, on independence, practically every Third World country set about building a modern sector in its biggest cities, constructing Western-style factories and Western-style houses and developing Western-style medical and educational services. They were helped along in this by the major international development agencies and donor governments. Western 'experts' toured the world, advising developing countries on how things were supposed to be done. And there was, of course, only one way to be taken into consideration. External advice coincided with and reinforced internal inclination in fostering Westernization.

The new rulers did not have the funds to transform the whole country overnight, so they began on a small scale, hoping that the dynamism of this sector, and the income they hoped it would generate, would rapidly spread to cover their entire societies. It did not work. The modern sector did prosper, and produced high incomes for many of those lucky enough to be employed in it; but it remained isolated, and often flourished at the direct expense of the farmers and poor consumers, who directly or indirectly financed the investments and subsidies involved, and the traditional artisans, who were flung out of work by competition from mass-produced goods. As population grew, poverty, landlessness and unemployment spread. The neglected rural areas stagnated and the favoured cities grew bloated with refugees from the land who settled in slums and shanties. After one, two, three and even (in Latin America) fifteen decades of independence, the majority remained victims of hunger, disease and ignorance.

There were many, especially among Third World leaders, who were not deterred by this. Development, they would say, involved national sacrifices, patience, a necessary degree of temporary suffering. Industrialization had never been a Sunday school tea party – one only had to look at the miseries of the people in nineteenth-century England or Russia in the 1920s and 1930s. You had to pass through purgatory to reach paradise. The poor would have to wait, their turn would come to inherit the earth. Some might have to do without bread today so that everyone could have jam tomorrow. This way of thinking was not necessarily wrong: the benefits might well, eventually, have trickled down. It was only a question of how long this would take, and how tolerable it was, morally and politically, that the majority should pay the price while a minority cleaned up the benefits. The élite, after all, seemed to be having their jam today.

Meanwhile, the atmosphere had changed in the supposedly advanced countries. In the late sixties and early seventies, with rising unemployment, crime, drugs, terrorism and the youth revolt against materialism, the West was losing its arrogant self-confidence. The ecology movement gained ground. The impending oil shortage brought into question the philosophy of eternal growth. For all their increased wealth, people were plainly not getting any happier; indeed in many countries the point seemed to have been reached where further increases in material wealth brought an actual decline in human welfare. The Western model no longer seemed such a desirable goal to aim for. At the same time, as Western growth rates slowed, concern for social justice came to the fore, as the poorer groups aimed to get from redistribution the extra income they could no longer hope for from growth. Trade unions and neighbourhood groups increasingly sought improvements in the quality of life and work as well as purely material advances. Community activists rebelled against the entrenched authority of experts, bureaucrats and 'representatives'.

This groundswell of disenchantment with growth in the West came at precisely the same time as awareness was growing that, despite the massive national and international development effort, poverty and inequality were actually increasing in many if not most developing countries. It was this conjuncture that formed the background to the new approach to thinking about development, which began in the early seventies and became almost a new orthodoxy towards the end of that decade.

The approach to development of all the main agencies and aid donors underwent a sea change during the Second UN Development Decade. One after another the United Nations Conference on Trade and Development, the International Labour Office, The World Bank, UNICEF, the World Health Organization, the United Nations Environment Programme and UNESCO came out with their own brand new blueprints for the millennium. The multiplication of models, the plethora of new slogans, was bewildering: the New International Economic Order, growth with redistribution, basic needs, basic services, participation, eco-development, endogenous development. Each had a slightly different emphasis, but all had a common ground of values based on the idea that growth, pursued regardless of who benefited from it, was making little impact on the poverty of nations and of people.

All the new models were motivated by a desire to make sure that the poor benefited from development, not just in another century or two, but within their own lifetimes, through improved incomes, more jobs, better health, nutrition and education. They were all concerned with eradicating absolute poverty, and as redistribution seemed essential if this were to happen, they were also concerned with social justice and with increasing equality – or, what is the same thing, with reducing inequality, both within nations and between nations.

The protagonists of redistribution from the rich nations to the poor were the countries of the Third World, with the moral backing of the oil producers, UNCTAD and other major agencies. Boiled down to essentials, the New International Economic Order is a call for an end to the inequities of the prevailing system and for an increased transfer of real resources from the rich countries to the poor. A new and more equal international division of labour would replace the current division into industrial nations and producers of primary commodities. To speed this up, an increased transfer of real resources from the rich countries to the poor would be needed. This would involve greatly increased aid, perhaps in the form of a sort of international taxation system levying a tax on the rich and giving it to the poor. To improve the Third World's ability to earn its own keep, the price of commodities, subject to wild fluctuations and a gradual decline in value, would be stabilized and perhaps indexed to the price of manufactures. The West would help build up industry in the developing countries by opening its door to Third World manufactures. The Third World would produce goods needing more labour, such as textiles and clothing, while the West would specialize in high-technology products.

Soon after the developing countries began to clamour for international justice, a parallel cry for justice for the poor *inside* these countries was raised both by leading international agencies and by aid donors. The donors' motives were not entirely disinterested: aid was no vote-getter in most Western countries, and governments felt the need to prove to their publics that assistance was going to help the poor and not to make the Third World élites better off. Moreover, Western governments were calling for national reforms in developing countries while refusing to concede international reforms. But the development agencies had no ulterior motives in their call for a new model of development, other than the realization that the old model could not eradicate poverty in the foreseeable future.

Redistribution with growth: the World Bank

The idea that growth could be combined with increased social justice, and had to be so combined if the plight of the poorest was to be improved, was promoted by the World Bank. In the 1950s and 1960s the bank was riding at the front of the growth bandwagon, lending heavily for large, often capital-intensive projects in power, roads and industry. But after Robert McNamara became president in 1968, the bank became a surprisingly radical force. It now tries to target many of its loans specifically to the poorest groups, the marginal farmers, landless labourers and shantytown dwellers, lending massively for rural development and the improvement of squatter areas.

The new thinking emerged from the realization, as more and more confirmatory data came in, that despite the rapid growth in total national incomes in many developing countries, the poorest 30 to 60 per cent of the population were often not getting any better off, indeed in some countries were getting poorer. The benefits of growth concentrated in the modern sector were not trickling down to them, or at least were trickling so slowly that it would be a century or more before their descendants benefited. Their poverty could be eradicated more rapidly if some of the gross inequalities and inequities in the Third World could be reduced, if the assets that produce wealth, from land to government infrastructure, were redistributed to give the poor a better chance to help themselves. But reform alone was not enough. If all the wealth of the poorest countries were shared out equally and the incomes equalized, the majority would still not be lifted out of their grinding poverty. Growth *and* redistribution were both essential.

An earlier generation of development economists had considered these two incompatible: rapid development demanded a high level of investment, which, unless you wanted communism, could only come from profits and the savings of the rich. Development seemed to require inequality. But the experience of several countries like Taiwan, South Korea and Costa Rica, which grew fast and improved the relative share of the poor at the same time, showed that social justice need not be sacrificed at the altar of growth.

The new theory is best expressed in the book *Redistribution with Growth*, produced jointly by the World Bank and the Institute of Development Studies at Sussex, England. The book proposed that the growth of total gross national product should be dethroned as the prime measure of progress. In the typical developing country the richest 40 per cent of the people got 75 per cent of the national income, so it was quite possible for GNP to grow while the incomes of the poor actually fell. The aim of development policy, the authors proposed, would be to maximize the growth of incomes for the poorest groups in the medium term. In practice, this would mean a series of measures targeted to benefit the poor, from land reform to a shift in government spending on roads, power, health, education, credit and other subsidies, away from the cities and large-scale industry towards rural and marginal urban areas, small farmers and small-scale enterprises.

Meeting basic needs: the International Labour Organization

The concept of basic needs is a further refinement of the idea of redistribution with growth. It was developed primarily by the International Labour Organization and adopted officially by governments, employers and trade unions at the 1976 World Employment Conference.

Basic needs means a concern not just for improving the *overall* income of the poor, but with making sure that they get all the essential elements for a life of dignity freed from absolute need: adequate food, clothing, shelter, health care, education, employment, and the right to participate in making the decisions that affect them.

Development planning, this approach holds, should set minimum targets in each of these fields and pursue policies to achieve them.

The first set of needs involves a basic level of private consumption consistent with survival, good health for work and school, and dignity. A minimum diet would vary, according to region, between 2,180 and 2,380 calories per person. Every family should be able to afford a basic range of household equipment: pots and pans, stove, table and chairs, bed and a minimum amount of clothing according to the climate and prevailing standards of public decency. For example, Azizur Khan has calculated that a Bangladeshi woman could not appear in public unless she possessed a minimum of two short, coarse cloth sarees, which would require 12 square yards of cotton per year. Each household needs shelter adequate in space and protection against the elements. Again, this will vary according to general standards and weather hazards. The World Employment Conference proposed a space standard of 5·25 square metres per person in Asia and Africa and 7·5 for Latin America (the average slum family in a single room will have perhaps only 2 square metres per person or less).

These minimum standards of consumption might, in some cases, be met by public distribution of goods. More usually, governments would have to calculate a basic needs income, which could purchase for the average poor family the required quantity of goods. Economic policy would then have to be directed at pushing enough employment income to the poorest 20 per cent, to make sure everyone was raised above this poverty line. In some cases this could not be done within the existing social structure. For example, if all unemployed labourers in Bihar were to get jobs, the wage rate – already below the poverty line – would have to fall even further. Guaranteeing the basic needs income here would require major social changes such as land reform. Industry, currently geared to meeting the needs of the better-off, might need to be replanned so that it could manufacture enough of the basic goods.

The second set of basic needs is the essential services that government provides: clean water and sanitation, health services, public transport, education (see page 269 for a definition of basic education), and an important one the World Employment Conference did not mention: family planning. These needs are largely unmet for the majority of the rural and even urban poor in the Third World because of government discrimination in favour of the modern city sector. In this field, minimum standards would need to be set in terms of a certain percentage of households with access to each service, target levels for infant mortality, life expectation, disease incidence, or enrolment at school. In each case performance would be measured area by area, social group by social group, to make sure that averages did not conceal large inequities.

The final, and perhaps central, basic need is for productive employment paying an adequate income. Employment is the cornerstone of the basic needs approach. Without much fuller use of their underemployed human resources, poor countries will not be able to produce enough wealth to meet basic needs. And without jobs poor people will not be able to earn the money to satisfy their basic needs.

Employment generation had earlier been a development model of its own. In 1969 the International Labour Office set up the World Employment Programme, aimed at making the creation of jobs a central goal in development efforts. Before the late sixties development projects and investments had set out to achieve 'results' of production or profit – in the same way that nations aimed at increasing GNP – regardless of how many people they employed or put out of work. With the new employment focus, agencies and governments began to choose approaches and technologies that created jobs as well as wealth. (On appropriate technology, another key idea, see Chapter 6.)

Basic needs is a useful concept because it allows for the setting of precise goals and target dates for precise groups, and gives governments far less room for empty rhetoric about progress in the abstract. It concentrates the thoughts of planners on meeting the real needs of the poor. But the approach is not entirely problem-free. The statistics and statisticians required to measure performance do not exist in many countries. The question of who should set basic needs standards, and at what level (since human needs, beyond survival, are relative), is an open one. There is disagreement, too, as to just how much government intervention is needed to meet food, clothing and other private needs.

Despite these difficulties, the basic needs approach is now widely accepted as a philosophy, if not as a detailed planning tool, by several UN agencies including the World Bank and UNICEF, and by the Organization for Economic Cooperation and Development's Development Assistance Committee, which includes all major Western aid donors. But the greatest handicap of the approach is that it is viewed with suspicion by many Third World governments. They tend to think, wrongly, that it is opposed to growth. On a political level, many see it as a neo-colonialist intrusion into their domestic affairs and a diversion from what they see as the main task of getting a more just international economic order. For some governments these arguments are no more than rationalizations, and at bottom they are unwilling or unable to set about the social and economic reforms that would be necessary. But there is an element of truth to the point of view. It ill behoves Western governments to give Third World leaders lessons in concern for their poorest, when Western aid has sunk to abysmally low levels. At the same time as the US Congress was pressing in 1977 for aid to be restricted to countries pursuing basic-needs policies, US aid had reached its lowest recorded level of only 0·22 per cent of GNP. Basic needs, in other words, are not only a task for Third World governments. If they are to be met within any reasonable time span, then massively increased transfers of real resources from the rich countries to the poor will be essential.

Basic services: UNICEF and the World Health Organization

The next of our general models tries to answer the question: How do you satisfy the basic need for essential public services – health, family planning, education – which the poor require to alleviate suffering and to improve their productivity? The methods used in the past have demonstrably failed to reach the poor majority, especially in the rural areas. Western models of health care and family planning, based on hospitals, clinics, expensive hardware and expensively trained experts, could not reach poor, scattered populations lacking the time or the money to attend. Similar considerations prevented the poor from attending, or remaining long enough, at formal schools. At current rates of expansion, it might take four or five generations for these services to extend to the rural majority.

Such services may at first sight seem peripheral to the development effort; parts of a welfare state that might be expected to grow up much later, when countries were better off. In reality they are just as important as the bread and butter issues of employment, food production and industrialization. They obviously improve the quality of life by enabling people to reach closer to their full human potential. And they can achieve a rapid impact. Whereas radical improvements in private consumption depend on higher incomes, these public goods can be provided cheaply by governments even while average incomes are low.

But they can do much more than this. The most precious resource any country possesses is its people – indeed some of the most successful of the developing countries, in south-east and east Asia, have little else. Agriculture and industry both depend not only on machinery, materials and land, but also, and heavily, on the vigour, skill and adaptability of the people who work in them. Poor nutrition and bad health both drag down a worker's productivity – better health and nutrition services can improve productivity, increase production and boost incomes. New and improved techniques can also increase productivity – but people need education and training to use them.

Basic services aim to improve the quality of human resources in developing countries. They can quickly pay for themselves through increases in productivity. Even in the very short run they may save money by providing services more cheaply than

33

existing methods. Piped water for urban areas, for example, can be provided for one tenth of the price the slum dwellers are often paying for dirty water from vendors.

The basic services concept has been developed primarily at UNICEF and at the World Health Organization, and is being applied by those and other agencies to the fields of health, sanitation, housing, out-of-school education, nutrition and family planning. It is based on the idea that expensive technologies or highly-trained experts are not the only way of providing such services, nor the best way for poor countries. A wide variety of low-cost technologies exists in the fields of construction, water supply, sanitation and health. A modicum of education or experience, plus a modest, effective training, can equip people to give out contraceptive pills, weigh babies and teach mothers what to feed them, give first aid, prescribe basic medicines, run a nursery school or teach literacy. Previously governments have asked the question: Given our resources, how many people can we provide with services at the usual high (that is, Western) standard? The basic services viewpoint asks instead: Given our resources, what standards, what technologies, what level of training must we adopt so we can reach everyone within a decade or two? The village or poor slum, in other words, no longer needs to wait for the far-off day when the government can provide municipal housing and hospitals for everyone. They can have adequate shelter and basic health care now. A modest level of provision is better than none – and can be improved on later.

With low-cost solutions, harnessing community participation, the people themselves can help to solve their own problems. In this task they will be aided and guided by grassroots community workers: non-professionals, men or women of the people, chosen by the people, to serve the people. Grassroots workers have to have a minimum level of education, but standards are set low enough to guarantee candidates from the local area. They are put through a brief training course – anything from a day or so for family planning distributors, to a few days for nutrition cadres, to three or four months for health workers. They are paid a modest salary or commission, or may often even be unpaid volunteers. Often they are only part-time, continuing with their normal occupations for most of the week. Their equipment, if they have any at all, is basic, simple and cheap. Barefoot technicians have many advantages over their expensively shod professional counterparts. They speak the same language and share the same culture as their clients. They enjoy their trust. They understand the people's problems, because they share them. They do not pose as omniscient, omnipotent experts, and their most fundamental task is to help people to help themselves.

The spread of basic services does not mean that the professional services, the hospitals or family planning clinics, become redundant. They have to be remodelled as back-up services, directing, supervising, training field workers, providing technical support, transport, communications and supplies, and dealing with the more complex cases which the village worker cannot cope with.

There are several other areas where the concept of basic services could be extended. Agricultural extension workers are, in practice, a kind of barefoot expert and might benefit from being elected by their clients. Villages could do with barefoot technologists who would help people to improve their tools and techniques at home and at work. Small-scale businesses of every kind could benefit from barefoot management consultants trained to teach the rudiments of accounting and marketing. And, as the law is so often in the pockets of the rich in the Third World, every village could do with its own barefoot lawyers and probably a barefoot court as well.

Popular participation has become an important element of basic services programmes. In most of them the client communities have become involved to varying degrees. They often elect the village-level workers democratically. They may pay their wages through either insurance systems or modest fees. They may help to build the necessary premises and any environmental improvements they are persuaded are necessary. And they often elect and staff committees which support the barefoot experts, help to spread the educational messages and express the communities' needs to them.

Participation in development

The ideal of participation is gaining much wider currency in all spheres. There is a growing consensus that development can be accelerated if the energies and resources of the people are mobilized, and that the poor have a basic human right – hitherto denied them by unequal power structures – to take part in making the decisions that affect their lives and livelihoods. This idea was incorporated in the International Development Strategy for the United Nations' Second Development Decade, adopted in October 1970, which affirmed that 'every effort will be made to secure the active support and participation of all segments of the population in the development process'.

Participation should occur at each stage of the development process: before, during and after. In setting the goals and making the decisions that affect the community; in carrying out the plans; and in sharing the benefits. Most of the projects with which this book is concerned involve some element of participation. In many, the people have a voice in deciding what improvements are needed, and do not simply have to accept what is decided for them on high. In many, the people contribute their voluntary labour, tools, transport and funds. Often a grassroots democratic institution – a local health or nutrition committee or a farming cooperative, for example – is set up around some particular issue, and can later be generalized into something like an all-purpose village development committee.

The potential benefits of mass participation are immense. Participation in implementing projects reduces their cost by mobilizing unused local resources and free human energy. Participation in decision-making provides planners with much better information on people's wants and dislikes. It helps to avoid the kind of disastrous errors, failures and white elephants with which the history of development is littered, usually because the supposed beneficiaries were not adequately consulted. Participation in productive enterprises is increasingly fostered by way of service or producers' cooperatives. In this context it can boost morale, increase productivity and reduce negative and destructive conflicts between managers and managed, from go-slows to sabotage. In many places the poor live in a state of passive inertia because of their total powerlessness in the face of entrenched élites: this inertia affects not only their involvement in public life, but infects even their family and home life. For these people, participation is an educative process. It can give them confidence for the first time in their ability to control circumstances instead of being controlled by them. By broadening the base of decision, it reduces the chances of development strategies being adopted which benefit only a small minority, and hence improves the chances for the adoption of the new egalitarian and poverty-oriented approaches.

Finally, participation can contribute to political stability which is so often in jeopardy in the Third World. All too often, in poor and polarized countries, the sectional interests of family, tribe, religion or faction come first and the state is seen as a means of advancing them – or, where it stands in the way, as an obstacle to be cheated, defied or swept away. Dictatorship – the prevalent form of government in the Third World, in varying degrees – encourages these attitudes. But where decisions have been arrived at in consultation with the people, they are more likely to be accepted without the need for coercion. Widespread participation makes for a state where the government has high legitimacy and for citizens able to consider the good of society as a whole as well as their own interests. In history, a high level of participation has normally emerged in economically advanced societies, along with the growth in education, literacy and communications. However, experience in poor developing countries such as China, Tanzania and Guyana suggest that participation can be fostered before development has advanced very far, and in its turn can help to speed up development.

Increased participation will mean a considerable measure of self-help. But there are dangers in taking this approach too far. The masses usually lack much of the necessary technical skills, materials and finance. Participation from the base has to be accompanied by material and technical help from above. Self-help of the poor and uneducated cannot go far unaided. What is required is what might be called 'assisted self-help'.

In poor countries this must mean the mobilization of all possible resources and skills to help the poor. High-level skills are in short supply – and yet medium-level skills may often be underused. One of the most intriguing new ideas is the massive mobilization of the modestly trained to educate those with no training at all. In Mozambique, drained of technical manpower by the departure of the Portuguese, this has been developed into a national system. So first-level secondary school pupils are being used to teach in primary schools, second-level to teach first-level secondary. University students in all relevant fields spend vacations in the villages: agricultural students teach better farming methods, medics provide health care, while law students train villagers to administer popular justice.

Eco-development: the United Nations Environment Programme

One of the most distasteful aspects of the Western model of development has been its appalling arrogance, in the face both of nature and of traditional cultures. The rape of the earth has been central to the past progress of Western industrialism: the plunder and waste of irreplaceable resources, the poisoning or destruction of fragile ecosystems, the belief that man can mould nature with no need to take account of nature's reactions to such a violation. Disdain for traditional cultures and social systems was a fundamental characteristic of all modern European empires, and this attitude spread to the new ruling élites who had adopted Western ways. As a result one development project after another triggered irreversible changes in local habitats. And the whole development process did not build on the foundations of traditional society but fell on it like a nuclear bomb and blew it apart.

The concept of eco-development, or ecologically sound development, has been developed by the United Nations Environment Programme. Its basic principles are simple. Development should respect the local ecosystem. It should conserve resources, using renewable resources wherever possible. It should minimize waste and recycle as much as it can. And it should respect local social and cultural patterns, by involving the local population in deciding on the style and pace of development.

In practice, eco-development is not easy to carry out. It demands careful study of the local ecology of man and nature, and often there are not enough trained people to do this even for major projects, let alone minor ones. Technologies using renewable energy sources and conserving and recycling other resources are now emerging, but they are still in a primitive stage compared with the technologies of large-scale waste. Moreover, not everything in traditional culture is wonderful: some practices such as destroying forests for firewood, or farming techniques that accelerate erosion, are as destructive as anything industrialism can offer, and social institutions such as the place of women and the treatment of minority castes or tribes have to be modified.

Apart from these quibbles, eco-development is no more than a sensible precondition of sustainable development. It asks no more than that we should live today with tomorrow in mind, that we do not snatch a momentary prosperity for ourselves at the expense of the very survival of our children.

Ultimate values: Cocoyoc and UNESCO

Third World leaders frequently refer in their pronouncements to national values and aspirations and to the uniqueness of their local cultures; but these ultimate ends are generally ignored in practice. With a few notable exceptions, development has been a piecemeal, pragmatic endeavour, aimed for the most part at the multiplication of material wealth. Basic values such as justice, cooperation, charity and respect for nature have not only been subordinated to that, but are often trampled underfoot in the gold rush.

Values are implicit in the new development models outlined so far, as we shall see in Chapter 15. In addition, there are two general statements which explicitly offer a framework of values. The first is a Cocoyoc declaration, adopted in October 1974 by a symposium convened by UNEP and UNCTAD, on patterns of resource use, environment and development strategies. This is one of the most sane, enlightened and humane statements on the goals of development. The second statement is contained in UNESCO's medium-term plan for 1977–82, officially adopted in 1977. The UNESCO plan puts forward the idea of 'endogenous development', planned and carried out by each nation in line with its own choices and in accordance with the authentic values, aspirations and motives of its people. The values that inspired development in the early years were exogenous – imposed by or copied from outside from the West, whether capitalist or communist. What is needed is a new, authentic style of development emerging from within each culture, inspired by values derived from the people's deepest roots. UNESCO implies that this will be different for each nation, but one of the purposes of the present book is to show that there is a common ground of values in all Third World cultures from which a general model of development can be derived and applied to developing capitalist and communist countries alike.

Both documents emphasize self-help, self-reliance, self-improvement. 'Development must be designed, even at the humblest level, as a process of ensuring the advancement of man through his own endeavours,' says UNESCO. The multiplication of material wealth has to be dethroned as the purpose of development. 'The goal of development should be not to develop things, but to develop man,' says Cocoyoc. 'Development must be aimed at the spiritual, moral and material advancement of the whole human being, both as a member of society and from the point of view of individual fulfilment,' says UNESCO. For example, the right to work, Cocoyoc suggests, involves 'not simply having a job but finding self-realization in work', and implies the right not to be alienated by production processes that use human beings as tools.

The model of development as material growth gets most of its fuel from the Third World's desire to close the wealth gap with the West, in a possessions race almost as futile as the arms race. The Cocoyoc participants rejected the idea of gaps: 'The goal is not to catch up, but to ensure the quality of life for all.' A primary aim, naturally, was to meet the basic human needs of the poorest. But once these 'inner limits' had been passed, mankind had to beware of overstepping the 'outer limits' set by the world's resources and ecological balances. A certain minimum of consumption had to be guaranteed for all – but there was also a maximum, set by the carrying capacity of the biosphere, and by man's own limited ability to absorb material goods without damage to his physical or mental health. This part of the Cocoyoc declaration was addressed primarily to the West, but it also has a lesson for the élites of the Third World.

The new model of development has aroused some consumer resistance among many Third World leaders. Some see it as a new Western stratagem to make them accept second best, to make them dismantle their modern sectors – a new sort of foreign model which neo-colonialists are trying to impose as they see the developing world about to 'take off' into sustained growth. Those who reject it often use elements of the rhetoric of the new approach, such as the right of each nation, implicit in the idea of endogenous development, to choose its own path.

Telling enough, these arguments were rarely raised when all the aid effort really was pushing Westernization. Those who now raise them against the new style of development do so because they want to push on with the old model. It is this latter model that ensures continued mimicry of the West, and continued dependence.

The new model has nothing to do with the perpetuation of Western dominance. It aims at developing the capacity of individuals, communities and nations to provide for themselves. It is essentially of the Third World, consistent with what is valuable in cultural roots, and derived from pioneering experience in individual developing countries. While some of its details remain to be worked out, and adapted to each country, its basic framework and foundations are clear, offering a rough blueprint for guidance in the Third Development Decade of the eighties. In the following pages we shall see how its outlines are being filled in in concrete programmes across three continents.

3 Land to the tiller: the brown revolution

Puwokgahena estate, in the lush south of Sri Lanka, was a wilderness before the Baddegama Land Reform Cooperative Society took over. Four hundred acres of neglect, with weeds waist-high along the roads and the stubby tea bushes drowned in overgrowth, unfertilized, unpruned and unweeded by its former owner ever since the first rumour that land reform was in the air. At the best of times, it does not look like ideal soil. The steep hillsides are dotted with rounded outcrops of basalt, like plum puddings.

After Sri Lanka's land reform of 1972, all this changed and there was a palpable atmosphere of bustle and business about the place when I visited it in 1975. Talking to the workers here was like hearing a Chinese moral tale of black and white, before and after, evil capitalism and benevolent socialism. They tell you how, before the takeover, they used to get only three or four days' work a week and earn thirty rupees a month. The younger ones recall bitterly their years of unemployment, sponging off parents. Before the takeover, the estate was employing only about thirty workers. Now there are 400, working seven days a week all the year round and making 170 rupees a month. In the first fourteen months, besides growing a lot more tea, the workers built a new nursery school, a volleyball court, and a canteen where they can eat jakfruit, bread and tea under straw sunshades, and started building new houses to replace the infamous lines – rows of one-roomed, windowless cells shared by families of two to ten people.

Near the tea-weighing shed a huge board (erected with the estate's first profits) proclaims in curly red Sinhala characters:

'Guard this estate, this is your property. These hundreds of acres formerly belonged to two capitalist families, but now you are the owners. It belongs to you and your future generations. It is your duty to protect and safeguard it from the capitalists.' On the hillside overseeing the plantations, in a shrine painted with blue clouds, a serene statue of Buddha meditates in lotus pose, painted, appropriately, in red lacquer.

The estate superintendent, Amris Silva, works as hard as if the millennium had to be finished by the end of next week. A slender, toothy and tousle-haired figure, he is like a father and mentor to the workers. At this stage worker participation (which Silva advocates passionately) is only a slogan. The reality is a benevolent dictatorship in which his plans are automatically nodded through: before the workers can control operations here, they need a great deal of education in farming and management, and motivation for collective self-improvement. Silva was providing this by way of Marxist indoctrination, of the more benevolent Trotskyist kind represented by Sri Lanka's Lanka Sama Samaj Party. In the corner of his house there is a white alabaster statue of Buddha scattered with frangipani and hibiscus flowers; next to it, a bronze bust of Lenin. Silva sees no incompatibility here.

Puwokgahena is in Galle district, on the southern tip of the island. Industry is practically non-existent, apart from fishing from wooden canoes with outriggers, converting coral, chipped from the offshore reef, into lime, and tapping toddy from the pinnacles of the tall coconut palms that line the coastal roads. Even in Galle town, a fishing port that was once the capital of the Dutch colony on the island, there is only a cement works and some fish processing. Increasing agricultural employment was thus of crucial importance if Sri Lanka's problem of endemically high unemployment was to be attacked. For Puwokgahena, land reform has meant vastly increased employment, higher incomes (and these, when spent, will stimulate greater demand for local manufactured products) and increased output.

Of all the wide range of changes needed to benefit the poor of the Third World, land reform is perhaps the most important and the most necessary. The World Bank has estimated that 85 per cent of the very poor in the Third World live in rural areas. In most of sub-Saharan Africa rural poverty has more to do with primitive techniques, and excess population on poor soils, than with landlessness. But in Asia, the Arab world and in Latin America almost all the rural poor are those who are either landless labourers or tenants, or who own plots too small to support them and depend on employment to supplement their incomes. Unequal and inadequate access to land is the prime cause of their poverty. Unequal access to other factors needed in agricultural production – water, credit, fertilizers, market outlets, expert advice – may aggravate the poverty of the small farmer. But this, in turn, is often due to unequal land-holdings, as the big landowner translates his economic power into political pull and monopolizes any benefits the government is handing out.

Just how needed land reform is, is shown by figures on the distribution of landholdings collected for the last World Census of Agriculture in 1960. Worldwide about 1 million holdings of more than 200 hectares – less than 1 per cent of the total number – occupied two thirds of the farm land. At the other end of the scale, 109 million holdings of under five hectares (79 per cent of the total) were cramped on to 7 per cent of the land. Since 1960 the situation has almost certainly got a lot worse. The extent of inequality varied between the three continents. In sub-Saharan Africa, excluding the white-dominated South, communal forms of landownership still predominate. In many areas they are breaking down into small individual private holdings, but pronounced inequalities and widespread landlessness have not yet had time to develop. Asia is characterized by apparently moderate inequality, with the top 0·2 per cent of owners holding only 9 per cent of the holdings larger than one hectare. In Latin America the top 3 per cent of landowners held

90 per cent of the area. In the late 1960s, around one third of the active population in agriculture in Latin America, Asia and the Middle East were landless labourers, while the proportion of tenants and sharecroppers ranged from 31 per cent in Latin America, through 33 per cent in Asia, to 61 per cent in the Middle East and North Africa. On all continents, but especially in Asia, landlessness and rural unemployment are on the increase, as population growth has led to the shrinkage of the majority of smallholdings below subsistence level and owners have had to sell out to pay off debts or keep alive. The new profitability of farming with green revolution techniques has led to the eviction of more and more tenants, while mechanization wiped out many jobs, and the medium and large landowners were able to extend their holdings at the expense of the small.

The potential benefits of land reform are immense. The incomes of the beneficiaries invariably improve, along with their housing, nutrition and health. Better health and nutrition, in turn, improve their productivity at work and the ability of their children to succeed at school. The poor spend more on essentials, often giving a boost to local labour-intensive industries. In the most crowded parts of Asia, equal distribution of all agricultural land would still leave everyone with farms too small to support a family. Here rural small-scale industry and public works programmes will be needed to provide additional jobs. But even here, a large measure of redistribution would be valuable if only to smash the economic base of the local power of the 'big man'.

Land reform generates more employment. In the land reform areas I visited in Sri Lanka, Colombia and Peru everyone told me the same story: before the reform, they were working fifteen or twenty days a month, after, thirty days a month. Where land reform creates a mass of smallholdings (often worked cooperatively) this too increases employment. Small farms absorb a great deal more labour than large ones – thirty

Land to the tiller

to sixty times more man years per hectare in Latin America, for example. They also produce more food from a given area – three to fourteen times more in Latin America. In Thailand holdings of two to six acres gave yields 55 per cent higher than farms of 140 acres and above. Increasing food production and employment on limited land are the two most urgent tasks in the rual areas of most of the Third World.

As rural poverty and polarization increased and people's expectations rose, virtually every government in the Third World, outside black Africa where the question was less pressing, has enacted land reform legislation. In many, perhaps most, countries this has been ineffective, either because the legislation was not far-reaching enough, and was sabotaged in advance by exceptions and legal loopholes, or because local administrators and judges would not carry it out. But in several countries it brought about fundamental changes in the distribution of wealth, income and power in rural areas. In Taiwan and South Korea, land reform practically wiped out tenancy and large landholdings, creating a mass of small property-owners.

Sri Lanka's land reform law, passed in 1972, aimed to increase rural employment and incomes and boost home food production. The ceilings were relatively high: private holdings were limited to twenty-five acres of paddy land per adult member of the family, or fifty acres of other land. As a result, the reform had little effect on the bulk of farmers, who are smallholders of paddy land, but it had an immense impact on the estate sector. A total of 560,000 acres were taken over between 1972 and 1974, nearly 14 per cent of all agricultural land in Sri Lanka. In 1975 Sri Lanka completed its reform by nationalizing all foreign and locally controlled company estates covering a total of 415,000 acres. The reformed land was divided up into four main types of holding. Some 84,000 acres were shared out in small plots of an acre or less to landless peasants, to be worked as smallholdings, in little 'colonies' that are not much more than allotments. Though their owners would still depend on labouring to make a living, the small plots were a worthwhile gesture, as they provided rent-free, secure housing and extra food for home consumption. But the bulk of the land taken over was in viable tea, rubber and coconut plantations which it was better to keep intact. Some of the best-kept estates were handed over to the State Plantations Corporation, and run as nationalized industries. Others, like Puwokgahena, were grouped under local cooperative societies, sharing supplies, marketing and higher management. A smaller proportion were transformed into collective farms known as *janawasas*, under the Land Reform Commission. They are similar in some ways to Chinese communes, but their progenitor, Chandrika Bandaranaike, daughter of the former prime minister and director of the commission at the time of my visit, told me she was not following any foreign models but was rather inspired by the village communes that were supposed to have existed in Sri Lanka before the era of empires.

The *janawasa* tries to combine an element of private smallholding with a larger element of worker participation in running communal land and sharing in the proceeds. The first of these collectives started in 1973, and by 1975 they numbered nearly 200, covering about 50,000 acres, varying in size from twenty-five to 4,000 acres, with anything from thirty to 2,000 members. In the ideal *janawasa* members get a quarter or half an acre for their own house and vegetable garden, in plots ringing the central area which is owned and worked in common. All the members meet once a month to discuss the running of the farm. Day-to-day matters are dealt with by a series of committees staffed by workers, covering planning, finance, supplies and marketing. The *janawasa* also sets aside funds for social insurance, culture, library and political education and administers a large measure of its own justice. Members get a quarter of the profits at the end of each financial year, the local village gets another quarter to help with schools, health centres and so on, while the rest goes to the Land Reform Commission to finance the opening up of new *janawasas*.

I visited one young *janawasa* in the Galle district, Walahanduwa. Half its 1,850 acres were under tea, the rest in coconut and spindly tangled rubber trees, around valley floors carpeted in the brilliant green of young paddy. On the highest hill, hidden among temple trees and flamboyant trees, stood the former owner's regal white bungalow, preserved like a people's museum of the bad old days. With its doric columns and moulded architrave, its spacious lounges and cramped servants' quarters, it now served the workers for social occasions. As on other types of land reform settlement, the workers were paid a basic wage of 5·60 rupees a day. At the end of the year they would get their share of the profits, which in the first year of operation were expected to be nearly 9 million rupees. The workers' share of this – about 2,000 rupees a head – would more than double their annual income. And this profit figure was after investment, including tractor, jeep, two lorries, re-planting of old tea bushes with high-yield varieties, and the turning over of some of the land to production of rice, fruit and vegetables to help make Sri Lanka self-sufficient in food.

Potential pitfalls

Several other countries have carried out land reforms on a really significant scale. In Iran the Shah began his white revolution on the land in 1962. At that time nearly two thirds of all land was rented from landlords, many of whom were absentees owning the entire lands of many villages. The first phase of the reform modestly limited owners to one village each. Subsequent phases compelled them to sell all their rented-out land to the sitting tenants and to divide up sharecropped land with tenants in the same ratio that each year's crop was shared. By the early seventies all of 50,000 villages had undergone land reform and 3 million peasant families had benefited. There were drawbacks: in particular the reform did not benefit the millions of rural families who were completely landless. It smashed the power of the feudal landlords, yet created another privileged class of small and medium landowners confronting an underprivileged and underemployed mass of labourers.

Chile enacted a vigorous land reform under the government of Eduardo Frei (1964–7). The ceiling on holdings was set at eighty hectares. As soon as the reform was announced, almost overnight the number of holdings sized between forty and eighty hectares mysteriously doubled – landlords were quickly dividing up their land among relatives and nominees to avoid expropriation. Despite these evasions, around 3·5 million hectares were taken over and handed to 27,000 peasant families. Allende's government of Popular Unity took over, between 1970 and 1973, a further 5·7 million hectares and gave them to 39,000 families. Most of these lands were worked as cooperatives.

The big landowners were among the groups whose agitation led to the military coup of 1973. Pinochet's junta halted all further takeovers of land and put the reform into reverse gear, restoring many estates to their former owners. Farms that had been worked collectively were split up into individual plots, as any form of social property was anathema to the new régime. A law which forbade peasants to sell land acquired through the reform (to prevent inequalities re-emerging) was repealed.

These examples show just how difficult is genuine land reform, how fraught with pitfalls. For if this is the single most important change that can benefit the poor in the Third World, it is also, by the same token, the most drastic blow to the economic and political power of the rich. As a result, land reform is fought bitterly before its introduction, and evaded widely when it becomes law. And even when it succeeds, serious inequalities can raise their heads in any number of forms. As land reform expert Erich Jacoby has written, 'Land reform is a continued uphill battle in which every step forward must be guarded against the opponents of change.'

To be effective, land reform must radically reduce rural inequalities, eliminating not only the very large landlords, but also the excess holdings of richer middle peasants. If it fails to do this, these, in their turn, become the new dominant class and monopolize the benefits of development efforts. It must benefit all major categories of rural poor, and in particular it should give land to the landless. It must be tightly and carefully framed, leaving no legal loopholes, for even if only one tiny pinhole is left, most landlords will find a way to crawl through it. It should have rigid ceilings, allowing of no exceptions, and applying to families, not individuals. The implementation process should be as speedy as possible, and peasants should be organized to help with the takeover and ensure the law is not evaded. Ideally, there should be no compensation, because the old landlords can simply use the funds to purchase other means of exploiting people, and the new owners will be burdened with debt before they start. But if compensation cannot be avoided, it should be in some non-inflationary form such as low-interest government bonds without any specific redemption date. Redistribution of land should go hand in hand with the introduction of extension services, credit programmes, supplies and marketing services to help peasants increase the productivity of their new holdings.

Division into smallholdings is generally a necessary first step to satisfy the hunger of all peasants for their own piece of land. But smallholdings become inefficient at later stages of development when machinery needs to be introduced. So ideally the initial redivision should be followed up fairly soon by organization of peasants into cooperatives, first for the purchase of inputs and the sale of produce, then for the actual working of the land. A few working estates may be retained as state farms to serve as models of technical development. But organization into co-ops should be voluntary: enforced collectivization of peasants who at first are bound to be individualistic tends to result in massacres.

Examples of radical reforms satisfying this demanding checklist are few outside the socialist countries. China's reform began with redistribution of land into smallholdings, then gradually introduced mutual aid teams, then cooperatives, then communes able to undertake non-agricultural works. Hungary placated the peasants' need for an area of autonomy by letting farmers retain an acre and a half of land for labour-intensive pursuits like livestock and chicken rearing, vines, bees or vegetables, while most of their land was pooled into cooperatives which reached a very high level of mechanization and technology. Japan and South Korea carried through two of the most radical land reforms in the world in the wake of the Second World War. In South Korea, in 1945, 70 per cent of farmers were tenants paying between half and nine tenths of their produce to landlords. By 1950 tenancy had been eliminated, and no one was allowed to own more than one hectare of paddy land. Japan imposed a similar limit.

Reforms with this much bite demand the right political and organizational conditions. The Chinese and Hungarian measures were backed by governments free from the obstructing pressure of vested economic interests, and there is no doubt that the lack of representative democracy of the Western kind helped to free them from those pressures. In the cases of Japan and South Korea, the necessary political muscle was provided by American armies of occupation, which insisted on radical measures to eliminate the sort of feudal conditions that had sped the Communists to power in China. In Japan the reform was supervised at local level by elected land committees, and effective unions of poor peasants ensured that these committees were packed with their own members. Any committee representative who acted against their interests was subject to recall and dismissal. But for this, bigger landlords would have seized control of the committees and perverted the reform.

Examples of reforms which did not go far enough are far more commonplace. Even Japan might have done better to introduce cooperatives, as the mini-smallholders were unable to mechanize fast enough to keep their incomes up with city incomes. Cooperatives allow mechanization without the inequality and upheaval that this can involve in large-scale private farming.

A half-hearted reform may provide short-term relief for some of the poor, yet make no fundamental and lasting changes. Between 1952 and 1963 Egypt enacted a series of land reforms which, in all, took over some 900,000 acres and redistributed them to 342,000 families – benefiting nearly 2 million individuals. On the face of it, this had a considerable impact. The proportion of farm land owned by holders of more than 100 acres fell from 27 per cent before 1952 to 6 per cent in 1965. The number of landless families fell from 1·46 million in 1950 to only 1·1 million in 1961. The average size of a smallholding rose from 0·8 acres to 1·2 acres. But the reform was not a radical assault on social injustice. Massive inequalities remained. In 1960 the bottom 60 per cent of rural households still owned only 3·5 per cent of the land, while the share of the top 20 per cent was still 80 per cent – only 12 per cent down from its level in 1950. In 1961 there were still over a million landless families, and their incomes barely improved at all. New cooperatives were set up, but the bulk of the benefits accrued to the larger farmers. By 1972 the number of landless families had risen again to 1·5 million, and the number of rural families below the poverty line shot up from 900,000 in 1964 to 1·8 million ten years later. The reforms had provided only a temporary respite: they did not bite deep enough to change the basic structure of social and political power. So the old dynamics of increasing inequality continued from a new base line, and things slid back to where they were before.

One of the quickest paths to the undoing of reform is to divide land up into individual parcels and hand them over to people to farm individually without any restrictions on sale or division. Unless there are strong safeguards to prevent it, the engine of polarization gets to work again. People get into difficulties through natural or personal misfortunes, mortgage or sell part of their land, and before you know it things are back where they started.

I saw this sad process at work in a land reform dairy estate in Colombia. El Soche comprises 200 hectares of good pasture in Cundinamarca, with lush green grass rolling over hills and rocky outcrops and copses of tall eucalyptus. Workers' houses are scattered about in their own little vegetable gardens. Like so many of the land reform estates in Colombia, El Soche was bought by Colombia's National Institute for Agrarian Reform (INCORA) after repeated invasions by landless labourers. For the first couple of years the estate was farmed communally and the profits were shared equally. But tensions were building up. Some people worked harder than others, and resented that they got paid the same. Some of the men had turned to drink to forget the injustices under the old system, but even after land reform they were unable to give up their addiction and drank as much and worked as little as they could. But people were held together by the first president. When he was killed in a bar brawl the members decided they could not work as a cooperative any more. With INCORA's agreement the estate was divided into equal individual parcels and the herd of cattle split among them. In the next five years, starting from an equal base, huge inequalities built up. Jorge Salgado, a swarthy, fit man of thirty-five, had built up his herd through careful management to seven milk cows and seven yearlings that would start giving milk the following year. His next-door neighbour, Lisa de Gutierrez, a widow raising seven children on her own, had only four milk cows. I met another man strolling uphill leading a handsome pony by the reins. The smell of drink was powerful on his breath and he could not say much that made sense, but he did inform me as if he was proud of it that he had 'two cows and no more'. A little more neglect and he would have none, while Salgado would be needing extra land and the help of a labourer to look after his growing herd.

One of the most common criticisms of land reform programmes is that they have been known to lead to a fall in production. Many empirical studies show a rise, but whenever a drop happens it is seized upon by opponents of reform as proof that equality is incompatible with maximizing output and growth. It is certainly true that production does sometimes fall off. Part of the fall is due to the upheaval in social relations that land reform entails. But often a large part of any apparent loss in production is due to sabotage in advance. Land reform never arrives unannounced: election manifestos or junta pronouncements usually give landlords plenty of warning. If they cannot scupper or evade the reform, they invariably halt all investment and let their property deteriorate; indeed they often begin to disinvest and sell off everything that can be moved. In Sri Lanka the land reform was in the air for some time before it happened. As soon as they got wind of it many landlords stopped all investment and dropped all the work that ensures the long-term prosperity of a plantation: weeding, fertilizing, replanting worn-out bushes. Many estates became overgrown and the yield of bushes declined. All this lost ground had to be made up by the new land reform estates. Peru's landlords snatched quick profits before they were expropriated. In the sierra, they sold off and slaughtered up to half their herds of cattle, sheep, llamas and alpaca. New reform estates started life with depleted herds, which they had to build up by slaughtering fewer animals than usual. Outside observers took this as a sign that land reform led to reduced efficiency.

The new élites of land reform

Most revolutions promise equality, but inequality is a perennial weed with deep roots that often springs up again after it has been cut down. Yugoslav writer Milovan Djilas complained that a new class of party bureaucrats, holding economic and political power and enjoying higher rewards than the masses, had emerged under the Eastern European model of Communism. Land reform is a revolution of wealth and power relations on the land, and it, too, can easily give birth to a new class of rural privilege if it is not carefully designed.

Cooperative ownership and management does help to prevent the re-emergence of landlessness, at least among those given land, but it is no safeguard against other forms of inequality. Pronounced discrepancies can continue, both inside the cooperatives, between management and workers, and between the beneficiaries of land reform and smallholders, tenants or landless labourers who are excluded from the reform.

In Sri Lanka, on the nationalized and most of the cooperative estates, superintendents would remain in their comfortable bougainvillea-wreathed bungalows – or even move into the boss's home – while the workers stayed in their one-roomed cells. When I visited the estates, pluckers were earning around 170 rupees a month, while the superintendents were drawing 2,000 rupees and driving their own cars. They were unquestionably in charge. 'I give the orders now,' one of them told me bluntly. Local land-hungry villagers who had not benefited from the reform raided several of the new estates, believing they had become public property.

Precisely similar problems were emerging in Peru when I visited estates there in 1976. Of all Latin American countries, Peru was perhaps in greatest need of land reform. In 1961 the bottom 74 per cent of holdings occupied only 4 per cent of the land while 88 per cent of the land was held by only 3 per cent of the landowners. Just 1,000 individuals owned 60 per cent of all farm land in the country. In the mountains and high plateaux where most of Peru's population is concentrated, smallholders subsisted on minute parcels of land next to huge, spreading ranches. Under the slogan 'land or death', many of the peasants invaded the estates or were involved in rural guerilla activities. No one could accuse the Peruvian land reform, introduced by the military government of General Velasco which took power in 1968, of being a token measure. By 1976, when the process was slowed down under shortsighted pressure from the International Monetary Fund, the enormous feudal *latifundia* had been almost wiped out and one third of all farmland in Peru had been taken over and distributed among peasants. Only about 5 per cent was divided up into individual parcels, the rest was handed over to former landless labourers to be worked as cooperatives of various kinds. The constitution of the typical co-op is highly democratic. Workers have the right to elect a directing board which can hire and fire administrative staff. At their annual general meetings, they can fix relative salary levels and decide on how much of the profits will be invested and how much distributed among members.

The co-ops started life burdened with an army of problems. They had to repay loans from the state covering the cost of the land and machinery. Their constitutions required them to set aside half of their profits for education, social security and reserves. For co-ops already struggling to repair the damage done by saboteur landlords, there was little left over for new investment. But perhaps the most intractable problems were human. Even co-ops have to have someone who makes sure that the plans arrived at by democratic decision are carried out. Usually this function was taken on by the old management who were simply re-elected as no one else was qualified to do their jobs. But in many co-ops the old hostility between management and workers continued.

The tea-growing estate of Té Huyrof, in La Convencion valley near Cuzco, was the site of many bitter clashes between peasants and landowners in the early sixties. The administration clearly hoped that little would change under the new system. They continued to live in the decent houses the former owners had assigned them. A report by Peru's National Centre of Training and Research for Agrarian Reform found that they failed to keep workers informed of the progress of the estate and seemed annoyed when workers asked for information. They did their best to make sure that only lip-service was paid to democracy, cloaking a reality of technocratic command. They continued to believe that workers were basically lazy and that a hard hand was needed to keep them in line. The workers, for their part, still saw the management as representatives of the old landlord class, and felt allegiance to their trade unions or families rather than to the estate which was now, in theory, their own. They did not participate in meetings. They believed that only manual labour was real work, and that management ought not to be members of the new co-ops. After years of struggling for 'land or death', they were still preoccupied with getting their rights, and unwilling to fulfil the obligations that went with them.

The issue of discipline became the focus for these complex tensions. The administrators chafed under the powers of the general workers' assembly. 'Employees are there to obey, not to command,' said one. The workers, for their part, felt that now the bosses were gone no one had the right to control them. Every morning and evening a bell used to be sounded to mark the beginning and end of work. It was despised as a symbol of the old régime, and the workers voted to abolish it. But they did not propose any alternative means of checking on hours worked, and many people started to arrive late and leave early. Productivity fell, though everyone had voted themselves higher wages, so profits and investment suffered. Mutual jealousies broke out between groups of workers over pay differentials. The shambles was completed when two directors were charged with illicit appropriation of funds and the sole distributor of

Huyro Tea absconded with $10,000 of estate money. Everyone, it seemed, had put sectional interests first, seeing the estate as a kitty to be plundered for individual gain. No one had realized that the estate, if run on a democratic and egalitarian basis, *was* the people. The venture foundered on negative attitudes inherited from the old society that had developed into unshakable habits. It was as if the old order had sabotaged human beings as well as animals and machinery, bent and twisted the pieces as well as the board, to make sure the new game could not be played properly.

The case of Té Huyro is far from unique. Many cooperatives, in agricultural and other fields, have failed in similar ways. That does not prove that land reform or cooperatives cannot work. It simply shows that much more is needed for success than simply the formal change in ownership. Members need training and retraining for their new responsibilities and relationships; workers need training in management so they are not at the mercy of the professionals. People from every new cooperative need a grounding in everything from production, marketing and accounting to the conduct of meetings. Participation, unless it is firmly based in information and readiness to accept the will of the majority, can end up as the chaotic clash of individual and sectional egoisms.

Picotani estate in Puno province, Peru, seemed well on its way to solving these problems. Isolated and windswept, high in the *altiplano*, Picotani spreads over 94,000 hectares of rolling, treeless hills and moors. Packs of llamas and alpacas tear at the spare clumps of wiry *ichu* grass and stare at you, camel-like, moving off if you approach. It is a harsh climate, 4,400 metres up in the Andes, and the air is cold and rarefied – after a slow climb of only fifty yards I was as breathless and exhausted as if I had run half a mile at top speed. When we arrived at the estate headquarters, sheltered in a deep valley, the alpacas were being sheared, at the rate of 1,000 animals a day. Elegant and fleecy white, they waited, wide-eyed, in pens, sighing nervously with a high-pitched whine. From there they were dragged off one by one to the shearing machines, where one worker held them down with a foot on their necks while another clipped them quite bare. They emerged naked, skinny, ungainly, confused and terrified.

The president of the workers' assembly at Picotani, who holds power in theory, is Epiphanio Desa, a middle-aged chauffeur with the tanned, wrinkled face of the Sierra Indian. I asked him who ran the estate, management or workers. 'The boss has to obey our orders,' he answered without hesitation. The boss in question is Jaime Barreo, who used to be manager under the old owner, but that does not seem to have counted against him. Barreo has entered into the proletarian spirit of workers' democracy – he often goes around in blue dungarees, heavy black working boots and three days' growth of beard. He agreed that the workers were in control of the estate. 'But who prepares plans for the future?' I asked. 'I do,' said Barreo. 'Have the workers ever rejected any of your plans?' 'No. But sometimes they demand extras like new houses, and I have to work out how we can get the money for that from somewhere.' On many estates, workers' assemblies used their new powers to cut the salaries of administrators, many of whom resigned. Barreo told me that perhaps a third of Picotani's workers wanted all incomes to be equal, but the majority were in favour of differentials for responsibility. Barreo was earning 33,000 soles a month (at the time about $600), while an ordinary herder got only 5,000 soles. 'Some of them criticize me about my salary. Then I say, OK, you draw up the plans and accounts and I'll look after the alpacas. That soon shuts them up.'

Picotani has had to battle against the problems that crippled Té Huyro. Some of the new members came from neglected estates where the owners had just left them to their own devices, and these men found it hard to keep regular hours. Under the old system every herdsman used to have his own herd of private animals, and naturally put most of his effort into looking after these. Even under common ownership they tend to do this, so the estate is planning to buy out the private herds to end this conflict of interests.

At Picotani, efficient management has been combined with a democratic spirit and genuine attempts to educate the workers. Barreo says he is training them so as to put himself out of a job. The estate puts out a little newsletter in Spanish and Quechua. 'What is participation?' one issue asked. 'It is to know the facts, to criticize the good and the bad, to take part in decisions and realize organized action to solve the problems.' Picotani also has a social development officer, Soraya de Campos, whose job it is to mobilize the workers and overcome the obstacles to cooperation. I visited the estate with the military governor of the region: the children staged a revolutionary play and sang revolutionary songs and then Soraya addressed the meeting on the new man needed in cooperatives: 'We need people who have something to give, not people who want only to take.'

Participation and training can overcome divisions *inside* the new land reform estates. But often, in a land reform that does not cover everyone, there are conflicts with those who have not benefited and who may, in fact, be the majority. Land reform beneficiaries as a whole can become a new rural élite, enjoying more land per head, more state assistance with credit and expert advice, more inputs of seeds and fertilizers than the rest. The excluded may be the landless, as in Iran, or they may be smallholders outside the estate system, as in Sri Lanka. In southern Peru the beneficiaries were mainly the landless labourers who used to work on the expropriated estates – in Puno province, they made up only about one seventh of the rural population (in Peru as a whole, 28 per cent benefited). The mass of smallholders derived little benefit, though many of them had also worked as casual labourers on the *latifundia* and had joined the invasions and occupations of estates in the days of agrarian unrest. They felt entitled to a share of the land, and had little respect for the new legalities of the situation. Many of the reformed estates included former village lands taken over only a few generations earlier by the landowners, by purchase, real estate fraud or force. So all over Peru the land reform estates found themselves being reinvaded by smallholders driven by land hunger.

Picotani did not escape. 'The place is so big that a little more, a little less won't matter,' neighbouring villagers remarked. Soon after the takeover some forty families tore down the steel fences around Picotani, built houses for themselves and started farming the land and grazing their animals. Open hostilities broke out and one man and many animals were killed in the exchanges.

An effective land reform must benefit all the rural poor, including the landless and the owners of parcels too small to survive on. Some land reforms include mechanisms whereby some of the profits of new land reform cooperatives are channelled to associated villages and go to build schools, health centres, roads and so on. But this does not confront the central poverty problem of excluded groups.

Smallholders need a land reform of their own, to save them from sinking into collective ruination. This may involve, for example, consolidating a man's land, fragmented into several scattered parcels through inheritance and marriage, into a single viable holding. More ambitious schemes involve pooling the land and working it as a cooperative, taking a share of the proceeds in proportion to the land owned. Whatever the method, smallholders have as much right to government services to boost their productivity as the new model estate sectors.

The new frontier

Land reform involves the redistribution of property in settled areas. Yet throughout Africa, Latin America and south-east Asia there are vast stretches of empty or underused land, inhabited only by sparse populations of pastoral nomads or primitive shifting agriculturalists. Worldwide the total area of potential farmland amounts to at least 2,500 million hectares, but of this total only 1,430 million hectares were being farmed in 1970. More than a billion extra hectares could thus be opened up, and nearly nine tenths of that in the developing countries. About half of this underused land, some 459 million hectares, lies in Latin America, where the farmed area could be expanded to four or five times its present extent. Another 260 million hectares are in Africa, where farmland could be doubled or trebled. Asia, the most crowded continent, can add only another 52 million hectares (or 19 per cent extra) to her present cropped area, and most of this lies in south-east Asia.

The migration of peasants into these areas is inevitable, whether or not governments encourage and help them. Rural poverty in settled areas, whether due to soil degradation, land fragmentation or unemployment, drives out the surplus population. The majority migrate to the cities, but many make for the empty quarters where they know there is land for the taking. Like waggon trains moving west, they head for their new frontiers in a movement of great daring and risk. Estimates indicate that they may be settling anything from 4 million hectares a year upwards. Three out of four of them are moving and starting up fresh under their own steam, while one quarter get government help.

Latin America has seen the biggest colonization movement: settlers leave the exploitation of feudal *latifundia* or the barren poverty of smallholder areas and move into the empty grass-lands or the vastnesses of the Amazon basin, flinging up tiny homesteads in defiance of hostile nature. They invariably run into difficulties. The state of land titles is often in chaos and real estate fraud is widespread. Conflict with Indians is endemic. For the Indians, the settlers are intruders onto tribal lands, while many settlers regard Indians as dangerous vermin, to be exterminated on sight. As if these human problems were not enough, settlers often have to cope with ecological disasters of their own making: rapid exhaustion of soil fertility, erosion in hilly areas, waterlogging.

In the Sahel, the dry region stretching across the south of the Sahara, a quiet migration is going on of peoples driven by drought and the slow advance of the desert. Pastoral nomads who lost their herds are building villages and turning to the (so they hope) more reliable business of agriculture. Thousands of farming families in the drier areas are leaving the lands of their ancestors and moving to better-watered lands in the south. Many of the better agricultural areas in Upper Volta, for example, are underpopulated, while the semi-arid northern regions are overcrowded. Mossi migrants from the poor districts head for the lands to the west and south, belonging to the Gurunsi, Lobi, Turkan and other tribes.

Most governments have a stake in the settlement drive. Every Latin American government with a slice of the Amazon basin has a colonization programme. Settlement schemes are common in Africa. In West Africa the eradication of river-blindness (see page 247) will free around 70 million hectares of fertile land near the rivers for intensified use. In East Africa, Kenya, Rwanda, Malawi and Zambia have extensive resettlement programmes. In Asia, Malaysia, Indonesia and Papua New Guinea have the biggest schemes.

Settlement programmes are no more free of problems than land reform, though they are politically much less explosive. Everywhere, land titles and conflicts with aborigines are a problem. But the principal dangers are ecological, arising from the interaction of natural conditions, prevailing technology and the social and economic situation of the settlers. The central problem of settlement is this: if, at this advanced stage in human history, large agricultural areas remain underused, it is for the very good reason that farmers cannot make a living out of them with the techniques they are familiar with. Some areas

– such as parts of the alluvial plains of the Amazon – may be unused because they are inaccessible, others, like the river-blindness zones, because of disease. But the vast majority of possible settlement areas are either dry zones, swamps or rain-forest. Most of them are ecologically precarious.

If settlers use their traditional methods, developed for areas with different ecological characteristics, the dry areas will become desert and the leached, infertile soil of the rainforest degrade until a survival yield can no longer be wrested from it. The only way these areas can sustain farming is with an im-proved technology. At the very least this involves retraining farmers in soil management, erosion control, use of fertilizers and so on. Often it may involve heavy investment in irrigation works or drainage. Hence almost all settlement schemes have to negotiate between the devil and the deep blue sea. On the one hand, if not enough help is given, settlers may sink into deepen-ing poverty and permanently ruin the area of colonization. On the other, they may be given too much help, cornering scarce funds and personnel that could be better used in other rural areas.

The swamp farmers

There are no roads to Delta Upang in Sumatra. To reach it, you have to catch a motorboat from the crowded wharves of Palembang and head down the broad Musi river, past the flares and cracking plants of Pertamina, Indonesia's oil company, between endless banks of jungle surrounding the odd logging mill or stilt villages, dodging fishing nets stretched across the river on bamboo frames, and then up narrowing creeks until you come upon the new settlement. Upang has the feel of a frontier town. Its muddy wharf bustles with launches and dugout canoes loading with cargoes of dried cassava, firewood, bananas, rice. A busy market has sprouted up, selling anything from hoes to batik dresses. A gang of settlers are vigorously digging a new road, others building timber-framed houses, while hordes of children play boisterously in the new school.

Delta Upang is one of dozens of new settlements that the Indonesian government is opening up on Sumatra and on Kelimantan (Borneo). The central problem Indonesia's transmigration programme is trying to alleviate is that Java, with only 7 per cent of the country's land area, has 65 per cent of the population. The average density on Java in the mid-seventies was 660 persons per square kilometre, while on Sumatra, for example, it was only thirty-eight. Land fragmentation on Java has reached levels found in few other parts of the world. Landlessness is increasing rapidly and almost every farmer has to spend part of the year in the cities earning extra cash. But population is concentrated on Java for a very good reason. Her soils are extremely fertile, thanks to a range of volcanoes along her spine that have spewed out mineral-rich ash and lava. These have been washed down on to the plains as alluvium. Irrigated paddy farming has worked these soils for centuries with no loss of fertility. The outer islands, by contrast, suffer from excessively high rainfall and are covered in rainforest and swamp. Once the forest canopy is removed, the heavily leached soils quickly lose what little fertility they have. Aboriginal farmers here use the only form of farming such a system can support without fertilizers: shifting cultivation, clearing and burning a bit of forest, growing mixed crops or dry rice for a year or two, then moving on to another patch to let the used bits recuperate for a decade or two.

Resettlement in Indonesia started under the Dutch as early as 1905, when Java, with less than half its present population, was already considered to be overpopulated. Independent Indonesia's first president, Sukarno, pushed resettlement hard. But the early schemes involved no technical surveys of soil suitability or legal surveys of land titles. They provided no roads, no schools, no health facilities, no clean water, no agricultural supplies, credit facilities or extension. Settlers used their old farming techniques brought over from Java, but without fertilizers or irrigation yields quickly fell. They saw all their great hopes evaporate, and degenerated into subsistence farmers. Land was subdivided among children, indebtedness and landlessness reappeared. The situation on Java was being reproduced on Sumatra's poorer soils. With endemic malaria, settlers were lucky to survive, let alone prosper.

Sukarno was ousted in a military coup in 1966, and under the new president, Suharto, a new generation of technocrats gained influence. No transmigration project is now undertaken without a thorough survey. Settlers get not only land, but houses and the essential back-up services of roads, credit, seeds, fertilizers, tools and extension workers.

Delta Upang is one of the new-style settlements, now a growing municipality of 7,500 souls, located on a wedge-shaped island of 26,000 hectares between the Musi and Upang rivers. There is rainfall all the year round, and the soil is a beautiful dark brown peat rich in humus and enriched with minerals washed down from volcanic areas. Until 1969 the area was a forested swamp. The bold idea behind the project was to turn the low level of the land to advantage, using the sea tides to raise the fresh river water above the land, so paddy fields could be irrigated. Primary canals were excavated to link the two rivers, with secondary and tertiary canals to carry the water on to the fields. A series of simple flap gates allowed the water to be retained on the land after the river level had dropped, and drained off as required. The river level is high enough for irrigation for four months in the year, long enough for a crop of high-yielding rice. The rest of the year, rain-fed crops can be grown. Each new settler at Upang is given two hectares of land, a house, tools, seeds and enough food for his first year or so, until he can get his land into production.

In theory, farmers could do quite well for themselves. In practice, considerable problems remain, which show the dangers inherent in even the best-laid settlement plans, and the difficulties of getting farmers to change ingrained habits. On the best seventeen hectares of land in the delta a plush research station was set up to find out the best ways of farming this land. As we sat in his luxurious bungalow, the station director told me he was recommending that farmers should keep up the organic content of the soil by digging in all waste plant material and by practising mixed farming with livestock. If they followed these guidelines, two crops of rice could be grown in a year, a wet one of two or three tonnes and a dry one of one or one and a half. This would give the farmers an annual income of 250,000 rupiahs (about $700 or £350) which could be augmented by growing cassava, bananas and so on. Then why, I wondered, did most of the farmers seem to be ignoring this guidance and remaining at subsistence level? Why were yields so much lower (typically about two tonnes per hectare per year) and ecological dangers much higher than they need be?

To find out, I talked to some of the individual settlers. Jasmo Suwito came to Upang from central Java eight years ago. His father had been a landless labourer. After several years of fruitless search for casual work on the land, Suwito joined the exodus to the cities and became a rickshaw driver in Jogjakarta. There he heard about the government's transmigration programme. At the time of my visit, at the tail end of the dry season, he had only one fifth of his two hectares under cultivation, growing cassava. He and three of his six children were hacking back the growth of weeds from the rest of his land, ready to plant rice in time for the high tides that would irrigate the fields. I asked him if he would dig the weeds in (as the station recommended). He said he would burn them. Why? Because it would take too much work to dig them in and he couldn't afford to pay labourers. I asked him why he farmed so little of his land during the dry season. It was too much work, he said. Why so – he was going to clear it now to plant rice, why couldn't he manage to do that twice in the year? It wasn't worth the effort, he told me. The rats would eat whatever he planted and he couldn't afford poison. So what, I asked, did Suwito do during the dry season if he wasn't farming his land? A bit of construction work for the transmigration department, a bit of tree felling in the forest around, to get firewood for sale at three rupiahs a stick. Neither of these activities would continue for long.

The basic reason for all the settlers' deviations from recommended practice was their poverty. They were unable to pay for the inputs of pesticide or extra labour that would be needed to get the higher yields, and this, in turn, kept them poor. Instead of conserving the soil, they were mining it and, as rice yields fell, switching to cassava (which gives more calories per hectare than any other crop). The organic matter in the soil was shrinking by five centimetres a year and would be exhausted within a decade or so. The settlers are allowed to sell their plots after a certain period: already some have done so and moved out, while others have acquired two or more plots, and employ landless labourers to work them. Java is reappearing again on Sumatra, despite all the effort put in.

The opposite extreme of this danger of regression into poverty occurs when lavish settlement programmes create a new élite of rural privilege. Brazil's Amazon settlements provide farmers with huge 100 hectare spreads and create a new kulak class employing, and exploiting, landless labourers. The average incomes of settlers on projects supported by the World Bank were over three times higher than rural averages for the countries involved. Official settlement programmes are often very expensive. One Zambia project cost a staggering $67,730 per family. Costs on other World Bank supported projects varied from an unobjectionable $820 on a Rwanda scheme to $23,400 in Keratong, Malaysia.

The ever-present danger is that settlement programmes can eat up large chunks of scarce agricultural budgets and siphon funds away from the rural majority towards the creation of small rural élites in isolated pockets. Malaysia, for example, spends half her agricultural budget on resettlement. Usually sponsored settlers are provided with a level of services – schools, roads, health posts, agricultural extension, credit and so on – far above the average for the country. And the returns are often disappointing. Michael Nelson, who studied resettlement schemes in Latin America, concluded that few spheres of development had a history of failure to match that of government-sponsored colonization in the humid tropics. Land reform expert Erich Jacoby comments: 'The history of human settlement reflects an endless waste of human and material resources.' Often the money is better spent in developing existing areas – a World Bank survey found that this gave a rate of return on investment 50 per cent higher than in resettlement. Moreover, settlement rarely absorbs more than a fraction of the surplus population from dense areas. Even if Indonesia, for example, succeeds in its aim of resettling 100,000 people a year from Java, a rate that it has never approached in the past, that will only amount to about 7 per cent of the island's annual population increase. Official schemes in Latin America are calculated to have created jobs for only one in fifty of the extra rural workforce created by population increase.

All in all, the majority of settlement schemes so far have been either human and ecological disasters, or diversions from the central task of improving already settled areas. Yet, whatever one may think of the way it has usually been done, resettlement is probably inevitable. The Food and Agriculture Organization's Indicative World Plan for Agriculture states that new land will have to be opened up at the rate of some 10 million hectares a year if food production is to keep up with population increase. If settlers are left to their own devices, traditional techniques get transplanted to areas where they can do irreparable ecological damage. Governments have to get involved, if only in directing settlers to the most suitable areas and providing them with agricultural advice and inputs. Settlement should not divert funds, scarce experts or attention from existing areas of poverty. It should not be used, as it often is in Latin America, as an alternative to land reform. It should not create a new rural élite privileged by higher rates of investment and better services than everyone else. It ought to respect existing ecology and indigenous peoples. Provided these requirements are met, settlement can have a valid place, opening up new areas, exploiting underused resources and providing land for some of the landless.

Access to land is central to the attack on rural poverty. It is a necessary condition of progress – but it is not, in itself, sufficient. Other factors are essential if the land is to be made more productive. It is to these topics that the next chapter turns.

4 The green, blue and other revolutions: developing rural areas

Ramdullah's great walled compounds are scattered widely across the red, parched land. Each one is a tiny fortress as complex as a miniature city, with a high wall encircling a maze of round huts and pointed straw roofs, and granaries and dividing walls, tracing in space the convoluted family relationships of the seventy-odd people who live in each compound.

The soil in this northern region of Upper Volta, as in so much of the tropics, is poor. In the short, four-month wet season torrential rains tear off the topsoil in sheets and wash away the valuable plant foods, leaving an excess of aluminium and iron, whose oxides give the earth its rusty hue. The traditional technique of cultivation, common to sub-Saharan Africa, is slash and burn. A patch of bush is cleared and fired, cultivated for one year or at most two, then left to recuperate for six to twelve years. But the growing population has meant that fallow periods have been cut back and soil fertility has no time to be restored. Yields are falling, plant cover is slowly thinning out, erosion is worsening. Already near-by patches are becoming hardpans of dead earth. Though some locals own cattle, they are pastured by a nomad tribe, the Fulani. Their dung and draught power is unavailable for manure or ploughing, while their trampling hooves and hungry mouths aggravate the problems of erosion. The situation here is typical of sub-Saharan Africa: primitive techniques that are degrading and destroying the soil, little or no use of fertilizer, no water control, no mixed farming.

Driving to Ramdullah down a bumpy dirt path intended only for foot, we passed through desiccated, barren lands where even the shrubs had died. The southward creep of the Sahara was almost palpable. Yet suddenly, rounding a bend, we came upon an astonishing, incongruous sight – a bright green sea of potato plants, with dozens of men in kaftans rushing up and down the rows, a watering-can in each hand, to and fro from a new concrete well. A market garden was flourishing here, in the parched Sahel, in the depth of the dry season when normally there is no work to do in the fields.

Ramdullah is one of the many scattered places known locally as *bas-fonds* or swampy bottoms. It lies at the lowest point of the surrounding area. Rains wash down the gentle slopes and gather here before they seep into the earth. Much of the topsoil that the downpours carry away settles here, so the earth is darker and more fertile. Yet the villagers of Ramdullah never cultivated this richest portion of their lands. In the dry season there was no water, and in the wet there was too much and the hollow became a swamp. The solution would hit any Asian farmer in the eye: irrigate in the dry season, grow rice in the wet. But the idea is as exotic to the local Mossi tribe as space travel. They have never practised these things, and do not know how to. They do not possess the necessary equipment, or seeds of suitable crops, and have no surplus funds to buy them. They could not, unaided, break out of the technology trap that condemned them to a low and dwindling subsistence.

To help villages like Ramdullah, Upper Volta established a Rural Development Fund with the help of loans from the World Bank and grants from other aid agencies. The fund decided to avoid large-scale prestige projects and to concentrate on cheap, small-scale improvements that could benefit a large number of villages: wells that could tap the groundwater far below; better storage facilities to save the harvest from the ravages of termites and other pests; modest feeder roads linking villages with the main highways to allow them to get their produce to market more easily; and hundreds of minor land and water improvements, from erosion control earthworks to small dams. The idea was to do the job with an absolute minimum of equipment and as cheaply as possible. Each village had to agree to the proposals after officials of the Regional Development Office had explained them to local chiefs and notables. Some were unconvinced and unwilling to take on the extra work that would be required. Others were won over after being shown around pilot villages where the new techniques were being tried out successfully. To prove their commitment, villagers had to provide free labour for the improvement works, which helped to reduce costs even further.

Ramdullah was willing to give it a try. The work started before the rains of 1975. A young extension worker got the villagers to build low dikes to hold and control the water. They were given rice seeds and fertilizer and credit to buy them with. Some villagers got cold feet at the risk involved and the back-breaking work required at the busiest time of the year, but most opted in, and within a couple of months this bit of the African scrubland was looking like the plains of the Ganges. Had the crop been a failure at this point, the project would have been doomed and the villagers would never again have listened to an outsider trying to get them to experiment with new methods. But the harvest was good enough to allow every participant to pay off the seed loan and pocket a decent cash surplus. That convinced even the waverers. Tradition is sometimes a barrier in development projects. But most Third World peasants are adaptable pragmatists. They are willing to adopt any innovation so long as the risk involved is not too high and they are convinced it will help them survive and prosper.

The following dry season, when they would normally have been idling their days away or patching the odd crumbling mud wall, the men of Ramdullah dug out a deep well which was lined with concrete. They were provided with seed potatoes and watering-cans on credit, and every villager was allotted his thirty rows in the neatly enclosed field by the well. The potatoes would be ready for lifting in March, a few weeks after my visit, and they looked very healthy plants. The local Regional Development Office had set up a marketing cooperative grandly named the Voltaic Union of Horticulturalists, which sold potatoes and the other vegetable crops such as beans and onions to the European market, where they would arrive in the shops just when prices were highest. With the proceeds of the sale, the villagers would be able to pay back their loans. The development fund would be topped up again and become a revolving fund, so that the progressive improvement of the first wave of villages could be used to finance development in the next group.

The innovations had brought about a metamorphosis for Ramdullah's hundred families. The dry season was no longer a dead time of chronic underemployment, when young men would migrate to the Ivory Coast in search of work. The village's unused human and material resources were being exploited to give a massive boost to local subsistence incomes. All this had been effected at minimal cost, most of which would be repaid by the villagers from direct cash benefits which they had begun to reap within six months of work commencing.

The introduction of irrigation was putting Ramdullah through Asia's earlier agricultural revolution. The next phase – about to begin when I visited Upper Volta – was to take her and the other villages through Europe's agricultural revolution, based on mixed farming and crop rotation. Families with the biggest area of land (which, as land is allocated by the chief on a basis of so much per head, were also the biggest families) were to get loans of about $500 each to buy two oxen, a plough, a little cart and a harrow. The plough, combined with the use of fertilizers plus the manure from the cattle, would enable them to farm the same plot of land permanently, so they could farm a larger area. Crop rotation would be practised: the staple millet, followed by a cash crop, cotton, followed by groundnuts, a protein-rich legume whose root nodules put nitrogen back into the soil. The whole experiment would mean a lot more work, but it would produce a correspondingly higher income. There were fewer takers for this offer, which involved greater risk; but it was hoped that other families would follow suit when they saw the benefits to be reaped. One danger about this scheme is that it could produce, in the relatively egalitarian society of the African village, new divisions of rich and poor families.

Ramdullah is an excellent example of the new style of rural development. In the older version, still pursued in most countries, the priority was boosting agricultural production in the fastest possible time: extra food production would save foreign exchange on imports, extra cash crops would earn more foreign exchange from exports. The foreign exchange would then be spent, not on the rural sector, but on building up the modern industrial and urban sector. Ideas of how production was to be expanded were imported from the West: mechanization and commercialization were desirable, and for that purpose larger farms were better than small. Government investment, expert advice, credit and supplies were concentrated in the best-endowed areas which would show the quickest return. Within these areas, the larger farmers were favoured, if not officially, then under the counter because of their political influence over local government employees. Where public works, dams or roads were necessary, large-scale projects were all the rage, and Western machinery and usually Western contractors would be imported to execute them.

Little or no thought was given to the social effects of this approach. Larger farmers and favoured areas raked in all the benefits, earning enough extra money to buy out the poor and make them landless. Poverty and inequality tended to increase. More food was produced, but the poor could afford even less of it than before. Plenty and want grew in parallel.

The new strategy for rural development is based on the premise that the situation of the poor can be improved now – not after a century or two of intolerable sacrifice. It is based on the belief, backed by much solid evidence, that food production can be increased in ways that also reduce poverty and inequality and distribute widely the extra income needed if the poor are to buy the extra food produced. In other words, growth in rural areas can be combined with social justice. The strategy aims to help primarily the small and marginal farmers and the landless labourers, on the assumption that the rich will manage to help themselves. It means providing equal access – or preferential access – for the poor to credit, supplies and extension. It aims to reach the widest possible number, and that means it has to be cheap. And it tries to create the maximum amount of employment, so public works are labour-intensive and often small-scale, carried out with large armies of labourers rather than a few gargantuan earth-movers. In these ways the benefits of extra production are spread as widely as possible, so the maximum number are involved in both creating and enjoying the fruits of growth, and so the poor will have the money to buy some of the extra food, and not be condemned to starve in the midst of plenty.

Palms and progress: outgrower schemes

The road to Ehania roller-coasters up and down through dense rainforest, layered from undergrowth to towering *iroko* and ironwood trees, held up with buttresses like the fins of space rockets. Creepers clothe everything, even the telegraph poles, and crawl along the wires. Until the early seventies this southeast corner of the Ivory Coast was an underdeveloped, inaccessible region with poor communications and scattered villages of subsistence farmers.

The jungle clears, and is replaced by a disciplined, neatly spaced forest of oil palms, not the tall spindly village variety but a new, high-yielding breed with short trunks, designed to come into production much earlier. Cattle are grazing among the ferns and grasses that grow under the trees, making double use of the land, and a hawk takes off from the crowning fronds of a palm, in search of snakes or bush rats. The plantation, run by the state-owned company Sodepalm, spreads for miles, like waves of a dark green sea, washing over the gently undulating terrain to the horizon. We pass a neat modern settlement where the plantation labourers live – most of them are migrants from Upper Volta. Two plumes of smoke, one steam white, the other black, announce the oil-pressing mill at the heart of the plantation. Here heavy bunches of palm nuts, yellow, orange and deep scarlet, arrive in lorries for boiling and pressing. Their oil is stored in tall cylinders ready for transport to the bottling factory or the wharves in Abidjan.

The most intriguing feature of Ehania is not the factory or the industrial plantation, but lies outside the borders of the 12,000 hectare company estate. The factory also serves as the nucleus for some 2,400 smallholders, most of them local villagers, who have started to plant the new varieties of oil palm on their land and will soon have almost as big an acreage as the company. Ehania is the centre of an outgrower scheme, a new style of egalitarian cash crop development, vastly preferable to the old style of plantation with its gross inequalities, exploitation and rigid authority structure – and more efficient than West Africa's traditional network of independent small planters. It is a neat way of improving small farmers' techniques and materials and boosting their incomes. The factory provides local farmers who wish to take part with improved seed stock and inputs such as fertilizer, credit and extension advice. Every farmer who participates gets attention, however small his farm, and those who opt out soon join in when they see the money that is to be made. The factory also provides a guaranteed, close-at-hand market for the farmer's production, which it collects at regular intervals from his farm.

The potential incomes are high. When I met Ido Ibrahim, a slender, Western-dressed Gurunsi from Upper Volta, on his farm, he was cutting bunches of nuts with a matchet mounted on a long bamboo pole, while his two wives looked on. For twenty years Ibrahim had been a chauffeur in Abidjan, the Ivory Coast's racy capital, earning good pay but spending a lot of that in extortionately high rents for a modest lower-class flat. The promised earnings from the outgrower scheme were attractive enough to make him leave the city for the land, proving that if rural incomes can be improved, the usual direction of migration might be reversed. He was now earning about 80,000 francs CFA a month (at the time about $360 or £180), a very handsome income by local standards.

Several local villages had joined in the scheme. The coastal settlement of Aby used to make a passable living from subsistence farming, cocoa, coffee and fishing. When I visited the place the chief, sixty-seven-year-old Kossi Bile, grey-haired and green-robed, husband of two wives and father of twelve sons and daughters, greeted us, had some chairs brought, glasses wiped and beer got out of the fridge, and explained how the village had profited. When Sodepalm's extension workers had come round to persuade them to join, the villagers had decided to go softly softly, and had started with a small area first to assess the situation. They soon saw it was good, and planted more, so the average family now has four hectares of oil palm each and can earn up to 100,000 CFA per month (about $450). As the palms can be cropped continually, the money comes in every month, regular and reliable, whereas the earnings from coffee and cocoa would arrive only once a year and they never knew for sure how much it would be. With the extra income an entire new village has been built on a hillside overlooking the old.

'The President (Houphouet-Boigny) has said we must transform the Ivory Coast, so we are doing it,' said the old chief. 'We have built a maternity centre, two new classrooms and a house for the schoolmaster so we can get a good teacher here. We were sleeping before, but we are awake now.' All over the Ivory Coast growing incomes from farming have stimulated a flurry of spending on village improvements which, in turn, has generated more local jobs in construction, transport, cement, furniture, sanitary ware, providing a local market for industry which would not have existed if the rural sector had been neglected.

Outgrower schemes in oil palm, similar to this one, have been started in Ghana, Nigeria and Cameroon. In Guinea the smallholders grow pineapples, in Tanzania and Kenya sugar. The pattern is suitable for a wide range of cash crops and allows for small-scale, decentralized agro-industry to be developed in the core plantations, canning fruit, ginning cotton, processing beverage crops, rubber or fibres.

The blue revolution: water

Wherever land is scarce, water can become a substitute for extra land. To irrigate dry land, or extend the number of months in the year when irrigated land can be irrigated, is like doubling or trebling the amount of land each farmer has, or like multi-storey building in crowded cities. Some market gardeners in Singapore manage to get eight successive crops a year from the same patch. The extension of irrigation, and the improvement of existing irrigation systems, can increase the yield of land more than any other change, and will be crucial in increasing the world's food supply. In 1977 some 224 million hectares were irrigated. Surveys indicate that perhaps another 270 million hectares, more than half of that in the Third World, could be added. Asia could nearly double her irrigated area, Latin America treble hers, and Africa multiply hers by a factor of seven.

Until recently the preferred manner of extending irrigation was through massive schemes, giant dams and giant expenditures. The great dams – like the Aswan, Volta or Kariba – had their social and ecological problems, but their benefits were indisputable: hydroelectric power, fishery in the new artificial lakes, improved river transport, greater control over flood and drought, irrigation. But the era when governments thought only of big dams is coming to a close, principally because the most promising sites were the first to be filled and fewer now remain. Emphasis is now shifting on to small-scale schemes that allow scarce funds to be spread more equitably over a larger area, that can more easily be built by labour-intensive methods, providing much needed work for the rural underemployed, and that are more easily and cheaply maintained.

Indonesia has embarked on a vast programme embracing hundreds of such small-scale works, both in rehabilitating and improving existing irrigation systems and in building small new ones. The Dutch started to build large irrigation systems here around 1820. When they finally pulled out in 1949, after fighting a losing battle against the national liberation struggle, they had done nothing to prepare Indonesia for independence and had trained no locals to understand and maintain the system. In 1949 there were only 2,000 university graduates, and a mere handful of them were engineers. Under Indonesia's first ruler, Sukarno, no funds were set aside for the upkeep of irrigation works, so they fell into disrepair. The canals silted up and floods became more common. The situation was aggravated as population pressure and land shortage pushed farmers on to higher and steeper hillsides in the watersheds. Trees were cut down and the rain washed more soil down, degrading the land upstream and ruining the irrigation systems downstream.

With the new high yielding varieties of rice, efficient irrigation makes a tremendous difference to the productivity of land. In most of Java, for example, there are only seven months of rain. Many of the new varieties of rice take four months to mature, so without continuous irrigation only one crop can be grown. If irrigation can be extended for only one extra month, two crops are possible, and three if it can be provided all the year round. Two or three crops means doubled or trebled incomes for farmers. It means that tiny plots that previously could not support a family suddenly become a viable proposition. And it multiplies the jobs available for the landless or land-hungry and spreads them more evenly through the year.

With the backing of massive loans from the World Bank, Indonesia is now putting immense effort into extending and improving the irrigation network. In 1968 only three million hectares, less than a quarter of the agricultural land in use, were irrigated and there had been no expansion of the irrigated area since 1940. Since 1968 the area has been increased by some 100,000 hectares a year.

The rural areas of Java are probably the most crowded in the entire world. Population densities are often higher than in Western cities and land is so scarce that even the narrow raised paths between paddy fields are used to grow groundnuts or cassava, with the roots sticking out of the sides. Many of the canal systems here had deteriorated seriously. The Dutch Van der Wyck canal, for example, could carry only 40 per cent of the water it was designed for. Sluice gates had rusted shut so silt could no longer be flushed out. Weirs and beds were worn through and leaked. Precious water that should have been carefully marshalled on to the fields was seeping away into the ground, or destroying crops in floods and running off uselessly into the sea. In a hungry area, water is as valuable as gold, and every drop needs to be devoted to the prime purpose of food production.

The Van der Wyck canal was rehabilitated in a project aided by Britain's Ministry of Overseas Development: the work was directed by British engineers, part of whose job was to train Indonesians so they could take over. The Van der Wyck had its beds dredged of silt and its channels widened to take more water. Aqueducts were built to carry natural rivers and streams, with their load of silt, over or under the canal. Great barriers were built to hold back freak flows of *laha* – sand and stones from Java's active volcanoes, mixed with flash floods, which flatten anything in their path. Modest improvements like these have led to increases in yields of anything up to 80 per cent.

Pulling all the stops out: integrated rural development

Farming is an immensely complicated business. It involves physical factors like land, tools, seeds, fertilizer, pesticides, water, roads to market; it involves the economics of credit, rent, prices of inputs and outputs; social patterns of land-holding, relations between landowners, tenants and labourers; and last but not least the farmer himself, his physiology and mental make-up, his knowledge and skills and his productivity as influenced by anything from the state of his health to what (if anything) he had for breakfast. Development projects have often failed because they concentrated on only one of these factors and ignored the rest. The most ambitious projects aim to transform the entire situation of the peasant, to remove every strand in the net that holds him in the poverty trap.

This approach is known as integrated rural development. In the most complete versions, farming techniques are improved by way of better seeds and tools and farmer education. The whole system of credit and supplies is revamped to make sure farmers can physically get hold of the things they need. All possible improvements are made to the land. Local health, nutrition and education services get attention, and there are often strong elements of grassroots participation.

One of the most comprehensive and innovative of these schemes was the Comilla project, set up in the east of Bangladesh in 1959 by Comilla's Academy of Rural Development. The project organized local smallholders into village cooperatives, which undertook to hold weekly meetings, keep accounts and adopt new agricultural practices. Instead of having government-appointed extension workers, each co-op elected one of its members to be trained in farming and management techniques and to act as their educator. Local youths were taught to drive tractors and operate pumps, literate villagers learned how to keep account books. Local education was improved, drafting pupils, teachers and villagers to extend primary school buildings and upgrading the little schools of village mosques which taught children to read the Koran.

Many integrated rural development projects focus on areas of high agricultural potential where quick gains in production can be expected. The Puebla project, initiated in 1967 with the support of the Rockefeller Foundation, deliberately picked a low-potential area in the rain-fed central highlands of Mexico, where subsistence farmers holding around two hectares each were scraping a bare existence out of the soil, using primitive techniques. Puebla was inspired by the researchers at CIMMYT, the International Centre for Improvement of Maize and Wheat, who were concerned that only large commercialized farmers were adopting the new seeds they were developing. They developed varieties specially designed for the conditions of the poor highland farmer. The project used extension agents trained at the local agricultural college, and organized demonstration plots on farmers' land. Credit – lack of which had been a major obstacle to technical improvement – was provided through local credit groups based on the farmers' own informal social gatherings.

But social justice in development is an elusive goal, and even integrated, poverty-oriented rural development projects can fail to benefit everyone. The landless, or owners of plots so small that they depend on paid labour, are often left out. In many Comilla villages, only half the farmers joined the cooperatives and the better-off ones benefited most. To prevent this kind of injustice, far-reaching national reforms may be required which many governments may be reluctant to enact.

Integrated rural development often also falls short of its potential because it is not integrated enough – in other words, because one or other of the factors that influence production and incomes is still left out. But perhaps the chief caveat about the approach so far has been its concentration, fostered by aid donors who prefer to see quickly visible results, on 'projects'. Most schemes involve selecting favoured areas and giving them hothouse treatment. They attract more than their share of national and international funds, absorb scarce qualified manpower in duplicating national services, pre-empt supplies and get first priority on funds for credit. Even if they succeed in distributing their benefits evenly to everyone in the lucky project area, simply to pick on a limited group of people for exceptional treatment is itself inequitable. The only really egalitarian rural development project would be one that embraced the whole country. It would, in the jargon, be a 'programme' rather that a 'project', benefiting all farmers regardless of their size or location. Programmes that promise the most widely spread benefits are research activities, developing new seeds and techniques suitable for small farmers of all types of crop, nationwide extension programmes teaching these innovations to all farmers, credit programmes enabling them to buy the extra inputs they need, and marketing and price systems that give farmers an incentive to produce more.

Phasing out the loan sharks

Poor farmers are often caught in a technological poverty trap: their land does not produce enough surplus for them to afford the new seeds, tools and fertilizers they need to make it produce more. Credit is the only way out of this trap: loans at reasonable rates of interest can easily be repaid out of the additional production they make possible. Yet throughout most of the developing world the credit system operates against the small farmer, perpetuating the poverty trap.

There are, it is true, many government institutions that lend at low rates of interest, usually between 6 and 15 per cent a year. In some cases their interest rate is lower than the inflation rate. On average, some 40 per cent of their loans are not repaid because of defaulting. So official credit often operates at a loss, and is, in fact, a disguised form of handout. Yet, for the most part, this subsidy only reaches the big farmers who need it least. In Africa, perhaps only 5 per cent of farmers get official credit, in Asia and Latin America around 15 per cent. One study in the Philippines found that less than a third of the farmers took up 98 per cent of the credit, while in Pakistan the poorest 60 per cent of farmers got only 3 per cent of credit between them. The larger farmers monopolize credit for a variety of reasons. They usually have social and political influence with bank officials. They can offer more land as collateral, and loans for the larger amounts that big farmers want are cheaper to administer and involve much less paperwork than a larger number of small loans.

So smallholders, and even more so tenants who have no land for collateral, are condemned to resort to another source of credit: the moneylender. In the commercial sector, interest rates are often extortionate. In thirty-three countries surveyed by the World Bank, rates averaged 44 per cent, ranging from a low of 20 per cent in Jordan, to 100 per cent in Bolivia, 150 per cent in Ivory Coast and 200 per cent in Nigeria. Moneylenders' rates are high partly because official credit is so scarce, while the demand for loans is strong because of poverty. At these rates of interest, private loans would rarely be used to finance an agricultural improvement, as few innovations would produce a profit good enough to repay the loan. So they are resorted to only out of dire necessity, to pay for food after the granaries have been emptied down to the last grain, or to cover inescapable social expenses such as weddings or funerals.

The newer style of official programme aims to make credit available to the excluded small farmers. The total amount of funds available can be increased by mobilizing the savings of farmers, which are often tied up in unproductive hedges like gold or excess cattle. This may involve creating mobile bank branches that travel round the villages. These also make credit more accessible to the farmer who may be unable to afford the fare or the time to visit a bank branch in a town twenty miles away or more. Credit can be assured for small farmers only by specifically reserving for them a large proportion of the funds available – in India, only small farmers get government credit. To help tenants and sharecroppers who do not own land, some banks now accept the eventual crop as collateral. The hardest group to help through an official credit scheme are the landless. Loaning to small farmers creates more employment than loaning to large. Banks should also (though few do) refrain from lending for investments that will reduce employment in labour-surplus areas. But the only way to break the back of the iniquitous rural debt problem that causes so much suffering and landlessness in Asia is to solve the problems of inadequate incomes and inequality that give rise to it.

The power of knowledge: agricultural extension

Raimundo Roja owns 100 hectares of Amazonian jungle in Brazil, off the narrow dirt road that is grandly named the Trans-amazonic Highway. He works hard, but as he was a sugar labourer before joining the government settlement scheme he has little experience of the crops he is now growing: rice, bananas, coffee, cocoa and peppers. Like many local settlers, he made the mistake of growing too much rice in 1976. Local warehouses could not store all that was produced and stopped buying. Roja lost fifty-five sacks of rice, worth about $250. In 1977 the worst problem was with the cocoa trees: leaf-cutter bees had carved neat half-moons out of the foliage, and the pods were black with rot. The trees were not flourishing, he complained to the agronomist accompanying me. He had tried to put fertilizer on them, but it didn't work. Four large and expensive sacks of granulated fertilizer had been cut open and were dissolving away in the afternoon rains. The agronomist asked Roja where he applied the fertilizer. Round the trunk, said Roja. Ah, said my guide, you should have been putting it in a circle level with the trees' outermost leaves. That is roughly where their feeding roots would be.

All the new land, all the fertilizers and new seeds in the world are of little value if the farmer does not know how to put them to good use and cannot market the produce. On the other hand, a farmer who can be taught to improve his cultivation practices can often achieve tremendous gains in output at no cost beyond a little care and planning and a few hours' extra work. Agricultural extension, the provision of expert advice to all farmers great or small, is one of the most important of all the factors that can boost production. Knowledge is potentially the most egalitarian of all assets. It costs the farmer little or nothing, requires no credit or foreign exchange, and can be spread to the tiniest smallholder as well as to the great feudal landlord. It can also be a superb investment from the government's point of view. Costs can be as little as $1 per hectare and achieve yield increases worth sixty to a hundred times more – a cost-benefit ratio which no other kind of investment in development can hope to match.

Yet agricultural extension rarely fulfils its immense potential in developing countries. Typically the extension worker may have to service as many as 4,000 farmers scattered over a large area. The individual farmer sees him rarely, or often not at all, and has no chance to develop that relationship of confidence without which he will not accept new techniques. The extension worker, for his part, may have little more to offer than a stereotyped lecture that bears little relation to the ordinary farmer's problems. Usually he is not kept in touch with the latest conclusions of research. Underpaid, undersupervised, with no hope of improving his expertise and little feedback in concrete results, he may sink into demoralized lethargy, while the national agricultural research programme continues its investigation in a social vacuum, unaware of the real conditions of production.

A new model for extension work, able to reach large numbers of small farmers cheaply and quickly, has been developed by Daniel Benor and is now being applied in several World-Bank-assisted projects. At the base is the village extension worker, covering 800 or so farmers. Out of these he selects about eighty 'contact farmers' chosen in consultation with villagers – adaptable, trusted people whose example is likely to be followed by their neighbours. These contact farmers are formed into groups of ten. One day each fortnight, following a fixed schedule, the extension worker visits one of the groups and teaches them about the cultivation techniques that will be required in the following few weeks of the farming year. The worker himself attends training sessions one day a week, when he is taught, or refreshed about, what he will be teaching the following week. The contact farmers, in their turn, act as the unpaid bottom level of extension work, and undertake to try out the recommended techniques and to explain them to their neighbours.

An extract from the log of a typical extension worker gives some idea of what happens. In November 1975, Bimal Choudhury met eight of his contact farmers in Rokanpur School, Memari Block, West Bengal, India. The topic was potatoes. Choudhury explained how to apply soil insecticide before the final ploughing, how to cut seed tubers in the right sizes, keeping the eyes, how to treat them with mercury before planting, how much fertilizer to use. And, as the programme involves participation and not just a one-way flow of instructions from on high, the farmers in their turn informed Choudhury that that was all very fine, but they had to have water at the right moment and it would help if the irrigation and waterways engineers could start providing water when they needed it, instead of several days or weeks later. Choudhury agreed to tell the engineers about it and see what could be done.

The village extension workers are another type of barefoot technician: their education need be no higher than secondary level, though they should have some farming background.

Every eight workers are supervised and trained by an agricultural extension officer, who is a professional. He can call on the services of specialists in agronomy, plant protection and training in each district, whose job it is to keep in close touch with the findings of research programmes and to apply them to their own areas. Through a system of joint committees of research and extension services, the findings of research can be quickly passed on and be in use by every farmer in the country within a matter of months. Conversely, the extension services can advise the researchers on the concrete, day-to-day problems of farmers, so research can be geared to overcome these.

The training and visit system deliberately begins by advising farmers on their major food crops, and its first recommendations usually involve only improved cultivation techniques. These can produce sure results at no cost or risk to the farmer other than additional labour, so he develops confidence in the service.

The impact of this type of improved extension service can be considerable. In the Seyhan irrigation project in Turkey, farmers saw their profits from cotton soar by 1,300 per cent within five years of the start of a new training and visit extension programme, and methods spread widely and quickly from contact farmers to their neighbours. In the Chambal area in Madhya Pradesh state, India, the scheme boosted rice yields by 80 per cent and doubled mustard yields, and the performance of smaller farmers improved faster than that of larger operators. A team of bigwigs touring Chambal noticed one field with an excellent stand of crops, but could not find the farmer to congratulate him. Neighbours explained that he was now spending a lot of time at the temple giving thanks for the extension service: this was his first good crop in years.

What happens to the farmer's increased output, though, is just as important as his improved inputs and skills. All peasants are potential self-improvers, but they do need some material incentive before they will invest their hard-earned savings or extra sweat, or risk their families' food supplies, in some new method. Extra production that cannot be consumed at home or marketed, like the Amazonian rice, is a bitter harvest for the farmer. Governments also have to help small farmers to market their produce. This might involve setting up marketing cooperatives which cut out the parasitic middleman: one Peruvian village clubbed together to buy a truck to take its potatoes to the distant market town, and more than doubled its earnings. Small feeder roads have to be laid on, as well as prestige highways, so peasants can get their goods to market. The price of agricultural produce has to be fixed so as to give the farmer an incentive to produce more – all too often the city gets cheap food while the farmer pays dear for city products. And more government services – clean water, health, education – have to be channelled into the rural areas, as all are factors which contribute to productivity.

Helping the landless is a trickier task: only land reform can give them their own farm, or, where land is insufficient for that (as in the most crowded parts of Asia), at least their own house-plot and if possible a vegetable garden. Apart from this, the task is to increase the demand for labour in rural areas, in relation to the supply. Population programmes can help to reduce the supply of surplus labour, which keeps wages down. Demand can be increased by discouraging those types of mechanization which, on balance, reduce the need for labour in labour-surplus areas, and by encouraging labour-intensive methods of cultivation. Even then, the land itself cannot employ all the rural population, so governments will have to encourage the development of rural industries and carry on labour-intensive programmes of public works.

The small-scale irrigation programme in Indonesia, for example, uses as much labour as possible. In Bali I saw women repairing roads by hand, laying down rows of selected cobble-stones as carefully as if they were a mosaic. Others were digging out deep, long tunnels with pickaxes, removing the debris in basketfuls on their heads. A new weir across a river was getting a meticulous finish of tiny, smooth pebbles, set one by one into concrete. My Balinese guide apologized for the primitive methods – and was greatly relieved when I commented that it would be much more primitive to use bulldozers and leave so many people without work.

These programmes of labour-intensive public works are often scheduled for the slack farming season when the landless can get little work. They neatly use up surplus labour to build up the capital of infrastructure that rural areas need for more rapid development. But there is always a danger that most of the long-term benefits of this type of project will go into the pockets of the better-off farmers. The labourers may collect modest wages for as long as the project lasts, but landowners will enjoy a permanent rise in the value and productivity of their land, and in their incomes – and the more land they own, the more they profit. These inequities are bound to arise in the absence of radical land reforms, but they can at least be alleviated if farmers pay progressive levies for the new services and if the funds collected are used to create permanent jobs for the landless in industry or services.

A revolution in the green revolution

The first wave of the green revolution, in the fifties and sixties, concentrated on ways of getting a quick return in extra production from the world's two major food crops, wheat and rice. Varieties were developed that were superbly efficient at converting fertilizer into foodgrain. They worked wonders on farms with good soil, plentiful water and enough capital or credit for fertilizers and insecticides. They brought immense benefits to medium and large farmers in areas already favoured by nature. But they did little to help small farmers, dryland farmers and cultivators of other staple crops such as pulses like beans or chickpeas, roots such as cassava and yam, and coarse grains – millet, sorghum and maize. Even within the favoured areas, the small farmers could not get the credit needed for the extra inputs the new seeds demanded. And hundreds of millions of peasants lived in areas that were not suited for the new varieties, in hilly, arid or swampy areas, with poor, leached soils, subject to droughts, or floods, or both. The green revolution sped past them, leaving them by the wayside, or even, at times, worse off than before.

I saw the contrast between poor dry and rich wet areas on Bali in 1977. Areas that are irrigated all the year round have a clean and prosperous look, bicycles and traders abound, family temples have fresh coats of paint and houses are being rebuilt in solid brick. Above the 500 metre contour, the land cannot be irrigated outside the rainy season, because the water table is too low. The crops here are rain-fed rice, soybeans, cassava and plantains. There are as yet no improved seeds for these, while Indonesia's credit and supplies system for intensifying rice production does not apply to them. So yields are low as they always have been, and the upland villages have a lean and hungry, rundown look. Compound walls are crumbling, temple paint flaking and fading, living-room walls are made of woven straw.

Inequality, and poverty for the neglected groups, were not the only result of the earlier approach of research. As all the emphasis of government programmes was put on cereal production and inputs for this were often supplied to farmers at artificially low prices, production of protein-rich legumes and pulses fell off everywhere. So while the green revolution allowed food production per head to remain more or less static despite population increases, the quality of nutrition may have actually declined. And the extra food production did not provide the urban and rural poor with enough money to buy themselves a better diet. It became clear that the balance of food production, and the distribution of income to buy it, were as important as increasing the sheer quantity of food.

There were ecological and economic problems too. The new varieties were less resistant to local pests and diseases, less tolerant of drought or flooding. The extra fertilizer and insecticide they needed brought pollution problems. Worst of all, after the first heady three or four years, the rapid initial spread of new miracle varieties was slowing down and grinding to a halt. They had come up against a barrier of poverty among farmers whose land, or whose pockets, could not accommodate the new seeds and all that went with them. Eventually, the green revolution looked as if it might no longer be able to produce extra food faster than population was growing.

A revolution in the revolution was urgently needed – a second green revolution, bringing benefits to the groups that the first one neglected. The small farmer, the poor regions, had to be brought into the picture, not just because it was their right to benefit from progress, but even to keep food production growing ahead of population. That second green revolution is now in full swing, and has begun to breed a new generation of super-plants: plants that can do well on the poor soils and in the hostile climates that marginal farmers have to contend with; plants that cost less to grow, that need less fertilizer because they are biologically more efficient; that need less insecticides and fungicides because they are immune to many pests and diseases; that are more ecologically sound, because they minimize pollution and use of scarce resources; plants that will produce more food *and* raise the incomes of the poor.

The vanguard of the second green revolution, as of the first, is the network of ten major international agriculture research stations coordinated by the Consultative Group on International Agricultural Research and funded by a consortium of major aid donor countries, charitable foundations, development banks and United Nations agencies. Each centre concentrates on a different group of subsistence food crops (on the assumption that commercial interests will take care of the cash crops). They breed improved seeds and develop optimal farming techniques to go with them. And they have close links with the national research programmes of all developing countries, which test varieties in their local conditions and adapt the strains and techniques accordingly.

The International Centre for Tropical Agriculture (CIAT) at Cali, Colombia, founded in 1967, is one of the most important of these centres. Its objects and methods illustrate the new approach to agricultural research. From the road its 522-hectare estate and flower-wreathed, whitewashed buildings, nestling in the fertile Cauca valley between two arms of the Andes, look like any prosperous feudal hacienda. Only the peculiar way giant crops alternate with stunted ones, blooming, healthy plants are interspersed with crippled, disease ridden specimens, suggests its real purpose.

CIAT's burly director, John Nickel, explains that the centre aims to develop seeds that will flourish with little investment of purchased inputs, and to develop the kind of cheap, labour-intensive technology that is best suited for the small farmer's economic situation. 'For example, rather than change the acidity of the soil with extra chemicals, we would try to breed the kind of seeds that could do well on acid soil,' comments Nickel. Within its allocated sphere of lowland tropical agriculture, CIAT has been making progress towards its aims: low-cost protein from beans, cheap calories from cassava, and a generation of tropical legumes that could allow profitable livestock farming on vast neglected areas.

The runner bean *Phaseolus vulgaris* is widely grown by subsistence farmers in Latin America and is a valuable source of protein that neatly complements the maize with which it is usually grown. But disease and insect pests cut production way below potential. The average Colombian smallholder gets only half a ton per hectare, where CIAT rarely gets less than two and a half and can achieve six tons per hectare. Common mosaic virus is one of the worst bean afflictions and can slash yields by 50 per cent. So CIAT is breeding beans that can resist it. In one of its fields stands an army of 100,000 bean plants, each one of which has been laboriously inoculated with the virus by hand. Many plants are dwarfed and twisted – but others are growing as vigorously as ever. These healthy, mosaic-resistant plants are chosen as parents for breeding – they will be crossed with high-yielding varieties to give offspring that are both productive and resistant. The cross-breeding is done in long tents with fine mesh walls to keep out insects which could play havoc with scientific pollination. Here skilled workers open each bean flower by hand and dust it with pollen from another strain of plant. The seeds of the pods that result are given a strain number, planted, grown, tested and measured by a dozen different criteria. Through painstaking work of this kind CIAT has built up a germ plasm bank of 12,000 varieties of bean – stack after stack of numbered plastic jars kept in a dark vault at below zero temperatures. This is the genetic reserve which can be raided to create hybrids with almost any combination of qualities you might desire. The characteristics of each seed are stored on a computer. When any national research programme wants some seed stock, the computer selects suitable seeds according to that country's day length, climate, soils and so on. Here one of the prime considerations is colour. Black beans yield most, but no self-respecting Colombian will swallow them. Mexicans and Brazilians cannot be persuaded to eat anything else. Peruvians prefer yellow beans, Chileans white, and central Americans red. All the research centres have to worry about aesthetic factors like this. The new seeds have to be not only prolific and economic, but culturally and gastronomically acceptable as well.

Making a plant disease-resistant is one thing. Making it insect-resistant another, and no easy task. Sometimes plants can be made physically resistant to pests. The parts where insects lay their eggs can be modified so that they can't lay their eggs there any more. The stems and leaves can be made as hairy and prickly as possible to stop insects crawling through.

The need for fertilizer is reduced, in the case of beans, by breeding more efficient strains of the nitrogen-fixing bacteria rhizobia. These live in the soil and in nodules in the roots of legumes like beans. They fix nitrogen direct from the atmosphere. But in tropical soils they do not work so well and are often completely absent. CIAT has been breeding rhizobia for adaptation to tropical soils. Its germ plasm bank of several thousand strains is stored in tiny ampoules in a small filing cabinet. Some of them are capable of fixing eighty kilos of urea per hectare – the equivalent of a massive dose of fertilizer – and can push up yields by 50 per cent. New techniques of genetic engineering hold out the possibility of developing rhizobia that could work even with cereal crops. Other fungi, known as mycorrhizae, may be developed that could improve plants' uptake of a whole range of nutrients in the soil.

Cassava, the shrub whose large starchy root looks like a dahlia tuber and produces tapioca, epitomizes CIAT's low-cost approach. Until recently it was disdained by research programmes because the edible root is pure carbohydrate, with almost no protein. It is a poor man's crop, grown for survival by subsistence farmers. Yet more of it is grown per person in Africa and Latin America than any other crop and, as land shortage progresses in Asia, it is spreading widely there too. The reason is that cassava provides more calories per hectare than any other food crop – 23 per cent more than its nearest rival, maize. You can get an unbelievable fifty to seventy tons of cassava per hectare. It may not provide protein in its roots, but the calories it provides at least save the body from burning up what protein it does consume, which happens when people don't get enough calories. Cassava's leaves – often discarded or fed to animals – are edible and contain protein, vitamins and minerals. Its final virtue is that it needs very little fertilizer to do well.

Farming practices are just as important as new seeds in

pushing up yields for poor farmers, and the research centres devote increasing amounts of effort to them. Traditional practices are not always wise. Latin American farmers plant their beans too late, for example, so they flower into the dry season, which makes them lose many more pods. CIAT has worked out the ideal planting time to get maximum yield in different regions. CIAT has also found that beans are best grown in association with maize. Weeds are kept down, the beans fix nitrogen for the maize and the maize stalks act as poles for the beans. Cultivation techniques can also cut diseases, reducing the need for insecticides. The ruinous cassava bacterial blight, for example, can survive in soil for up to six months and so get passed on from one season to another. Removing the debris and burning the plot after harvest can eliminate it. These techniques cost nothing in materials. They do involve extra labour – but that means more jobs for the rural unemployed.

The nine other research centres in the international network are working along similar lines to CIAT. Their prime target is the small farmer, working with problem soils, with little or no capital and a large amount of underused labour. The International Rice Research Institute at Los Banos, Philippines, fathered the miracle rice IR8 which formed the basis of Asia's green revolution and started to earn a fortune for rich and middle peasants in well-watered areas. But IR8 was of little use to poor small peasants, farmers of rain-fed uplands, coastal swamps or flood-prone river plains. So now IRRI is developing rice strains that will tolerate drought, varieties that can flourish in the salty soils of swamps and of irrigation systems in arid areas, and others that can stand the high iron levels of the laterite soils so common in the tropics. It is working to make strains with a built-in flood escape mechanism by cross-breeding high-yielding varieties with floating rice, whose stem can elongate up to twenty feet as waters rise. Other experiments are increasing the protein content of rice, normally 7 per cent, to 10 per cent.

Other cereals – wheat, sorghum, millet – are being developed along similar lines. CIMMYT, the International Maize and Wheat Improvement Centre in Mexico, is developing dwarf varieties of maize that can be grown with 70,000 plants per hectare, two or three times the usual density. The closer spacing keeps weeds down, produces more food and creates more employment for a given area of land. Breeding programmes are also working to boost the quality of maize protein, to make it almost as good as milk. This development, plus its high yield of calories per hectare, could make maize the crop of the future for improving the nutrition of the poor.

Potatoes, an upland crop, can – surprisingly – produce more protein per acre than cereals, and have a high content of B and C vitamins. The International Potato Centre in Lima, Peru, has developed varieties that can mature in 100 days – fifty to eighty days quicker than normal – and others that can grow in tropical lowlands in only sixty days.

Livestock is also getting attention: though the typical one-pound American beefsteak needs sixteen pounds of grain to produce, livestock need not always be so wasteful of world resources. There is an important place for cattle in poor soils that are unsuitable for crops, and in mixed farming systems in more favoured areas. ILRAD, the International Laboratory for Research in Animal Diseases in Nairobi, Kenya, is working hard to find ways of controlling the tsetse fly. The fly carries trypanosomiasis (which can also affect humans as sleeping sickness) and makes much of sub-Saharan Africa out of bounds for cattle.

Colombia's CIAT, meanwhile, is developing a legume known as *Stylosanthes* with which pastures in semi-arid areas could be improved. It resists drought, trampling and overgrazing, provides good-quality fodder for cattle and fixes nitrogen into the bargain.

Parallel with plant-breeding programmes, selective breeding of animals – of the kind that transformed European cattle – can vastly improve meat and milk yields. India's 180 million cattle have traditionally been a grossly underexploited resource. The country's nationwide dairy cooperative movement has dramatically raised the productivity of native stock by crossbreeding with improved strains. The poor peasant can upgrade his couple of cattle for the cost of a cheap vial of semen.

Fish farming offers another very promising way of increasing the consumption of balanced animal proteins. Fish grow fast on little food at tropical temperatures. Yet pisciculture is only in its infancy. It has barely begun in Africa and Latin America. Though Asia has an ancient tradition, her annual production of 4 million tonnes a year is only a fraction of the potential. Average Asian yields of only 200 kilos per hectare could easily be multiplied tenfold. Fish can be raised in enclosures in canals, rivers and seasonally flooded land, or in among the rice in irrigated paddy fields. Yet most inland water is not systematically farmed. Of India's 4 million hectares of village tanks, only half a million are used for fish culture, while the rest stagnate in deep shades of green. In Malaysia and the Philippines, research is developing techniques of breeding in captivity food fish, which so far have bred only in the wild, while India is experimenting with polyculture – combining three varieties of fish with different feeding habits – in the same pond. This has produced yields of up to nine tonnes per hectare.

Like CIAT, all the international research centres develop not only new breeds and seeds, but also a package of cheap, labour-intensive techniques to go with them, aimed at maximizing production and conserving the soil at the same time. The International Institute of Tropical Agriculture at Ibadan, Nigeria, is especially concerned with finding techniques that will allow Africa's farmers – accustomed to shifting their plots every year or two – to cultivate the same area permanently without degrading the soil. One promising line appears to be 'minimum tillage' – that is, farming with much less ploughing or hoeing, allowing plant debris to die back into the soil. This is now spreading even among commercial farms in North America. It conserves soil structure and retains the organic content, and appears to increase yields, too. Mulching – covering the soil around plants with straw, leaves or other organic material – is another hopeful practice for the tropics. It reduces evaporation, maintains an even soil temperature, controls weeds, prevents erosion in downpours, and provides extra humus.

Western agriculture has achieved its high yields by massive doses of fertilizer and a profligate use of energy. Every ton of food produced in the West requires 8 billion joules, nearly eight times as much as the Third World uses to produce the same amount. The future for agriculture in the Third World cannot lie down this capital-intensive and energy-intensive blind alley. It must lie in a new 'appropriate agriculture', involving intensive use of land and labour, minimum use of non-renewable resources, and soil conservation and creation.

The Chinese achieve the highest yields of any major region in the Third World, with a minimum input of energy, by organic fertilizing with everything they can lay their hands on: animal manure, ash, oil cake, mud dug from canals and fish ponds, green manure and the use of human excreta. This used to be dumped direct on to the paddy fields, complete with disease organisms, but is now fermented first to render it harmless. The Food and Agriculture Organization has calculated that in 1970–71 organic wastes available in the Third World contained 103 million tons of plant nutrients – eight times the amount of chemical fertilizer actually used. To capitalize on this wasted resource, every village in the Third World should have a sanitation system based on the collection and fermentation of human and animal wastes: this produces safe residue for use as fertilizer and, as an added bonus, methane gas for domestic use. The Third World's fuel crisis is the biggest single obstacle to the return of wastes – as fuelwood becomes scarcer, most plant and even animal wastes are burned as fuel.

New, non-conventional energy sources – fuelwood plantations, solar energy, biogas – will have to be developed before organic wastes can be used as fertilizer.

Prospects

It was Thomas Malthus who predicted, way back in 1798 in his *Essay on the Principle of Population*, that food production, in the nature of things, could not expand as fast as unrestrained population growth. History so far has proved him wrong, but may not do so for ever.

Food production in the Third World as a whole has managed to keep just a nose ahead of people production. In the 1960s per capita food production grew at 0·7 per cent a year. From 1970 to 1976, despite the green revolution, it slowed to only 0·2 per cent a year and in Africa actually fell by 1·4 per cent a year. The population of the Third World will probably go on growing at about 2 per cent a year for at least the rest of this century: that represents the minimum target for the growth in food production if malnutrition is not to spread. Whether large-scale famines can be avoided or not will depend partly on the weather, which man is as yet unable to predict, let alone to control.

But there can be little doubt that the world possesses the physical resources, and humanity the theoretical knowledge, to produce enough food to feed two or three times the present population, which is the level at which it will probably stabilize. But unequal social organizations are now one of the biggest obstacles to expanding production, as well as to distributing the extra production to everyone. The task now is to solve the production and distribution problems together. Achieving that will mean vigorous population programmes and a continued attack on all agricultural fronts, from land reform and extending the farmed and irrigated area, to new credit and extension programmes. Research will have to fight a permanent

The green, blue and other revolutions battle, both to increase yields and to keep ahead of insects and diseases which, almost as fast as ways are found of controlling them, evolve into new organisms that evade control. Malthus can only be kept at bay by radical reform and permanent vigilance.

5 The house that Jack built: Self-help cities

In the hot, milky haze, row beyond row of squat shapes climb the rounded hills. The squatter townships of Lima, Peru, with their simplified geometry of pure curves and rectangles, have a surrealistic aspect, like the tents of a numberless army camped outside the walls of the city. Their desert sites are inhospitable, dry and dusty. All but the oldest-established are without piped water, sewers, health posts, schools, paved roads or police. Yet the shantytowns of Lima offer some unique lessons for the cities of the Third World. Independently of the aid experts, the squatters here have discovered, spontaneously, many of the approaches that are now being built into the most progressive urbanization projects.

The settlement of Leoncio Prado climbs up the flanks and shoulders of a desiccated, ochre valley enclosed by high, stony hills. The highest houses, erected by the most recent arrivals, are no more than boxes made of six bamboo mats – four for the walls, one for the roof and one for the floor. These are slung on a framework of wooden supports to make a single room, no more than eight feet square, that must accommodate anything up to eight or ten people. Most of the inhabitants are young families who have migrated from rural areas. Many of them, before coming out here, will first have spent time paying high rents in crowded, filthy slums in Lima itself. Their move to the squatter areas is a refusal to pay any more rent, an act of self-liberation.

The first months or years in the settlement are squalid. But no one sticks with their straw tent any longer than the time it takes to save up for some building materials and make something better. If you follow the orderly rows of dwellings down the hill, you can see how people have gradually improved their houses as and when they could afford to. One by one the straw walls give way to wood — old orange boxes, motley collections of planks or old door panels — and wall by wall wood becomes brick or cement. Windows evolve from straw flaps, through wooden awnings propped open with sticks, to proper frames with glass. Roofs develop from plastic sheetings over bamboo joists held down with stones, to tarpaulin, corrugated iron and asbestos. Later, much later, the walls are cemented over and painted, solid flat roofs are added, and on to these, second storeys can be built as and when they can be afforded. Freed from restrictive building regulations, the squatters here have total housing flexibility. They can fit their house exactly to suit their pockets, their taste, the size of their family. They cut corners and costs are kept to a minimum, because the people themselves are paying, not some bureaucratic public housing authority. Makeshift materials, often recycled, are used wherever possible. Local craftsmen are hired by the day for the really difficult jobs, but most of the labour is free.

On a Sunday Leoncio Prado becomes one vast construction site. Piles of bricks, arranged in tall, precarious columns, litter the sandy streets like an obstacle course. Here one man on a shaky ladder is plastering his new brick wall. Across the street a husband, wife and children run relays from a pile of cement, scooping it up and dumping it with a splat into their new foundations. Next door four strong men are helping a neighbour lay his brickwork, their beer bottles balancing on a wall. No one here is handed the key of a ready-built house with a crippling mortgage or rent bill. They have the pride and satisfaction of building their homes themselves. The community strengthens itself by mutual aid. Men give their friends a hand for free, knowing that when they need it the help will be returned.

Though they must wait for the government to provide some services, like water, sewers and electricity, whatever they can lay on for themselves here and now, they do.

Justice, for example. The police rarely set foot in the *pueblos jovenes* (young townships, as the squatter settlements are called). They are not particularly welcome, because of their past record of persecuting squatters. Now some *pueblos*, faced with an epidemic of thefts and rapes, want police posts but can't get them. Leoncio Prado polices itself. Each household has a whistle, which it blows if there is trouble or a theft. Every able-bodied man within earshot then grabs a stick or cudgel and races after the thief, who is lucky if he survives the subsequent beating. I was assured by the president of the women's committee here, who seemed a very sober and sensible lady, that in the previous twelve months six thieves had died in this way. They had been buried, and a pole erected over each grave with a notice of what the man had stolen, as a deterrent. It is an indication of the degree of poverty in the settlements that thefts still continue in Leoncio Prado.

Other local self-help efforts are more unambiguously positive. Leoncio Prado has built its own community centre, which now doubles as a primary school in the day. When the settlement site was planned, a large space was left open and flattened to provide a play area and football ground. The day of my visit was the first round of the block championships. One team after another elbowed and fouled its way through in blue, pink, yellow or red shirts. Adjoining the football pitch is the site for the new nursery school. This is to be built and financed by local people, and staffed by a voluntary agency. That same day was also scheduled for the beginning of construction work. Sierra Indian women, their babies tucked into bright shawls on their backs, queued up to hand over the red bricks they were giving as their contribution. Some had even wrapped their brick in paper. A clerk ticked off their names from a list – everything had to be scrupulously fair and equal. A square of trenches had been dug for the foundations. The settlement committee secretary, Cesar Mendez, arrived. Everyone gathered round. He picked up a great hunk of rock and flung it into the foundation trench, shouting: 'In the name of the community I lay this first stone of our nursery school.' The clerk took a break from checking off brick contributions, and wrote down a minute in the committee's records, saying that the foundation stone was laid on such a date, in the presence of this person and that person 'and the English journalist Paul Harrison'. We all signed the book, myself feeling honoured at this sign of my brief passage.

The community association of which Mendez is chairman is the pinnacle of a pyramid of communal links of participation. Every twenty-five houses belongs to a *manzana* or block, of which there are thirty-seven in Leoncio Prado. The blocks hold meetings every week, which all heads of households are supposed to attend, to discuss neighbourhood problems and projects or ways of raising money, or to mediate in local disputes as a sort of street law court. Each household is saving up at twenty-five to 100 pesos a time, in special little savings books, to pay for electricity to be brought to the area. Again, this is done collectively, with everyone paying an equal share, and every household carries a responsibility to every other. Anyone who needs to draw out his savings has to put his case to the *manzana* committee and convince them that he has a genuine emergency to meet.

Each *manzana* elects one delegate to the central committee of the community association, whose executive committee and chief officers have to be elected once a year in a town meeting of every family head in Leoncio Prado. The committee has considerable powers. It allocates house plots to newcomers, negotiates with outside bodies, government and municipal authorities about provision of services, arranges community festivals (which are innumerable) and acts as a court of appeal from the *manzana* meetings, to which really serious disputes can be referred. This sophisticated local democracy is completely unofficial and unique to the *pueblos jovenes*, who enjoy democratic rights far in advance of those of the residents of the official, developed areas of Lima. Nothing is imposed on them from outside as a *fait accompli* – every household has a chance to discuss and vote on it.

This participatory, self-improving democracy emerged from the history of the *pueblos jovenes*, indeed it may even have its roots in the mutual-help traditions of the old Indian *ayllu* communities, some of which still persist. The first squatter settlements grew up in the late forties. At first they met with heavy police repression. The police would drive them off, beat them (sometimes fatally) and burn their shacks and possessions. So the squatters began to organize in large numbers. A site would be surveyed and selected, always on vacant public land, of which Lima, surrounded by desert, has plenty. Then up to 100 families would get together and invade the site all at once, turning up in vans and lorries loaded with straw mats and tools. The houses were rushed up on lots that had already been marked out in advance in an orderly street grid. Often the eve of a national holiday would be chosen to give everyone a clear day for building, and sympathetic journalists would be invited along as witnesses to deter police violence. The initial invasion required the creation of a tight, supportive organization, which was also needed after the event to prepare for self-defence against possible police attacks. This democratic organization persisted and adapted itself to later needs such as the provision of services.

The exploding shanty cities

As rural migrants left their exhausted soils, dwindling holdings and decreasing employment, the Third World's cities swallowed them until they were bursting at the seams. The urban population grew from 185 millions in 1940 to 792 millions in 1975, expanding at double the rate of the total population. By the early seventies some 12 million people joined the exodus from land to city every year, or 33,000 every single day. They were driven by poverty, but drawn, too, by the cities' promise of wealth, as average urban incomes are two or three times higher than in rural areas. It was the colonial powers who first built these enclaves of privilege, modelled on Western cities, and established high rates of pay for the higher government bureaucrats and managers who inhabited them. Independence brought no change of approach: the Westernized élites who ran the new governments had as their main ambition to extend the modern sector. They concentrated on modern capital-intensive industry, which cost a great deal and therefore could provide few jobs. In the housing sphere they built housing to excessive Western standards which only a small minority could afford.

And so the cities could not employ or house the millions which their privilege attracted to them like a magnet. Every Third World city is a dual city – an island of wealth surrounded by a black belt of misery. Outside the bright, shining modern city of skyscrapers, flyovers and desirable residences, the poor are camped in squalor, disease and neglect, in shacks and hutments of plywood, cardboard, mud or straw, usually without clean water, sewers, health centres, schools, paved roads or paying jobs. More than two fifths of city dwellers in developing countries live in squatter or slum areas, and these are growing at twice the rate of the official, modern cities they surround. Their residents live largely neglected by government. The informal trades and manufactures in which they employ each other have to fight against government indifference or even harassment. The shanties that house them get no services; indeed the response of many governments to the problem has been to demolish them, thereby destroying jobs and communities, and replace them with lower-density, higher-rent housing zones from which industry is banned. This conventional approach to slums attacks the symptoms, but leaves the disease untreated to break out again elsewhere. It is a strategy that cannot work.

The Third World Tomorrow

The most far-reaching solutions to the problem of urban poverty lie outside the scope of this chapter. The first is to halt the flood of rural migrants by channelling a far greater proportion of investment into the rural areas, to provide more amenities and to generate incomes that can compare with those of the cities. The second, for those already in the cities, is to create more employment and income by way of small-scale industries and labour-intensive techniques, which we shall examine in the next chapter.

Yet it is possible to do a great deal to improve the quality of life for the marginal urban masses, even in their present state of poverty. Governments have limited resources. The problem is not to see how many people they can house to uniform high standards, but how, given the lack of resources, a basic level of housing, services and utilities can be provided for all the urban poor within a short space of time. There are three possible approaches. First, the cost of new housing and services can be cut drastically by reducing standards to a realistic level that governments and people can afford. The second is to accept and legalize existing squatter settlements and to make them more habitable, by giving residents secure tenure and laying on the roads, water, light, schools and health centres to which they have as much right as the privileged inhabitants of the modern city. The third approach – necessary for new migrants and people rehoused from those shantytowns that are incapable of rehabilitation – is to provide a small, ready-serviced plot of land and leave new squatters to build their own houses. All three approaches are complementary, and succeed best when the people are mobilized to participate in improving their own environment.

Mud, mud, glorious mud

The public housing that governments have provided in the past has usually been beyond the means of the vast majority. A six-city survey by the World Bank found that between one third and two thirds of households could not afford to buy or rent the cheapest complete public housing units available.

An obvious answer is to cut the cloth to suit the purse, and adopt building standards according to the rents people can afford, rather than fixing rents according to desired standards. For the private sector, all that needs to be done here is to ease or totally abolish official building regulations for all self-built housing. For public housing, a bewildering array of low-cost building techniques has been developed by aid agencies and appropriate technology centres, to provide houses that cost less than Western ones, yet provide better and healthier shelter than traditional housing. These techniques have taken much of their inspiration from traditional methods, which were often ingenious and cheap ways of using locally available materials to produce shelter suited to the local climate and architecture in harmony with local social structure and culture.

Traditional housing often fulfils the requirements of good design, being both beautiful and functional. The haunting pyramidal houses of Lake Titicaca in Peru use domed mud bricks, supported by the walls in barrel vaults, to keep the interior cool in the day and warm at night. They cut out entirely the considerable cost of timber and tin for roofing. The interlocking cubes of north African hill villages make one family's roof another family's terrace for cooking, working or drying grain and fruits. Traditional housing design reflects daily living patterns and family structure. The walled Mossi compounds of Upper Volta enclose dozens of tiny circular huts. Each adult man has one hut, while each of his wives has a separate hut which she shares with her children. This provides privacy within a context of communality, and helps to avoid arguments between rival wives in polygamous marriages. Larger huts are for pottery and spinning, while square mud granaries keep the store of millet and sorghum. In the centre of the compound is a great round table of mud, with hard stones set all round the circumference, where women grind the grain together. The structure of the compound locates the individual securely in a supporting context of collective living.

It is sad to see this architecture of an older system of values disappearing before the advance of faceless Western designs, whose architecture, based on isolated cells suited for small nuclear families, tends of itself to smash the extended family of several generations and to undermine the open-air, communal style of living that goes with it. Unfortunately, very few of the new low-cost approaches to housing have tried to preserve the essence of traditional settlement patterns. The square box is the dominant form, and one has to admit that it is the form which most self-builders choose, because they are copying their own Westernized élites, because migration has already broken them into nuclear families or because there is no room for more expansive designs. But traditional materials and techniques have come back into favour, and are being improved to make them more efficient. They have many attractions, in that materials are cheap and locally available, and construction methods are labour-intensive and create the maximum number of jobs.

Mud is the cheapest and most accessible of all materials. British construction expert John Parry, of Britain's Intermediate Technology Group, comments: 'Mud is the only common substance which is generally freely available to people in need of building materials in a poor world. It is a principal base material for the development of environmentally sound technologies which will help communities to become self-reliant.' Traditional mud bricks are made of clay mixed with water, set in a rectangular wooden mould and left to dry in the sun. Their chief drawback is that after ten years or less of the battering of tropical rains, a living-room wall made of them is liable to collapse one stormy night.

Development efforts have aimed at strengthening the mud brick. One housing project in Upper Volta has developed a hand press that will make mud bricks with an admixture of 5 or

10 per cent of cement. This doubles the brick's normal lifespan. Asphalt residue and lime can also be used instead of cement. An Indian project has built a mill making good-quality cement out of lime mixed with the ash left over from burnt rice husks.

Not only mud, but even the split cane mats used for walls in many parts of the world can be greatly improved. In Dacca, Bangladesh, a rainproof and windproof home has been designed with walls made by sandwiching heavy-duty black polythene between two bamboo mats. Using this technique, one man can build a house in four days.

More savings in housing costs can be made by economizing on space and amenities. Reducing space standards can help considerably in cities with high land costs. For example, in an intermediate location in Mexico City, 69 per cent of families could not afford a shared services dwelling with ninety-five square metres of land, yet all but 28 per cent could afford one on only thirty square metres. Sharing toilets and water brings public housing within reach of a much greater proportion than housing with individual services, and this, in any case, has a value of its own in preventing isolation and developing community contacts. Further savings can be made by providing multi-family dwellings with shared outer walls, foundations, roofs and staircases, rather than free-standing individual units. When all these approaches are combined, the effect on costs can be dramatic: in Bogotá, for example, a single family dwelling with individual services would cost $2,884, against $1,107 for a multi-family unit with shared basic services. Only a quarter of the population could afford the first, but two thirds the second.

The final sphere of cost-cutting is in the location of the house – a site on the periphery can cost anything from 25 to 98 per cent less than one in the centre. But peripheral locations have their problems, especially the availability of jobs, and projects on sites at city fringes must also provide employment as well as houses.

Even if every single corner is cut and every mode of saving on costs exploited, there will still be a proportion of the people who cannot afford them. The World Bank Survey found that cuts of between 45 and 81 per cent in costs would be required for the poorest 10 per cent to be able to buy or rent public housing. This means that cheap public housing alone cannot solve the problem of squatter settlements. For a very long time there will be largish groups who either cannot afford the most rudimentary public housing on offer, or who have low-paid jobs in central areas and cannot afford either the rents near by or the fares to get there from further out. These people will go on squatting, and no laws in the world will stop them. So present shanties are likely to persist, or, if they are demolished, pop up again elsewhere, and new ones will join them. Getting rid of them is like trying to drain the ocean. The task is not to eradicate them, but to make them fit places for human beings to live in.

Calcutta crawls out of the abyss: slum upgrading

One of the most comprehensive assaults on urban squalor has been mounted where the human degradation of overblown cities reached its nadir: Calcutta. Calcutta, the human antheap, with its hordes of ragged street dwellers living in concrete tubes, under plastic sheets or under the sky; its *bustees* or slums with families of eight or more crowded into single rooms eight feet square, and disgusting, hole-in-the-ground service privies; its foetid canals, one bath and toilet for thousands; its rainy season floods of diluted human sewage, its sardine packed streets and trams, and its unemployment. In 1966 a city development plan was drawn up to solve these problems, and in 1970 the Calcutta Metropolitan Development Authority was created to put the plan into effect. Its brief: to unclog the sewers, free the crammed highways, end the flooding problem, put up low-cost housing, turn the slums into habitable dwellings and stimulate employment.

The activity which has had most immediate impact on the lives of its inhabitants has been the improvement and upgrading of the city's 3,000-odd *bustees*, where one third of the city's population of 8 million peope live. Rehousing $2\frac{1}{2}$ million *bustee* dwellers, even at the lowest possible cost of around $600 per family, would have cost impossible sums of money. It was lack of funds, more than anything, that pushed the CMDA away from the demolish and rebuild solution towards the idea of rehabilitating the slums. The CMDA's secretary, Sivaramakrishnan, told me: 'We decided simply to accept the *bustees* as part of the housing stock, and to try and make them habitable. We were forced into this approach by the sheer size of the problem. But now people are realizing that slums and shantytowns are also communities and places of work: demolition amounts to dehousing and destruction of jobs.'

Haransar Para is a typical old *bustee*, a motley assembly of single-storey courtyards and shaky two-storey structures of rusty corrugated iron. In the rains, many of the rooms here are two feet deep in water. The narrow, unlit muddy alleyways wind among the tenements. Some people use the filthy East Canal as a toilet rather than use the stinking service privies. When I visited it, the *bustee* was having a face lift. The alleyways were being lit and paved, and more water taps were being laid on. Storm drains were being dug, making the place temporarily even muddier than usual. The *pièce de résistance* which the residents led me to and displayed with excited pride, was the new toilets, two for each court – hexagonal concrete pillboxes raised like statues five feet above ground, with their own septic tanks attached. It would not be a paradise – large families would still be cramped in tiny cells – but at least they would not be breaking their legs in the dingy alleyways or getting sick every week or two from their poor sanitation. They had regained dignity – and retained the community contacts and jobs that rehousing would have destroyed. The total cost of these improvements was only 150 rupees (about $20) per head.

The Metropolitan Development Authority has been working hard to alleviate the other tribulations of Calcutta life. Formerly the sewers also served to carry off the water from monsoon cloudbursts and could not cope with the combined tasks – hence the floods, which the resourceful Bengalis tolerated with surprising good humour. A cartoon in the local paper had one umbrella-toting man commenting to another: 'Calcutta is beautiful – no garbage, no potholes.' Both were standing with floodwater lapping at their loincloths. Now separate storm drains have been dug, and waist-high flooding has gradually subsided to knee-high and ankle-high, before, hopefully, disappearing altogether. Four hundred new buses have been added to the city's stock, but they are still as full as ever because the latent demand – people currently walking because there is no place – seems virtually inexhaustible. Roads have been widened to cope with the throngs of pedestrians, rickshaws, taxis, trams, handcarts and goats who negotiate them, while the heroic Howrah Bridge, its girders creaking under the strain of being the only link for many miles between the two banks of the Hooghly river, is getting a companion bridge to relieve it. The CMDA is building 25,000 low-cost houses a year, many of them on reclaimed marshes now known as Salt Lake City. It has renovated 680 schools so they can accommodate twice as many pupils, while eighty new clinics and forty mobile dispensaries have brought health care for the first time within reach of the city's poor. Finally, to compensate for the prolonged recession that has plagued Calcutta since the mid-sixties, employment will be boosted in the informal sector (which employs nearly a third of the workforce) with a special credit scheme backed by a $33-million World Bank loan.

The CMDA has not worked miracles, and has been criticized for that. Its creation aroused high expectations from the long-neglected victims of the city's monstrosities. They believed that the millennium had arrived to save them from the armageddon of their daily lives, and were sorely disappointed when they realized it had not. Again, the cartoonists had a field day. A resident, shoes in hands as he wades along past neat signs saying 'CMDA', shakes his fist at the heavens and prays God to give him patience. A man who fell in one of the authority's myriad ditches and trenches lies in hospital with a plastered leg on a hoist. The doctor reasons with him: 'People sacrifice life for their country and for CMDA, can't you donate one leg?'

But once the exaggerated hopes had subsided, Calcutta's inhabitants undoubtedly began to value the real improvement in their material circumstances which the CMDA had brought about. The place is no longer the deepest abyss of hell, as it has been painted by so many visitors. It has a palpable feel of bustling optimism. I was shocked at the sheer density of humanity in the place when I first arrived, but when I left, against all expectations, I found that I had developed an affection for this place that Robert Clive, anticipating the sentiments of many later writers, called 'the most wicked place in the universe'.

The people as architects and builders

Popular participation in urban development can pay off perhaps more tangibly than in any other sphere. As the United Nations Centre for Housing, Building and Planning reported to the Habitat conference on settlements in 1976: 'Of all the resources now being devoted to improvement of conditions in slums and squatter settlements, those of the people themselves are by far the most significant.' The people represent a vast pool of labour, much of it already underemployed, that can be drawn on to speed up construction and cut costs. They have untapped reserves of savings, and will save much more given the incentive of improving their houses. These funds can finance construction and relieve the burden on government budgets. Not least, they are the world's greatest experts on their own housing needs and aspirations and on the kind of house and settlement design that can satisfy these.

Architects, of all the arrogant professions, have been among the most arrogant when it comes to dealing with the poor. If a wealthy client is footing the bill, his every whim will be humoured. But with the masses it is assumed that the architects and the municipal authorities who employ them know best. It is they, not the people who will live with the results for the rest of their lives, who decide how much space people need, what room layout is best, what standards of services and utilities are required, what community facilities are needed and where they should be located. Even in the advanced countries this assumption is dangerous and wrong, and there are millions of people paying for it in misery, stuck in heartless estates and tower blocks. In the Third World the architect is a member of the Westernized élite and can have little conception of the living patterns of the masses. People's participation in the design of houses and the planning of settlements is essential if these are to correspond to their needs. It is an important part, as Manila University sociologist Mary Racelis Hollnsteiner has pointed out, of the re-education of professionals and experts. It gives them a basic course in what they all should know about and all exist to serve, but almost all ignore or override: the felt needs of the people.

But participation in planning has to be meaningful. It is not enough to invite public comment from amenity groups, which are rudimentary in the Third World. Consultation has to be active and direct. The planners of New Bombay, a city that will eventually house 2 million people, decided they would place their plan before the public, but they published it in English only, so only the élite could read it. Then they hit on the bright idea of distributing a questionnaire with the daily newspapers, but once again, only the élite buy newspapers and only 1 per cent of the forms came back. Sample surveys are one way of discovering felt needs. All World Bank urbanization projects now involve a survey of squatters designed to find out what kind of services and/or housing they want, and how much they can afford to pay. The project is then designed accordingly, felt needs deciding what kind of services are provided, income determining the standard.

One of the most thorough attempts to consult the users of a new settlement was made by the Study Action Group of Ahmedabad in India. More than 2,000 poor families had been tempting destiny by squatting on the broad bed of the Sabarmati river, which was normally dry and one of the few pieces of land that belonged to no landlord who would evict them. But the river duly flooded, and the squatters were made homeless. The Study Action Group – made up of socially committed architects, doctors, engineers and social workers – first carried out extensive studies of family structure and family budgets. These revealed living patterns that would influence design, and income levels which would show how much rent people were able to pay and hence determine cost limits. Models of the draft designs were circulated among the people for their comments and modified accordingly, then eight demonstration houses were built for them to visit. The final settlement was an imaginative attempt to fuse the need for privacy with the communal, open-air patterns of traditional life. It followed a honeycomb pattern, with individual units arranged around small courtyards for cooking, laundry and informal socializing. But to prevent the courtyards becoming self-contained and isolated, they were all interlinked and people would pass through on their way to shops or work. As the preliminary surveys had shown up the tremendous poverty of the families, great emphasis was placed on creating enough extra employment to provide sufficient income for the rent levels. The Action Group stood as guarantors and helped residents to get bank loans for small enterprises, and they set up cooperative workshops for training and production. The community was also encouraged to organize itself to run facilities such as crèches and milk centres for children.

A further step in participation is to involve the people in constructing their own settlement, which ensures automatically that dwellings suit their lifestyles and their pockets. This type of scheme is known as the 'site and services' approach. The authorities provide the land, lay on some or all public utilities – water, sewage, electricity, access roads – and provide a plot on a street layout for houses. The settlers are left to build their own dwellings. Sometimes they are given technical help with construction, sometimes they are asked to comply with a set of basic requirements about ventilation, sanitation, alignment and so on, sometimes they are asked to follow one of a choice of model plans. The better schemes give settlers more flexibility to build what they want, and provide credit facilities so that the poorest can acquire the building materials. This approach cuts the cost to the public exchequer considerably. The cost per family in World-Bank-supported schemes, for example, ranges from $15 in Senegal to $350 in Jamaica, whereas the cheapest complete housing units in their six-city survey cost between $570 and $3,005 each.

The settlers themselves bear the cost of the house, but auto-construction can provide the same standard of building for half the cost of a public authority doing the work. The extra money is required to cover administration and interest charges with public housing, but with self-built dwellings these factors are not needed, as people draw on their savings. House-owners put an enormous amount of energy and investment into their homes: after twenty years of gradual additions and improvements, their dwelling may be worth as much as six times their annual income, much higher than the ratio with public housing. All this effort, though it is not carried in anyone's account books, is an investment as real as any tied up in factories or government buildings. It provides the family with extra income – equal to the amount they would otherwise be spending on rent – and therefore increases the prosperity of the country.

One of the cheapest ways of upgrading slums and improving housing is simply to regularize the tenure of squatter areas. The squalor of so many squatter settlements is one excuse governments use to keep them illegal. Yet often they are squalid *because* they are illegal. The self-build squatter will not waste money on improving his house if he is likely to be driven out or dispossessed at any moment to make way for some planner's dream or speculator's windfall profit. Providing squatters with security of tenure is enough to start them all off on a stampede of self-improvement. Lima's squatters have had security of tenure on public land since the 1950s, with results we have already seen. No one dares to call Lima's settlements *barriadas* (slums) any more.

Reshaping a shantytown

Cissin is a sprawling squatter settlement on the fringe of Upper Volta's capital Ouagadougou. Until a couple of years ago Cissin looked like any other squat – mud-walled, village-style houses had been built in a chaotic, unplanned muddle. The meandering, gulleyed paths were impassable to traffic. Poorly drained hollows became mosquito-breeding ponds in the rainy season. Most people had no latrines at all, and those who had dug pits for themselves usually placed them too close to the family well. In the dry season wells dried up and people had to buy water from vendors, peddling oil-drums-full on bicycle carts. In 1974 a project sponsored by the United Nations Development Programme set out to transform this quarter into a healthy, habitable environment, in a model scheme that involves all the elements of the new approach to urban problems.

The first task was to map the existing scatter of houses on

the basis of aerial photos. Some order had to be brought into this chaos to provide space for roads and drains. A plan was drawn up in consultation with local chiefs and community leaders. It was designed so as to cause an absolute minimum of disruption, but providing a clear path for roads meant that about eighteen houses and many individual huts that were part of other houses had to be physically shifted, demolished and rebuilt out of the way of the streets. The affected families did this work themselves. Every family was expected to build square walls round their individual lots (Mossi walls are usually circular) and to dig a household latrine to a specified depth. The individual family wells which most people had in their compounds had to be filled in – nine out of ten of them turned out to be contaminated by animal and human wastes. To replace these, deep concrete-lined communal wells were sunk at focal points, and would provide water during the dry season too, thus cutting out a heavy item on household budgets. Apart from this involvement in rebuilding their own homes, families were expected to participate in the collective work and costs, too. Every household had to contribute 15,000 francs CFA (about $60) towards the cost of laying out the streets, hiring a bulldozer to level them, building the wells and manufacturing concrete slabs, with a hole in the middle, to go over the latrines. Equally important, they chipped in 'sweat capital' to communal labour such as digging drainage ditches.

Residents had good reason to participate. In a cunning move, they were allowed to share out and keep the dirt dug out of ditches to make their own bricks with, or to sell it off at $2 a cartload. If nothing else, this ensured that the ditches were dug wide and deep. But their main incentive was that, at the end of it all, they were awarded the coveted urban residence permit. This gave them permanent security of tenure, made them owners of their little plot and freed them from the arbitrary power of police or local land chiefs to evict them.

The community organization and spirit that had been engendered during the rebuilding work were exploited to form more community groups – young people's clubs, women's co-operative workshops, and communal vegetable gardens in the marshy depressions. These groups would carry on with the further improvement of the area when the project team pulled out.

The overall result is not Beverly Hills or Mayfair, but it is sanitary, safe and secure. The city has gained an organized, planned and properly titled quarter with neat wide boulevards. The residents have gained a healthier environment, free water, rent-free accommodation and security of tenure.

Half a mile away from this restructured quarter, a new housing estate is being built on the 'site and services' principle. Future residents were chosen by lottery, and despite the fact that the poor were given more than equal chances to win, the preponderance of successful candidates were civil servants or soldiers. Residents have to contribute money to pay for materials and labourers to build roads, schools, health centre, market and community buildings, and must help out with some of the work. Every weekend they are all out building their houses. These have to comply with certain minimum standards of alignment, ventilation, sanitation and insulation. They are less vernacular in style than in the restructured district, and are almost all boring, uniform, tin-roofed boxes.

The process of building the new quarter and rebuilding the old one has been used to create a maximum of local jobs. Labourers were recruited from the local area, where one in four of the economically active are unemployed. They were trained in building skills which would give them a useful trade for when the project had finished. Local men who had saved a small amount of capital (around $120 was all that was needed) were helped to set up business as building contractors. The essential equipment was pretty basic – a press for making mud bricks strengthened with concrete, watering-cans, wheelbarrows, oil-drums, shovels and picks, and a donkey and cart.

With projected profit rates of 17 to 40 per cent, these little firms could earn enough to repay their initial outlay within six months.

The fighting communities

Effective public participation in cities involves the creation of active, lasting community groups which can provide for local needs and stand up for local interests after the project teams have packed up and left, taking their funds and expertise with them. Yet a spirit of community, cooperation and participation is one of the hardest things to develop among people who may be ethnically diverse and long accustomed to a total lack of power to shape their own futures.

Community organizations may crystallize around efforts to improve settlements. Self-provision of services is a strong tradition in Moroccan cities. In Rabat neighbourhoods finance and run their own nursery schools and koranic schools. They club together to build their own mosques. As squatter settlements are often considerable fire hazards, many of them have formed their own watch committees with wooden watchtowers. In Delhi local societies known as *vikas mandals* are involved in a long list of activities: repair and construction of latrines and water supply, literacy and craft classes, sports meets, educational tours, cooperative food shops. In Chile, during the popular political groundswell of 1969-71, the unemployed of the squatter settlements were organized into workers' brigades to build houses. Many squatter areas all over the world practise a more dubious form of self-help, getting local electricians and plumbers to rig up illicit pirate connections to electricity cables and water mains. It is a legitimate form of protest against official neglect.

Just as frequently a strong outside threat may gel a neighbourhood into a community fighting for its right to survive. One of the earliest community groupings emerged in the Tondo

Foreshore area of Manila, the Philippines' capital. In the early fifties the Federation of Tondo Foreshore Land Tenants' Associations was formed to press for security of tenure for squatters. In the late sixties Manila's planners came up with a splendid redevelopment plan which involved the total demolition of existing dwellings. New housing would be built at much lower densities – accommodating only one in three of the original residents. The rest would be moved up to thirty kilometres away, far from their jobs. The Council of Tondo Foreshore Community Organizations, formed in 1969, fought the plan tooth and nail and presented their own alternative plan. Eventually the Marcos government accepted a new plan which retained most of the existing structures but upgraded the area, providing paths, clean water, schools and so on. The very small number of families who could not be accommodated in the restructured area would be resettled close by.

The women of Alaska Beach, on the Philippine island of Cebu, battled with every demonstrator's tactic in the book. Alaska Beach is a former gamblers' haven on eleven hectares of shoreline south of Cebu City. When the tide comes in, the houses closest to the sea are flooded. But that, strangely enough, was one reason why squatters who had migrated from outlying islands, and refugees from evictions and fires in other settlements, chose to live there. As the women wrote in their manifesto: 'Because we thought no one could own the sea, we erected our houses on it.' But they were wrong. Someone did own it and had plans to redevelop, and in 1965 householders received notices to quit. A group of residents filed a case for the landlords' title to the land to be cancelled, but they lost. They appealed to the Supreme Court. But while the appeal was pending the landlords sent security guards to clear people out of their houses, offering them derisory prices for the buildings they had erected.

As a response to this immediate threat, the Alaska Beach Residents' Association was formed on 4 April 1972. On 21

April 200 women and children from Alaska marched to the consulate of the landlord, who was a foreigner, and invaded it. They could only be wheedled out when the city mayor offered to see them. They twisted his arm until he signed a commitment to buy the site from the owners. Then, fed up of waiting for a water supply, they marched on the community development agency's premises and proceeded to do their laundry there. Water was soon installed. On 10 July they moved on the City Council bringing along blankets, mats, cooking pots and children, ready for a long siege. The council authorized the mayor to negotiate for purchase of the land.

Meanwhile, the residents had lost their appeal to the Supreme Court and the landlords were again trying to clear the area. The women occupied one of the houses earmarked for destruction, hurled rubble at the demolition team and drove them off. While awaiting the final decision on expropriation, the women started up community projects to boost their incomes, and got aid from UNICEF to set up a fund providing loans for lamp-makers, fruit vendors and fish dealers. 'We would rather remain here than go anywhere else,' the women wrote to UNICEF. 'It is here that we have borne our children and here that we want to die. Until each one of us shall have acquired the title to his lot, we will not consider our long struggle to have ended. Without the security of ownership, we would never be free of the fear of being driven away from our residence at any time.'

Remaining problems

The principles of low cost, self-help, participation and poverty-orientation in city development are making headway. They have been adopted wholeheartedly by the major United Nations agencies involved in human settlements – the UN Centre for Housing, Building and Planning, the World Bank, UNICEF and the UN Environment Programme. These agencies are building in the new approach into their projects in more and more developing countries. But there are still many governments who persist in the old policies of neglect and harassment of squatters, demolition of slums and erection of high-cost housing. To provide services and security of tenure for squatters, they argue, would legalize and encourage squatting and make a mockery of urban development plans. Even where governments accept the new principles, the beneficiaries are not always the poor. Takers on some 'site and services' projects tend to be the better-off among the poor, as the really poor cannot afford building materials. Slum upgrading projects immediately increase property values in the upgraded areas, especially where roads wide enough for cars are provided. Existing residents often sell out at a huge profit and go and squat elsewhere, while the better-off, some of them with cars, move in. The more extreme forms of gentrification of upgraded slums can be avoided by providing only cement paths instead of roads, as Jakarta's Kampong Improvement Programme is now doing.

Apart from government resistance, the biggest single problem in urban development is providing employment which can pay enough for people to afford improvements in their housing. In many cities the available, affordable land for new settlements is on the outskirts of the city, many miles from the main sources of work. Poor residents then face hours of walking every day or several changes of bus, eating up a large proportion of their family income. If poverty is to be alleviated, residents have to have access to work without excessive transport costs. This can be achieved partly by reducing transport prices, improving public transport services, providing footpaths and cycleways and discouraging the private car which, incredibly, dominates the planning of many poor cities much as it has in Los Angeles.

In future, urban projects will attempt to create more jobs in and around the residential area itself. Some of these jobs can be in construction, and the building industry can itself become one of the leading sectors of the expanding city economy. It can have a similar effect in rural areas where the new approach to human settlements has equal validity. As the secretary of the Habitat conference, Enrique Penalosa, has said, 'The engine for growth can be centred on the construction and modernization of human settlements.' There is an immense latent demand for housing, which can be met with labour-intensive methods that do not require sophisticated skills or educational qualifications, and use locally available materials. The World Bank has calculated that every $10,000 spent on construction in South Korea, for example, creates fourteen additional jobs.

Calcutta's gigantic public works programme was costing $40 millions a year in the mid-seventies, and employing a huge army of 120,000 labourers. Indirectly, this has stimulated the emergence and prosperity of a host of small and medium firms in supply, transport and manufacture of all kinds of materials, bricks and granite from the local area, pipes and rods from the engineering shops of Howrah, raw steel from the Asansol-Durgapur steel mills or cement from factories in Bihar and Orissa. In this way the housing problem and the economic problem of developing cities can be exploited to alleviate each other. Surplus labour can be used to provide low-cost housing, and the housing needs of the poor used to develop local enterprise.

But construction is no perpetual-motion machine. A situation where one wave of migrants earns a living by building houses for the next is untenable in the long run. The people have to be fed, and the countryside has to feed them. The city's economy, if it is not to be parasitic, has to be based on a balanced trade with the countryside. It must provide goods to exchange for food, just as the land must produce a surplus to exchange for goods. This means that small-scale manufacturing jobs have to be scattered around in the upgraded slums and the self-built townships. Ways of encouraging this will be discussed in the next chapter: they include assisting the informal trades and industry that flourish in the slums, relaxing Western-modelled zoning regulations that keep industry and housing separate, and providing flatted factories and small workshops in among the houses.

Reforming urban landownership and the private renting of houses is also indispensable. Unregulated private ownership during rapid urbanization leads to riches for the few at the price of impoverishment and insecurity for the many – or exposure to grave hazards as people squat on rubbish tips, steep slopes or swampy areas which speculators have not bought up precisely because they were totally unsuitable for housing. At the very least, land taxes and rent controls are needed to reduce inequalities, improve tenant security, and acquire for the public the profits of scarcity. Ideally, all vacant urban land should be taken into public ownership, as happened in Manila in 1979. And the size and number of existing lots or houses that one person can own should be restricted – in 1976 India limited private ownership of vacant land in its largest cities to 500–1000 square metres, and the excess was acquired by the state.

The final danger is that the city's efforts to improve the housing and the incomes of its poor inhabitants may attract further waves of migrants from the rural areas and hence create the problem all over again. The situation can never improve if rural exodus and urban population growth continue faster than the cities can create jobs. The only long-term cure for the cities' ills lies on the land. Only if the land is made habitable and can provide adequate living can the city do so.

6 Working models: appropriate technologies

The tourist circuit through Agra, northern India, takes you by the broad sweep of the Yamuna river from the gleaming cupola of the Taj to the red sandstone walls of the fort and on to the air-conditioned restaurants and gift shops. But it will certainly not take you down the narrow, crowded streets of the real Agra to the quarter of Jagdishpura, where 2,000 cobblers and their families live and work. This former capital of the Moghuls is also the largest shoemaking centre in India, possibly in the world. An estimated 80,000 people out of its population of 650,000 earn their living from cobbling and turn out some 75,000 pairs of shoes every day. The vast majority of them work in their one-roomed homes. As in so much of traditional and informal industry in the Third World, they earn subsistence incomes. Their techniques of production are primitive. And their poverty exposes them to one of the most devious and persistent forms of exploitation I have come across.

When I visited Bagh Nanak Chand, he and his two teenage sons and orphaned nephew were handmaking black, wedge-heeled women's sandals. Inside the family, a rudimentary form of division of labour is practised. Chand and his elder son cut out the leather for the uppers and sew them by hand. The nephew fits them to the lasts, wets a finger in a pot of glue, sticks the underneath edges down and nails them to the last, then glues on the composite soles. The younger son squats by a charcoal fire and finishes the surface with a heated iron, then polishes them up to a bright, barrackroom finish. The shoes are neat and workmanlike, like most of Agra's footwear, testimony of considerable skill and craftsmanship. But these shoes will

Working models

sell on the lower, bazaar end of the home market and command
low prices. The reason is that Chand uses cheap, 9 rupee (60p
or $1·20) lasts made of unseasoned wood which shrink and start
to wear away after a couple of dozen pairs – he cannot afford
the 26 rupees for standard lasts. Chand tries to keep the shape
by tacking on bits of cardboard, but the result is that his shoes
do not conform to regular standards and vary somewhat in size
and shape. Chand's family workshop turns out twelve pairs of
sandals a day, or eight pairs of shoes. With suitable small-scale
machinery for stitching and sole-fitting, they could double their
output. But low productivity and poor product quality are not
the only causes of the vicious circle of poverty in which the
cobblers are caught. Like so many workers in cottage industries
in the Third World, they are trapped in a web of predatory
middlemen, moneylenders and raw materials suppliers. Although self-employed, the cobblers are exploited due to their
weakness in bargaining on the market. It is relative market
muscle, rather than supply and demand, that determines the
price they receive for their product.

At around 5·30 p.m. Chand collects the day's sandals into a
large flat wicker basket, covers it with a check cloth and goes to
the main road to hail a cycle rickshaw. He gets out at Hing Ki
Mandi, Agra's shoe market. The bustling main street is lined
with narrow booths where shopkeepers wait for customers,
squatting on piles of rubber and plastic sheet for soles, leather,
boxes of tacks and glue, and heaps of lasts. Chand carries his
load down one of the arcades where the middlemen, most of
them prosperously dressed, sit crosslegged surrounded by shoe-
boxes. Chand stops at the premises of a white-haired merchant
in his fifties, in Western dress, with gold-rimmed glasses. He
passes over the sandals, pair by pair, deferentially, while the
middleman, one hand in each shoe, twists and turns them to
check from every angle for defects and size. If he finds faults,
he will correspondingly reduce the price. A short haggle with
few words ensues – there's little point arguing with a middle-

131

man. Chand reluctantly accepts 12 rupees a pair. The cost of production, excluding labour, is 9 rupees, and Chand counts 2 rupees 50 paise for each pair as labour. That gives him a 'profit' of 50 paise a pair. Total owing from the middleman: 144 rupees (£9.50). If demand was slack, Chand sometimes had to sell shoes at a loss – by which he meant losing his 'profit' of 50 paise per shoe, eating into the labour cost. Neither he nor any other poor cobbler could hold back stocks to wait for better prices. He had to accept whatever the middleman was offering him.

The transaction that follows is the core of the system by which the cobblers are impoverished. Chand is paid – but not in cash. The middleman reaches down a pad of printed promissory notes (*purchas*) and fills it in for 144 rupees – postdated for payment three months later. This means that Chand is giving the dealer three months' credit. As Chand's family lives and works from hand to mouth, he has no choice but to seek out a special dealer in promissory notes, who will cash the *purcha* immediately. But he will deduct a discount of between 2 and 5 per cent for every month he has to wait for full payment from the middleman. Practically speaking, Chand, in his turn, is getting three months' credit, and paying the interest (annual rate: 25 to 60 per cent) in advance. For his 144-rupee *purcha*, Chand gets only 127 rupees, losing 12 per cent of the face value. But as labour and profit account for only a quarter of the selling price of the shoes, he is actually losing almost half his family's net income.

From the *purcha* buyer, Chand moves on to the raw material booths to get the supplies he will need for the next day's work. He complains that the traders always sell short measure, but as he is illiterate he has no way of checking what they are giving him.

Why do the cobblers tolerate this iniquitous system which cheats them of half their earnings? The fact is that they do not suffer it stoically. Three times they have gone on strike to try to change it, and three times they have been defeated by their own poverty. The last occasion was in 1976. All the cobblers in Agra stopped producing shoes, demanding that the *purcha* system be abolished. For poor, illiterate cottage workers with no trade union behind them, it was a remarkable feat of organization and solidarity. For fifteen days Hing Ki Mandi was closed. But the rich merchants simply lived off their fat and waited. The cobblers were all skin and bone. They had no strike pay or social security or savings to cushion them. Their children were starving, their wives pleading with them to go back to work again. Even so, surprisingly, no one broke ranks, but after two weeks they held a big meeting and decided they could not go on. The middlemen had won. Hing Ki Mandi opened again and again the middlemen paid for their shoes with credit notes.

Agra's shoemaking industry is typical of so much unorganized manufacturing in the Third World: primitive technology, low productivity, poor quality of product, poor access to markets, exploitation by middlemen and moneylenders. All these factors keep the price of the product low and trap the workers in poverty. For the past two decades a wide range of measures have been taken to improve the shoemakers' lot by working on each of these handicaps. They exemplify the new style of programme for industry, which pays much greater attention to small-scale, decentralized enterprises and to building on and upgrading traditional skills.

Since the 1950s India's Small Industries Development Organization has been trying to bring on the shoe industry. In Agra it has established a Small Industries Service Institute, working out of a converted Maharajah's mansion with twelve resident peacocks. Its super-efficient director, Mr Saha, has adorned its walls with slogans: 'There is no substitute for hard work'; 'Efficient management is the basis of success'; 'Observe honesty, integrity, punctuality, discipline, cleanliness'. SISI has helped hundreds of shoemakers to increase their efficiency and income. It has prepared projects for them to produce better-quality shoes for orders or specific markets. It has helped them to get bank finance at cheap rates, and to purchase machinery from its sister organization, the National Small Industries Corporation. It gives training in advanced craftsmanship, design and management. It helps with marketing, liaising with the State Trading Corporation, which handles outside orders for shoes, and with government purchasing departments wanting ankle boots or Oxford brogues for the home guard or the police.

On the outskirts of Agra SISI has established a last factory which turns out 12,000 pairs of precision lasts each year. These are of seasoned wood that will not shrink, and can make 100 identical pairs of shoes before they wear out. Shoemakers who use the lasts are able to produce a standardized quality product suitable for brand sales or export, which will sell at double the price of the bazaar shoe made on the bazaar last, and yield double the income for the cobbler. But resources have been limited, and so far only about one in eight of the city's cobblers have been helped.

Lack of adequate resources, equally, has restricted the impact of other efforts to help. In 1974 Uttar Pradesh state government set up the UP Leather Development and Marketing Corporation to act as non-profit-making raw materials seller, credit-giver and middleman. It provides cobblers with standard lasts and designs for orders it has received, inspects their products for quality, and pays cash on the spot so the cobbler loses nothing of his earnings. So far the corporation's capital of £300,000 ($550,000) has enabled it to deal with only 300 shoemakers.

Wanted: one billion situations vacant

In 1977 there were some 331 million people unemployed or underemployed in the non-Communist Third World – two out of five of the working population – according to estimates made by the UN-affiliated International Labour Organization. Forty million of these were wholly unemployed, most of them in the cities. The rest, overwhelmingly in the rural areas, were under-employed, that is, seeking additional work to make up their hours or their income.

Between now and the end of this century, the labour force of the developing countries will be growing faster than ever before. By the year 2,000, the ILO predicts, it will have grown to 1,927 million from 1,125 million in 1975. Adding to this the numbers currently un- or underemployed, this means that an extra billion jobs need to be created. Population programmes, however successful, will not alter this total much: the extra workers of twenty years hence have already been born. The larger part of the extra jobs – perhaps half in the poorer countries – will have to be in agriculture, through land reform, extension of irrigation and greater use of improved seeds and fertilizers. Another large section will be in services, including labour-intensive public works. But industry will have to provide a quarter or a third of the extra employment.

The strategy most countries pursued to create new jobs in industry was to build up manufacturing along Western lines, in large factories using imported Western machinery and technology. This technology was developed for the specific conditions of the West in the fifties and sixties, when there was a shortage of labour but ample amounts of capital for investment. In this context it made some sense to go for capital-intensive technology, using machinery rather than workers. In the context of poor countries with vast reserves of surplus labour and a shortage of capital, it was a recipe for disaster. It provided jobs for precious few people, but because of its high productivity it could pay them relatively well. It generated gross inequalities. Concentrated in the cities, it boosted city incomes and accelerated the migration from the land, all the more so as it attracted the lion's share of government investment at the expense of agriculture. This approach entailed heavy costs in foreign exchange, and increased dependence on Western know-how.

Industry grew rapidly: output expanded by 7 per cent a year between 1953 and 1975. But because the machinery used was getting more and more capital-intensive, employment grew much more slowly – at less than half that rate. Because it was starting from a small base, industry could absorb only a fraction of the increased workforce produced by population growth. Not only that, but with its mass-produced goods it helped to wipe out millions of jobs in traditional industries such as blacksmithing, pottery, and especially spinning and weaving.

This concentration on urbanization and industrialization, combined with poverty on the land, sucked the rural poor into the cities in vast numbers. There they could not find work in the modern sector. And so there grew up the teeming, motley circus of the unorganized or informal sector: hawkers, tailors, whores, rickshawmen, market mammies, fortune-tellers, watch repairers, bush garages, one-man engineering workshops. Enterprises of this kind employ as much as half the workforce in the typical developing city. They have much to recommend them. They require little capital, so anyone can set up in business. Their technology is labour-intensive, often using improvised or second-hand machinery, creating the maximum employment. The raw materials they use are cheap and locally available, often recycled waste. Their products and services are low-cost, within the budget of the urban poor who for the most part cannot afford modern sector goods.

Yet this great reservoir of savings, enterprise and inventivity has been, in the vast majority of countries, ignored or neglected by governments. It gets little or no official credit. Most of its capital is raised from family savings – the rest from moneylenders at exorbitant rates. It bumbles on, with inefficient management and *ad hoc* marketing. Indeed, it is often discriminated against or harassed. Official specifications and standards rule its products out of many markets. City zoning and licensing regulations make much of it illegal and hence subject to police prosecution. Informal enterprises often have to work in shantytowns, without light, power or water, sometimes even without a roof over their heads. Slum clearance programmes bulldoze away as many workplaces as homes.

Small is beautiful: appropriate technology

A new approach was needed. If developing countries were to have any hope of employing those extra billion workers, job creation would have to take the front seat in policy-making. The large-scale, centralized, Western-modelled approach had not solved the employment problem and had aggravated inequality and the urban explosion. What was needed was a new model of industrialization, starting with the small scale, building up indigenous technology, using local resources, employing people in preference to machinery – a decentralized form of industrialization, more evenly spread across the country, not one that created inhuman, polluted and polluting megalopolises with all their attendant problems, from traffic jams to social disintegration.

In 1961 India's then prime minister, Jawaharlal Nehru, invited Ernst Schumacher, at the time economic adviser to Britain's National Coal Board, to tour his country and advise the Indian planning commission on what to do with rural India. The visit was to lead to the birth of the idea of intermediate technology, which offered the hardware for the new humanized industrial revolution. Schumacher's brief was to try to identify non-agricultural activities in India's rural areas that could employ some of the surplus population that was moving to the cities.

I interviewed Schumacher a few months before his untimely death in 1977. 'Nehru realized his policies had had a certain effect on big cities like Bombay, but rural India had been bypassed and was dying,' he told me. 'Somewhere in south India the right question popped up in my mind, namely, surely the technology of Sheffield or Pittsburgh cannot fit into this region, because all the preconditions of infrastructure and education are absent. The question was: what would be the appropriate technology for rural India? And then the answer followed immediately: it would have to be something very much more productive than what they had, which was so miserable and kept them so poor, but something infinitely simpler and cheaper than the highly sophisticated capital-intensive technology the West would deploy. Yet between the 50-rupee technology of the village potter and the 50,000-rupee technology of the machine-minder on the industrial estate, there was nothing. The middle had disappeared. But without it there could be no hope for the poor. My name is that of a shoemaker. I realized that the modern world had produced only great big boots for the big feet of the rich, and no shoes at all for the little feet of the poor. If you throw these big boots at the poor countries, then only the rich people there can wear them.' Schumacher's report to the Indian planning commission recommended intermediate technology as a solution. Fifteen months later the commission convened a conference on it and the idea gained respectability. It began to be seriously applied in India, though at first only in a small way, in the second half of the sixties.

Schumacher, it has to be admitted, did not invent the idea of appropriate technology. Credit for that must go to Gandhi (see Chapter 1), whom Schumacher once called the greatest economist of the century. Schumacher was, in essence, a Gandhian gifted with a more scientific and pragmatic approach. His great contribution was in developing and fleshing out the principles and popularizing them in the development field. In 1965 he founded the London-based Intermediate Technology Development Group to start on the intensely practical and often humdrum task of identifying, developing or discovering particular machines and techniques, in every field from improved mud bricks to cheap do-it-yourself hospital equipment. The group tests and demonstrates intermediate techniques and publicizes them through its books and periodicals – such exotically named inventions as the treadle-operated peanut-thresher, the hand-pushed sod seeder, the bush ambulance or the pedal-operated cassava-grinder.

Addressing his last annual general meeting of the ITDG as its chairman in 1977, Schumacher was able to report on the continuing spread of intermediate or appropriate technology. United Nations agencies such as UNICEF, WHO, the International Labour Organization, the UN Industrial Development Organization and the World Bank officially encourage it in their projects. Appropriate technology research centres have been set up in Bangalore, Lucknow and Benares in India; in Bangladesh, Indonesia, Pakistan, the Philippines, Sri Lanka and Thailand; in Botswana, Ghana, Nigeria, Tanzania and Zambia; and in Colombia and Argentina; and research is being pursued at institutions and universities in the United States, the United Kingdom, the Netherlands and Canada.

The terms 'intermediate', 'appropriate' and 'alternative' are bandied around more or less interchangeably about the new soft technologies, and they do have a lot in common. But their connotations are slightly different. Alternative technology is the ecology, self-sufficiency and smallness-orientated version proposed to humanize industry in the West. Intermediate technology, as its name implies, aims to fill the gaping hole between traditional and modern machinery. Appropriate technology is a basket concept for all forms of small-scale hardware and software – including modern ones – which are suited to the economic conditions of developing countries. This is the term now most commonly used.

The name 'appropriate technology' conjures up images of exotic inventions, Heath Robinson-style contraptions made of only natural materials and using vast amounts of labour. The stereotype is misleading. AT is not a particular collection of rather funny-looking machinery – nor is it even a particular type of machinery. Large-scale, capital-intensive plants can be appropriate in the right contexts – for example, in oil-refining or the production of bulk fertilizers – either because they are the only possible way to achieve the desired quality, or because they are most economical in their use of capital. 'Appropriate technology' means simply any technology that makes the most economical use of a country's natural resources and its relative proportions of capital, labour and skills, and that furthers national and social goals. Fostering AT means consciously encouraging the right choice of technology, not simply letting businessmen make the decision for you.

In the majority of developing countries, the appropriate technology to use would look roughly similar. To soak up unemployment it has to create as many jobs as possible – hence it needs to be labour-intensive, using workers in preference to machines. It must be relatively cheap, because that enables the maximum number of jobs to be created with the limited funds available. But it must also improve income, so it needs to be more productive than traditional technology. And it must use scarce capital wisely, so it ought to produce as much output as possible for a given amount of investment.

As skills are usually limited, machinery has to be simple to run and repair. It ought to use as much locally produced raw materials and equipment as possible, thus saving on foreign exchange and creating more jobs indirectly. It should be of a scale suited to the local market, otherwise its capacity will be chronically underused – the usual story with much of Third World industry. Further, it should contribute to the development of broad-based technological skills within each country. This means that, except in strategic cases, it should not be too far ahead of local abilities to repair, copy and adapt, and should upgrade rather than destroy traditional skills. Environmentally, appropriate technology should be hygienic, conservational and non-polluting, using renewable sources of energy and raw materials wherever possible, with maximum reuse of industrial, animal and human wastes and farm residues (e.g., for paper, fibre, fuel or building materials). It should satisfy basic needs and involve popular participation.

Appropriate technology, in other words, is the hardware of the new development thinking and embodies all its major principles. But there is another more practical set of requirements without which all the other principles will remain pious hopes. Appropriate technology must be technically sound, economical to users and customers in comparison with the available alternatives, and socially acceptable in the light of local culture and traditions. Most of the failures of appropriate technology out in the field can be traced to these the lack of one or more of last three down-to-earth prerequisites.

Probably the vast bulk of appropriate technology in use today was not introduced from on high, but improvised by entrepreneurs and the self-employed in the unorganized sector. These people had never heard of the principle, but were driven to it by their need to improve on traditional techniques and their inability to afford modern ones. The rickshaw, for example, has been progressively upgraded from the slow, hand-pulled variety, to the trishaw – half a bike with a two-wheel passenger carriage tacked on; to the auto-rickshaw – a scooter with a canvas-covered cab attached. The auto-rickshaw is an ingenious adaptation of a cheap piece of Western technology to Eastern needs. Intensifying the use of advanced machinery also counts as appropriate technology – the battered Morris 1000s that rattle around Nigerian cities, picking up one fare on top of another until the chassis is scraping the road, are making more economical use of scarce resources and bring the price of taxi fares within range of the poor. Another area where the people are way ahead of the experts is in the use of second-hand equipment. As technology advances, Western machines are becoming more and more productive and capital-intensive. One study by the International Labour Organization found that a 1950 spinning plant could employ twenty times more people per unit of capital than the 1968 version.

Appropriate technology of the kind introduced by expert outsiders takes a variety of forms. It may involve improving an existing traditional technique, modifying a modern machine, inventing a new one from scratch, digging out a piece of antique Western technology from industrial archeology, or finding a particularly ingenious bit of indigenous wisdom working in a small area and spreading it abroad.

We have already seen some of these technologies in the realm of construction, and we shall meet others in food storage and preparation and in health. In villages throughout the Third World small, inexpensive adjustments in the technologies of everyday life and work are improving productivity, easing the burden of housework on women, cutting living costs and safeguarding the environment. In north-east Kenya windmills based on Cretan designs are being used to pump water for irrigation, instead of diesel pumps that used to break down too often. Elsewhere in Kenya, cement water jars collecting rainwater from tin roofs are saving women the long trek to the well. In Guatemala, where firewood can cost a quarter of family income, a mud stove moulded from soil, sand and water retains the heat and circulates it through ducts, halving the consumption of fuel. In transport, cheap, energy-saving vehicles can meet the needs of the poor, from more efficient backpacks and bullock carts to tougher bikes and utility vans. Roads fit for these can be built cheaply, linking up villages that could wait decades for conventional roads.

Renewable sources of energy are being harnessed to replace dear oil, dung needed as manure, or wood cut without replanting. Solar energy technology is still in its infancy, but clearly has a big future in the tropics where sunshine is plentiful. In the Mauretanian village of Chinguetti, deep inside the Sahara, solar energy was used to work a gas expansion engine to pump water from underground. The simple solar reflectors were built into the roof of a school, which, as an added bonus, they helped to keep cool. Pedal power – harnessing the mechanical efficiency of human beings through modified bikes – is becoming a popular way of driving all kinds of machines. Animal power is being pushed to new efficiency by improved harnesses and gear systems. The energies of wind, water and the earth's inner heat are waiting to be harvested.

Fuels of the future

Finding appropriate solutions to the fuel crisis is becoming an important priority, both in alleviating poverty and in preserving the precarious environment. The world's tropical forests are being felled at such a speed that at present rates the forests of the developing countries could well disappear within a century, and more than four fifths of the wood that is cut is being used for fuel. As population expands, the task of gathering fuel has become increasingly time-consuming and exorbitantly expensive. The resulting deforestation is stripping soil of its cover, accelerating erosion and the spread of deserts. Thus the poor are driven by their sheer poverty to destroy the environment they depend on for a living – they are buying short-term survival by committing long-term suicide.

Yet the vast bulk of national investment and international aid in the energy field has gone into the construction of massive conventional electricity-generating projects and distribution networks. As most villages still lack electricity supplies, and the poor cannot afford domestic connections, this is no answer to their energy needs. A study by the International Institute for Environment and Development found that less than 1 per cent of the funds of development finance agencies between 1973 and 1977 went into non-conventional energy projects.

Until breakthroughs in photo-electric cell technology make solar energy competitive, fuelwood plantations are likely to become the most significant of the appropriate energy sources. One hectare of land planted with a fast-growing species like eucalyptus (which can grow up to twenty times faster than many local species) can provide enough fuel for up to 100 families if combined with fuel economies from improved stove designs. In the new science of agro-forestry, trees can be combined with food crops, intercropped on the same plot, or included as part of a systematic crop rotation to maintain soil fertility. Fuelwood plantations have been spreading in the Third World. By 1978 the World Bank had initiated or planned twenty fuelwood projects. In the Philippines 32,000 hectares of trees were planted to provide pulp for paper, leaf-meal for compost or leaves for livestock fodder, charcoal, fuel and poles for building. Plantations can also halt or reverse land degradation. In Senegal and other Sahelian countries plantations of acacia trees are providing fuel and helping to halt the spread of the desert.

Another appropriate fuel with considerable potential is methane gas from the fermentation of animal and human wastes. Where forests have been depleted, dung from livestock is often dried and used as fuel, instead of as manure to maintain soil fertility. One third of India's billion tons of cowdung is burned as domestic fuel each year and meets more than half of household fuel needs. This is a tragic waste of the equivalent of more than India's total production of chemical fertilizer. If applied to the fields instead of going up in smoke, it could produce an extra 10 to 14 million tons of food grains. It took India three decades of experimentation to come up with a biogas plant that really works in village conditions: the gobar gas plant developed by the Khadi and Village Industries Commission. By the end of the sixties only a few hundred of these were in use. But the oil crisis transformed the economics of fuel and fertilizer use and put a new urgency into India's programme. The number of plants installed rose from 6,000 in 1973 to more than 60,000 in 1978.

The plant is a deep pit lined with brick and concrete and divided into two chambers, capped with a steel gasholder which rises and falls as gas is generated and used. Cattle dung is fed in at one inlet, and flows down a long pipe to the bottom of one of the chambers. As it progresses upwards, over a divider and down the second chamber, saprophytic and methane bacteria digest it into methane gas (CH_4) and carbon dioxide. The methane burns with a pollution-free flame, converting into water and carbon dioxide. The slurry passes down to the bottom of the second chamber, by which time digestion is completed, and is pushed up out of the outlet pipe, so the farmer can transfer it to his manure pit for drying and composting with other wastes. The gobar gas plant neatly resolves the Asian farmer's great dilemma: whether to use his cattle and buffalo dung as farmyard manure, or as fuel. Now he can do both, and both in greater measure than before. One kilo of wet dung, processed through a gas plant, produces eight or nine times as much usable heat as when dried and used as fuel. Moreover, the same amount of dung produces 43 per cent more manure than if left in a manure pit, where decomposition is more complete. The gobar gas scheme's research station on the rural fringe of Bombay has now developed a mantle lamp which gives light equivalent to a forty-watt bulb; industrial burners that can be used for village industries like soap and sugar making; and modified petrol and diesel engines that can run off gas.

So far all the plants installed have been purchased by private individuals, and only the better-off farmers with sufficient cattle have been able to benefit. To solve the fuel problems of small farmers and landless labourers, community gas plants are needed. These could also make use of the wasted resource of human excreta. But Indian culture and politics have proved formidable obstacles. The villages are fragmented into rival factions, cutting across caste lines, which compete for advantage with embittered hatred. Farmers who own cattle are reluctant to hand over their dung for the benefit of the community, as the opposing faction would also benefit. The fear of pollution by human excreta has also hindered progress – fortunately other countries are not so handicapped.

The potential of biogas is considerable. If all the dung of India's livestock, and all human wastes, were fermented, this would meet the domestic fuel requirements of three out of four families and the savings in manure or fuel could be worth $1 billion a year or more. Other countries are now realizing the importance of biogas. China, which does not have India's cultural and social obstacles, uses biogas widely; in 1977 around 5 million plants were in use.

New tools for industry

Finally, there is the important sphere of industry. Here the most appropriate technology will not always be small-scale or labour-intensive. With petrochemicals or fertilizer, for example, bulk production offers huge economies of scale and saves on energy. But even within large-scale, capital-intensive enterprises there is an important place for labour-intensive methods. Often the mistake has been made of thinking that the entire production process, from raw material to finished product, is an inseparable whole. In fact it is usually possible to break down every production process into stages, for some of which capital-intensity might be best, while for others labour-intensive methods make economic sense.

The United Nations Industrial Development Organization, for example, recommends that fertilizers should be produced in bulk. But they could be packed into blends of nitrogen, phosphates and potash, suited to local crops and soils, in small units decentralized to rural areas. Jumbo plants may be needed to crack ethylene, but much smaller plants can process the bulk raw material into PVC chips, synthetic fibre or polyethylene sheeting. In turn, scattered workshops with cheap injection-moulding machines costing as little as $400 can make these intermediate materials into end products for the local market, such as grain storage bins, plastic sheeting for pond lining, or domestic ware.

Sometimes the choice of appropriate technology faces planners with a difficult dilemma. There are several possible criteria: creating the *maximum number of jobs* per unit of capital; producing the *maximum output* per unit of capital; turning out the *cheapest possible goods* for the consumer; or providing the *greatest profit* for the entrepreneur. These criteria often point in different directions. For example, labour-intensive technologies may sometimes produce goods that cost more. In other words, consumers at large would be paying a hidden tax to keep the producers in work. But if the price difference was small and could save a lot of jobs, this would be well worth while. Cheap goods are of little use to people who have no money because they can't get work. The best technology for a situation will usually be the one that, for a given unit of capital, achieves the best balance between creating a maximum number of jobs and producing maximum output. Often a careful search of possible alternatives will unearth a technology that is both efficient and labour-intensive. One International Labour Office study, for example, found a semi-automated can-making technique in Thailand that produced cans three times more cheaply than a high-speed automated technique being used by a large multinational – and created five times as much employment for a given amount of capital.

Another example is provided by the small-scale crystal sugar plants developed by the Planning Research and Action Institute at Lucknow. Previously, crystal sugar had been produced only in large, modern mills. These paid a good price for sugar cane, but their large capacity (over 12,000 tons a year) meant they had to cover a huge area to get enough sugar to process. The resulting transport problems stopped them from taking produce from more than a third of the farmers, and the other two thirds got much lower prices for their cane from makers of crude village sugar. So the PRAI developed a small-scale plant that turned out 640 tons of sugar a year. In place of the large expensive vacuum pans of the big mills, the small plant uses open pans to concentrate and evaporate the cane juice. These plants are cheap to build, and create many more jobs. For the price of one large mill employing only 900 people, forty-seven small mills can be built providing 10,000 jobs. And the economics of the operation are very favourable – an essential requirement for the adoption of AT. A hundred kilos of sugar could be produced for less than 236 rupees, against 250 rupees for the big plants. The small operations could provide cheaper sugar for the consumer, more jobs for the under-employed, and extra profit margins for the entrepeneur. So the mini-mills proliferated. By the mid-seventies there were over 1,200 of them, producing 20 per cent of India's sugar and employing 100,000 workers.

Public works are another very promising area for labour-intensive appropriate technology. In the bad old days Calcutta's new underground railway would have been built using some futuristic mechanical mole to carve out a tunnel. Instead thousands of workers in loincloths and headwraps are digging out immense pits with picks and shovels, removing the debris in straw baskets on their heads, and will fill them in again when a concrete tube has been inserted. Avoiding use of mechanized methods saves huge numbers of jobs. A cement mixer replaces five to twenty men, a crane thirty to forty. A bulldozer demolishes seventy to ninety workplaces, while a big excavator makes up to 160 labourers redundant.

Cautionary tales

Unfortunately, appropriate technology is still very much thinner on the ground than inappropriate technology. The amount of research being done is minimal. The Organization for Economic Cooperation and Development estimated that in 1975

AT institutions were spending, worldwide, less than $5 million on developing and diffusing appropriate technology, against some $60 billion spent on developing new modern technology.

More than anything else, this shortage of research funds and personnel accounts for appropriate technology's numerous failures in the field. Take the case of the cow-dung cooker developed by Lucknow's Planning Research and Action Institute – an earlier attempt at the problem successfully resolved by the gobar gas plant. PRAI developed and sold these plants to individual farmers, but a year after their introduction only one in five were still in use. They had become clogged with vegetable matter, and moisture in the gas had rusted the fittings and pipes. The flame was uneven and took a long time to cook food. The plants were not producing enough gas to cover family needs. The efficiency of the plant in field conditions turned out to be only half of what was expected, because the working temperatures were too low.

The project failed, quite simply, because not enough preliminary research had been done. Villagers have a right to expect technical perfection before a new machine is tried out on them at their expense, because they have too little surplus income to waste on failures. A single failure of this kind in an area will permanently undermine the credibility of the institution that is pushing it.

Other appropriate technology projects have failed for complex economic and social reasons. Water-purifying systems using cheap filters of local materials were abandoned in favour of the traditional polluted waterhole, because a water charge was imposed that the poor villagers preferred not to pay. In Orissa, India, moulded concrete latrines were produced and sold at only $1 each, but only a few villagers bought them and only a third of those who did ever used them. The fact was that the new conveniences were a huge inconvenience. Women had to fetch a lot more water to flush them. Men usually did their daily defecation in the fields, where it did some good, and would not come all the way back home just for that.

The average piece of academically researched appropriate technology, in other words, is no more likely to succeed just because of its noble intentions than any other backroom inventor's brainchild. The only sure test is if it works in field conditions, and if it is widely adopted and used. Appropriate technology has to answer a felt need. It has to make sense from the users' point of view. So research is not enough. It can all too easily be pursued in a social vacuum, unconnected with the real needs of farmers and manufacturers. Many, if not most, AT inventions moulder away in college backyards or are applied only in a few lucky (or sometimes unlucky) villages. This is merely tinkering about. It does not become appropriate technology unless it is considered appropriate by the eventual users. In other words, systems have to be set up which allow the users to participate in deciding what technical gaps exist, and to cooperate in ensuring that proposed solutions take their real economic situation into account.

Appropriate technology research must be closely linked to agricultural extension services and to programmes encouraging small-scale and rural industry, so the activities of research institutions can be harnessed directly to the needs of the small farmer, the small businessman or co-op. A pioneering scheme along these lines is India's network of District Industry Centres, set up in 1978 to unite under a single roof all the services a small enterprise might need. One of the centres' key functions is to find out from local entrepreneurs what their technical problems are and to commission local colleges and universities to research solutions for them.

Correct government policies are essential if AT is to spread. Given enough help, incentives and training small entrepreneurs will invent for themselves and disseminate more new inventions than a thousand academic researchers could dream of. The biggest boost to AT would be to foster small enterprises.

Technological dependence – or independence?

Despite its clear social and economic advantages, appropriate technology faces an assault course of hurdles and obstacles which must be removed before it can progress far.

First there are what economists term the factor price distortions of the typical developing economy. The factors involved here are capital and labour. Governments, concerned to encourage rapid industrialization, have often provided cheap credit, tax concessions for investment, lower duty rates and cheaper foreign exchange rates for machinery imports. These things have tended to make machinery artificially cheap in comparison to labour, and encouraged capital-intensiveness. Restoring the true price would mean abolishing tax and customs concessions, raising interest rates and perhaps devaluing the currency. This would encourage greater use of labour – and also promote the growth of a local machinery industry, one of the prime necessities of a solid industrial revolution.

Another factor encouraging capital-intensiveness as well as technological dependence is the way aid is usually organized. In 1977 more than half of Western aid was tied or partly tied to purchases of goods or equipment from the donor nations. Moreover, most aid programmes, national and international, are willing to finance only the foreign exchange costs involved in projects, and not the local costs. Both of these factors encourage developing countries to hunt around for projects that will involve imported equipment. This ties them in to Western technologies and to particular suppliers. If local industries and technological abilities are to be fostered, then aid will have to be increasingly untied and ready to finance local costs. This may mean that aid does not result immediately and directly in more exports for donors; but indirectly, through the boost it gives to local industry, it may generate more export orders in the longer run.

One reason commonly advanced for using inappropriate

Western technology is that it is the only efficient technology there is. It is certainly true that the world's patrimony of productive technology for sale is dominated by the West. It has been estimated that only 2 per cent of the world's research and development expenditure is made in developing countries. Studies by the United Nations Conference on Trade and Development have revealed that in 1972 only 200,000, or 6 per cent, of the world's 3·5 million patents were held in developing countries. Of these only 30,000 – less than 1 per cent of the global total – were held by nationals of these countries. The other 170,000 were held by foreigners, usually multinational companies. By and large, the industrialization of most Third World countries has taken place with imported Western technology rather than technology they have developed for themselves. Most countries have simply purchased the hardware, and not the knowledge of how to make their own hardware – so, like drug addicts, their dependence has been strengthened and they have been forced to return again and again to the pushers for further supplies.

Western technology is controlled by the great transnational companies. Whenever these firms set up branches of their own in developing countries they tend to use the same capital-intensive technologies they would use back home, the same standard factories. They adopt the same high levels of quality control which usually push towards capital-intensiveness, as machines turn out a more predictable and uniform product than humans do. They appear to waste no time researching into locally available alternative technologies, though these may often be capable of cutting production costs. Even when multinationals are selling to local companies or governments, the technology they sell is often excessively capital-intensive, wrapped up in package deals which often include elements that could be provided by local firms. Most contracts for technology transfer commit the recipient to purchasing spare parts, other equipment and even raw materials from the supplier or his nominees.

However much they focus in the future on technological self-sufficiency, developing countries are likely to go on wanting certain kinds of Western know-how. But there are ways they can control the transfer to ensure it increases national technological capabilities, rather than boosting dependence. Attempts to draw up an effective international code covering technology transfer have been foiled, because Western governments have been unwilling to make it binding on the multinationals. Hence developing countries must impose their own controls, individually or, better still, collectively. In India multinationals have been forced to make most of their purchases locally, even for machinery, because of stringent import controls and foreign-exchange restrictions. This has helped built up indigenous technological capacities, as the multinationals are compelled to give technical help to their subcontractors to make sure they can meet specifications. Several national governments in Latin America have introduced legislation to control technology transfers. In 1974 Argentina set up a National Register of Contracts, and required all agreements to be registered before remittances of payments abroad would be allowed. Contracts are not sanctioned if they involve tied purchases, 'packaged' technology or use of technology that is locally available. Colombia's Royalties Committee has cut down tied purchase clauses by 90 per cent. Countries with large home markets, such as India or Brazil, can afford to be exacting. But smaller countries that get tough on their own may simply find that the multinational sets up shop in a neighbouring country with less stringent regulations. For this reason, the majority of developing countries will have to cooperate regionally if they want to control the import of technology without damaging investment.

But the blockage against appropriate technology goes deeper

still. It comes from the infatuation with Western lifestyles and Western techniques. Third World élites often have an insatiable taste for high-quality Western-style goods, and as they have the purchasing power they may constitute the most profitable market for manufactures. In many countries some of the first large-scale factories to open produce consumer durables such as cars or fridges to cater for élite requirements, and the quality expected can only be provided by using capital-intensive technologies imported from the West.

The problem has two roots: on the one hand, the existence of gross inequalities that give the élite their disproportionate purchasing power and political pull: on the other, the obsession with an alien culture. Inequality can be tackled by redistribution of wealth and income to the poor. The basic goods they so desperately need can usually be produced using much more labour-intensive methods – they cannot afford to be too concerned about quality. India's planning commission has calculated that every million rupees (£65,000 or $120,000) of income transferred from the rich to the poor creates an extra twenty jobs.

The fatal infatuation with the West is a harder nut to crack. Western technology is productive, powerful and seductive. It is also the ground out of which military strength grows. Hence it is easy to justify a fixation with Western technology as a desire to obtain the best for your country, so as to make it strong militarily and economically. And so, paradoxically, an obsession with Westernization can be passed off as a fervour of nationalism. In this spirit many Third World governments have poohpoohed appropriate technology as a neo-imperialist plot dreamed up by Western-dominated development agencies to keep them backward and subservient. At the World Employment Conference in 1976 many of the most vociferous and influential governments spoke out against AT. In a typical comment, India's Sanjivan Reddy remarked that 'no nation could afford to lose the long-term advantages of modern technology. Excessive dependence on labour-intensive technologies would deprive the Third World of its right to the patrimony of mankind.'

The nationalism expressed in the now growing resistance to appropriate technology is taking a misguided path. The way to build up an independent national industry on a secure base is not to import the building blocks ready made from the West or Eastern Europe. An industrial revolution surely cannot be made like a Lego outfit or bought off the shelf. It is not a matter of importing some impressive bits of hardware and training up a few privileged workers to run them – more of knowing how to make your own hardware and creating an economic climate in which it will flourish. The idea that a minute advanced technology sector, light years ahead of the rest of the economy, can somehow pull the whole nation's technology up by the bootstraps is as wrongheaded as the idea that prosperity for the élite will quickly trickle down to the masses.

A truly national industrial revolution, therefore, must build on existing technological abilities and resources, upgrading them as rapidly as desired and as possible, but on a very wide front. It involves widespread technical education, not just in a few institutions but in a more practical emphasis in all aspects of school and adult education. It means helping out all forms of small-scale businesses and crafts. And it means creating a buoyant local demand for manufactures by improving the incomes of farmers, as demand has always been the strongest stimulus to technological innovation. Some aspects of advanced Western or East European technology may have a definite role to play – but it will only be a positive role if they are very closely related to local technological capacities.

The technologies that emerge naturally from this broad effort will also be more appropriate. They will promote gradual social and economic change, instead of the explosive impact which alien technologies have had. Authentic nationalism, and concern for the poor and employment creation, therefore, both point towards the same kind of solution. Industrialization in most of the Third World has so far been exogenous, pulled from outside. To avoid dependence, it must be endogenous, fuelled from within.

7 From little acorns: small-scale and rural enterprise

Technology never exists in a vacuum. In the everyday world it is applied through social organizations, and the managerial context has a strong influence on the kind of technology chosen. So appropriate technology must go together with an appropriate form of management. That form cannot be large-scale enterprise, with its penchant for capital-intensive technology. It must be small-scale enterprise, which has a natural affinity with labour-intensive technology. Even in the West small businesses are enjoying a new vogue and, despite a lower level of government help, appear to create a major proportion of new jobs. They are more human in scale. Relations between workers and management are face to face. Labour is less minutely subdivided and specialized. Work is likely to be more varied, less alienating. Power is less concentrated.

Small enterprises, whether modern, traditional or makeshift, employ anything from one third to four fifths of the non-agricultural labour force in developing countries. That alone ought to give them a central place in government efforts to develop industry. And they have other points in their favour. It costs between four and nine times less to create a job in small-scale industry than in large firms – hence a given outlay of scarce development finance can generate much more employment. Small businesses tend to use a greater proportion of unskilled workers, because their machinery is less sophisticated. This helps the poor urban masses whose lack of skills is one of their greatest handicaps in finding a job. Small-scale industry creates more jobs indirectly, too. The big modern firm in the Third World tends to be isolated in a privileged enclave, cut off from the rest of the local economy. Far more of its machinery and materials tend to be imported, and it has few links with smaller local enterprises for supplies or subcontracting. By contrast, the little workshop may have immense problems getting hold of foreign exchange, and so is forced to use local materials, to buy machinery from local suppliers or to get an engineer to fiddle around with a second-hand machine so that it suits their requirements. Where the big factory creates orders for the capital-goods industries of the advanced countries, the small firm helps to boost the early stages of a local machinery industry. In the development of the Western economies, small companies usually preceded large ones. Henry Ford's beginnings in a tiny workshop, with improvised and gradually upgraded machinery, are the classic example. Countries who want their industries to start off big are forced to import them ready-made, and that perpetuates their technological dependence.

Small-scale industry produces less output per worker than large – that is why it generates more jobs – and so it cannot afford to pay such high wages, and does not give rise to the inequalities that large-scale industry creates. Yet, surprisingly, many studies suggest that this sector often uses capital more efficiently than large industry, turning out more goods for a given amount of investment. A four-country survey by the World Bank found that small firms produced between 80 and 300 per cent more output per unit of fixed capital than large firms. This fact has very important consequences for the growth of incomes in poor countries, which have lower rates of investment than richer ones. The lower the amount of capital needed for one unit of output, the more production a country can achieve from its rate of investment and the faster the national income will grow. And, as small firms use more labour, this extra national income will be more widely and fairly distributed. Smallness, in other words, can accelerate economic growth *and* ensure that the benefits of growth are equitably shared.

There are other advantages, too. Small firms need less infrastructure (power, water, roads, etc.) and so do not need to be concentrated in the biggest cities. They provide a cheap, on-the-job school for vocational and entrepreneurial skills. They encourage and mobilize family savings among poorer groups. Some of these advantages arise because small firms are using appropriate technology on a vast scale, quite spontaneously and usually without any help from governments. They use it mainly because they lack the funds to buy more sophisticated, capital-intensive equipment.

Against all these virtues of smallness, big industry has clout and political pull. Once a country has made the mistake of fostering it, this bias is difficult to correct as so much appears to be at stake. So, typically, big industry has been favoured with government concessions, while the small firms, often operating completely outside the law, have been starved of assistance.

In effect, because they are small and cannot afford the specialized departments of the large firm, small enterprises need more help, not less. The first of their needs is credit. Banks prefer to lend to a few large borrowers: they involve less work in appraisal, bookkeeping and monitoring than a larger number of smaller loans. Some of the World Bank's most recent loans to development finance companies now reserve specific amounts for small-scale businesses. Governments can induce private banks to lend to the small entrepreneurs by guaranteeing their loans to them. The Philippines and Cameroon governments have set up special funds which guarantee 80 per cent of the loans made to small businesses.

Technology is the second headache of the small company. Traditional technology is uncompetitive, while the typical Western-produced machine is too expensive and has too big a capacity for the small firm's requirements. The small businessman has not got enough turnover to finance a research and development section – often he may be too small even to employ a production engineer or product designer. If the productivity and product quality of small businesses are to improve, they need a government technology consultancy service. This may be no more than a centre they can visit to get information on all the available machinery, with catalogues of appropriate technology equipment and second-hand machinery, as well as the price lists of conventional machinery suppliers. At a higher level, such centres could commission or carry out research to solve the small businessman's technological headaches.

Management is the third problem. Small business in the Third World is invariably a family affair. Entrepreneurs often have no formal education, let alone any training in management, accountancy or marketing. The Lagos car repair shop may keep its accounts on the back of an envelope or in the boss's head. The Calcutta engineering workshop will have brothers, sons or nephews working all hours of the day, without counting their labour as a cost. Most entrepreneurs are satisfied with a modest income that does no more than provide them with a living wage. They have no real idea if they are making a profit or not. One man will probably be filling all the chairs of managing director, accountant, personnel manager, salesman. Small businesses need a management consultancy service that can show them how to make the most efficient use of their scarce resources of cash, hardware and manpower. Such a consultancy service can be quite modest: you do not need PA or McKinsey to advise Das Engineering of Dharamtolla Road, Calcutta. British management expert Malcolm Harper has developed a course by which unemployed school leavers can be trained as barefoot management consultants in only six months. That way they can provide a straightforward, unsophisticated but effective service on a large enough scale to make a difference.

Quality control, design and marketing is the fourth major headache. Here the small firm is at a considerable disadvantage. It hasn't got the manpower to build up a wide network of sales outlets. It can't afford advertising to create a brand image. Its products may not be standardized or fashionable.

There are other areas where official help is required. Workers may need training in more advanced skills. Official standards and regulations about quality and safety of products may need relaxing so that small firms can compete with large-scale industry. In fields where small firms can produce goods more efficiently than large, governments could profitably give them a monopoly. Examples of this are machine tools or machinery, where small numbers of items or one-off jobs are required, or products that can be produced in small batches and are not needed in bulk, such as most drugs or laboratory chemicals. Even where large-scale operation is really the only way, or by far the most efficient way, of making a finished product (as, for example, with cars), many aspects of the work can be subcontracted out to smaller enterprises. All too often in the Third World large-scale modern industry makes all its own inputs, or buys them from other large-scale firms or from abroad. But several industrialized countries – Japan is the prime example – have preserved a large small-scale sector by promoting subcontracting links between large and small industries. When the bigger firm helps the small subcontractor to meet the quality control it requires, it can quickly upgrade the small firm's technology and skills.

Halting the technological juggernaut: India's programme

Many developing countries are now realizing the potential contribution of small-scale enterprises and have set up programmes for them: Indonesia, Singapore, Philippines, Kenya, Tanzania, Ghana, Ivory Coast, Upper Volta, Cameroon, Colombia, Mexico and Venezuela. Some countries have made token gestures with a few miniature industrial estates, modest special credit schemes and lightweight training programmes. India has now totally committed itself to developing small-scale, labour-intensive and rural enterprises. It is the largest and most significant of such programmes in the world.

At the end of the seventies India faced what was probably the world's biggest employment problem. In 1978 she had the equivalent of 21 million unemployed out of her labour force of 265 millions, and 6 million new workers were coming on to the labour market each year. Her sixth five-year plan, for 1978–83, had to face up to the problem of how to create 50 million new jobs. Almost half the new jobs were to be created in agriculture, through land reforms and extensive small-scale irrigation works. Another 17 million jobs would be created in services – many of these in labour-intensive public works building up rural infrastructure. And 9·4 million jobs would come from a rapid growth of labour-intensive industry in the small-scale and village sectors.

India's small-scale sector was already booming. Registered small-scale units employed an average of eleven workers each and had average capital investment of 80,000 rupees ($10,000) in 1977. In 1976, though they represented only one tenth of the capital investment in industry, the 2·9 million registered small-scale enterprises provided two fifths of industrial jobs and two fifths of the production. For one unit of scarce capital they created six times as many jobs and six times as much output as large-scale units. The total numbers employed in the whole small-scale and village industry sector in 1978 was 18 millions – three times as many as in the factory sector.

In recent decades, as we have seen, industrial employment in developing countries has grown only about half as fast as industrial output, because machinery has been getting more and more capital-intensive. The startling decision India took in 1977 was this: in future, employment in consumer goods industries would grow faster than output. What this means, bluntly, is that normal ideas of technological progress would be put into reverse. Machines would be introduced that produced less output per worker than before, that were more labour-intensive. The great juggernaut of technological change – which has been trundling forward all over the world with no regard for its human and social consequences – would be reined in and led at a pace consistent with guaranteeing productive employment to everyone. Job creation would for once be put before the creation of extra material wealth.

In December 1977 George Fernandes, India's minister of industry, laid before both chambers of parliament a statement on industrial policy which was nothing short of revolutionary. What it proposed in essence was that the last should henceforth come first and the first last. Small-scale industry would now get priority in growth. Large-scale enterprise would no longer be specially favoured and sheltered – indeed in some respects it would be discriminated against. Most official credit would be reserved for small-scale and rural industry, while the big industrial houses would be expected to finance any expansion from their own internal sources. To slow down the urban explosion, no more licences would be given to new industrial units in urban areas with populations above half a million. The move to smallness would be speeded up by encouraging large firms, including public sector enterprises, to hive off parts of their business as independent ancillary units run by small entrepreneurs.

'Whatever can be produced by small and cottage industry must only be so produced,' the document stated bluntly. A list of 504 products was reserved for production in small-scale units (that is, with capital investment below 1 million rupees – £65,000 or $120,000). No large-scale factory would be allowed to expand its capacity in these goods. The list, as in 1977, ran to twenty-six pages and covered an immense range of goods, including some highly sophisticated items. A sampler: fireworks, hypodermic needles, paper bags, rivets, toothpaste, cycle tyres, small diesel engines, hearing aids, polystyrene foam, moulded plastic goods, sweets, footwear, toys, cheap radios, TV games, digital clocks, wooden furniture, dustbins and wheelchairs, razors and table fans, chest expanders and dumb-bells. In addition, there are 241 different products which the government will buy only from the small-scale sector – from ammunition boxes to leather belts, boxing boots to mosquito nets, padlocks to pillows. In other products, tenders from small-scale producers are accepted preferentially even if their price is up to 15 per cent higher than the large-scale offer.

Reservation of products acknowledges an important factor that most government programmes ignore. Small-scale industry, especially in the early stages, is highly vulnerable to competition from large firms who enjoy all the economies of scale in production and marketing. If small enterprises are to prosper, they may need protection against the big league in the same way that budding national industries need tariff protection against foreign competition. Ideally, such protection will not be permanent, otherwise it might amount to a mollycoddling of unviable firms producing overcostly products. It would be temporary, designed to help small firms reach the stage where they can hold their own. Hence protection needs to be paralleled by technical assistance aimed at boosting efficiency. With this in mind, India's Small Industries Development Organization runs a network of service and extension centres throughout the country. Typical of the help these offer is the work of the Small Industries Service Institute for Haryana state and Delhi, on the southern outskirts of the capital city. The institute has 220 staff. It provides technical consultancy to small firms, advising on suitable machinery, designing tools and dies where necessary. It prepares feasibility reports and project appraisals to help with applications for bank loans. It may suggest potential new products and markets, provide product designs, drawings and blueprints. It has a quality control testing centre where entrepreneurs can send their products for chemical, electronic or physical checks to see they comply with standards and regulations. On the premises there are extensive workshops providing the kind of expensive facilities a small entrepreneur may not be able to afford on his own, such as heat treatment or special lathes and cutting machines to make tools and dies. The institute provides a management consultancy for new or established firms. It runs training courses for skilled workers and managers in marketing, production, finance, cost control, personnel, work study and market research. Finally, it administers India's entrepreneurship development scheme – an imaginative approach to the problem of educated unemployment. Unemployed graduates who have promising business projects are trained in management, given expert help with their project, and provided with unsecured loans up to 200,000 rupees (£13,000 or $25,000).

SISI's deputy director, Nanak Singh, has sorted out the management, marketing and accounting problems of dozens of small firms. He was called in, for example, to help a cooperative making clothing, which had been formed by 200 workers after a factory closure, but had started to lose money heavily and faced bankruptcy. Singh himself was co-opted as a director to save the situation. He found that the firm was dispersing its energies in an excessive variety of products from bras and blouses to skirts and suits, selling to a very large number of down-market outlets. The place was top-heavy, with supernumerary managers drawing excessive salaries for little work. Singh began, in somewhat draconian fashion, by sacking all the managers and slashing back the product lines to just two profitable items: ordinary shirts and safari shirts. He secured a few large contracts for these from bus companies and government departments. The co-op's main men's shirt, brand-named Captain, had been poorly packaged and sold at 11 rupees a time, giving a profit of only 1 rupee. Singh tarted up the pack, changed the name to Major, and upped the price to 15 rupees, giving a 400 per cent increase in the profit margin with no loss of sales.

Many of the 200 small companies housed at Okhla estate, across the road from the institute, testify to the value of its work and show the tremendous vigour and vitality of small industry in India. There are companies here making dolls, cycles, fans, microscopes, felt pens, razor blades, batteries, gas compressors and even calculators and TV sets, with all components except the picture tube made in India. Most of these firms, with the technical help of the institute, have developed their own products and much of their own machinery. Allied Cables and Industries, which started from scratch in 1958, now employs thirty workers with a turnover of $500,000 a year, producing a variety of wires, cables and aerials. Inside its modest premises you can see clearly that small firms are quite capable, with training and help, of pulling off the kind of indigenous technological development that is essential in every country wishing to industrialize.

The story begins with copying. There is a row of machines weaving plastic insulation around wire with a set of rotating bobbins. The parent machine at the end of the line bears a little label that states, revealingly, 'Made in Occupied Japan'. The rest have been copied from it nut for nut and bolt for bolt, with a fine disregard for patents and licences. Next comes adaptation. The director, Krishan Kumar, wanted to make aerotone aerials, long sleeves of open weave copper wire which improve radio reception. So he took an old imported hosiery knitting machine, reduced the number of needles and made them of stronger steel to cope with wire. Kumar's younger brother, Kamal, an engineering graduate, took ACI's small industrial revolution one step further, designing new machinery from scratch. The *pièce de résistance* is the wire coating machine: four strands of wire unwind from reels into a box where PVC, melted by a simple blowlamp flame, is coated on, then cooled in a trough of running water. The cost of the machine was a mere

£650 or $1,300, and all the parts were made in India. The Western machinery which would otherwise have been bought cost five times as much, in scarce foreign exchange.

Factories in the fields: rural industry

Smallness is not enough. If the new small-scale industries are located in the major towns, they will do nothing to alleviate rural poverty and may even encourage further migration to the cities. To reduce inequalities between town and country, and between different regions of the same country, industry has to be much more widely dispersed.

Non-agricultural employment is still important in many rural areas in the Third World. Non-farm work may employ anything from a quarter to a half of the rural workforce. In the slack season, when there is no work to be had in the fields, it may take up as much as three-quarters of working hours. It helps to even out the work available over the year. And it is particularly important in maintaining the incomes of small-holders and the landless.

Industry in rural areas suffers from greater handicaps than most small industry. Markets are dispersed and infrastructure is underdeveloped. In 1971 only 12 per cent of villages in the Third World were electrified; in Africa the proportion was only 4 per cent. The staying power of tradition in all spheres, including skills and technologies, is stronger in rural com-munities. And rural industry is carried on in much smaller units than the average small industry in an urban area. Typically, it operates at family level, inside the home or farm. Producers are poor and widely scattered. As a result, many cottage industries, like the shoemakers of Agra, suffer under the middleman system, especially in Asia, North Africa and the Near East and parts of Latin America. The middleman supplies the raw materials and credit to buy them with – both at inflated rates – and buys back the finished products at low prices, creaming off a fat profit as his reward. He is not entirely parasitic: he does perform some managerial functions (purchasing, marketing) which the individual family does not have the time, skills or contacts to do for themselves. He may even, to some extent, develop product style and quality, supplying different materials and ordering different designs according to market tastes. But he does little to improve production technology, and because no one is performing this function for much of rural industry, many trades are caught in a trap of technological stagnation at extremely low levels of productivity.

For these reasons traditional rural industries find it even harder than small urban enterprises to compete with large-scale modern industry, despite the fact that their workers' incomes are appallingly low. Everywhere in the Third World traditional rural industries are being wiped out and the workers remaining in them pauperized. This dwindling of non-farm work adds to rural poverty and fuels the exodus to the cities. Traditional industry in its original form is, without doubt, doomed everywhere to extinction. But it does not follow that those who now work in it must sink into poverty or seek their fortune in the cities. What is needed is to adapt traditional skills and products to changing market needs, and to develop appropriate technologies so they can improve their productivity. Yet even fewer countries have any kind of programme for rural industry than in the case of small-scale enterprise.

Existing skills in rural areas are a valuable base that should be built on, not allowed to die out. Most rural communities have their blacksmiths, builders, potters or weavers, familiar with at least some aspects of consumer needs, design, materials and technology. With government help, they can be transformed into small-scale rural entrepreneurs, rather than uprooted, deskilled migrants to the cities.

Several countries have programmes for retraining blacksmiths, who are perhaps the most skilled of the rural craftsmen. It is a sensible measure. On the one hand demand for village-made machetes and other tools is declining as farmers prefer the stronger steel of factory-made products. On the other, tractors and ploughs stand idle for want of a drop of oil or a spot of welding. Several countries have programmes to retrain rural craftsmen in more relevant skills. Senegal set up regional centres for rural artisan training, taking in craftsmen for one-year courses designed to make them into an élite cadre of rural artisan-entrepreneurs, able to tackle any job required in their home areas. In the first months they made their own set of tools – carpenters made planes, chisels and jigs, blacksmiths made cutters, tongs and measuring instruments. Then they were trained to do the kind of jobs they would face later. In the classroom they were taught basic literacy and how to keep accounts.

Industry in developing countries has typically been built from the top down – that, indeed, has been the root of most of its problems. But it is possible to build from the bottom up. The United Nations Industrial Development Organization has put forward a model scheme for rural industrialization. This is based on what UNIDO calls Rural Workshops and Industrial Centres (RWICs), set up in centrally located villages and covering six or more other villages. The purpose of these centres would be to spread the knowledge and use of machine tools, to upgrade local technologies and train rural artisans in new skills. Each centre might accommodate around 100 trainees, who would also do productive work. They would service agricultural and transport machinery, which usually has to be taken long distances to towns for repair. And they might manufacture a limited range of products such as tools for farming and handicrafts, improved stoves to consume less fuel, storage, containers to cut down grain losses, devices to cut down the burden of domestic labour on women, and so on. Each centre, built on free land using local labour, might cost only from $22,000 to $100,000, complete with machinery. Equipment would be simple to begin with. More sophisticated services could be provided at a smaller number of more central rural foundries and toolrooms. The RWICs could be cooperatively run and owned. But naturally they would have to be set up with government finance, training and technical expertise.

It will not be possible to set up industry in every village. A greater potential lies in selecting small rural towns – markets, crossroads, railway stations – as growth points where small industry can be fostered, creating alternative magnetic poles to draw migrants away from the great metropolises. Many branches of manufacturing could be successfully set up in such rural centres: agro-industries, processing agricultural products that are by nature dispersed, oil extraction, sawmills, charcoal-making, leather tanning, stone quarrying. They could provide products that are in local demand, hard to transport or easy to produce on a small scale: bread, ice, furniture, wooden and cardboard boxes, agricultural implements. These industries, in turn, would create demand for light engineering repair shops, which could later blossom into manufacturing.

Several countries are consciously trying to build up local centres of small industry in rural areas. Pakistan's integrated rural development programme of 1972 provided for the creation of *agrovilles* – small towns which would be provided with urban amenities and developed as marketplaces, centres for processing of agricultural products from cotton ginning to rice husking, and for repair of agricultural machinery. At a higher level *metrovilles* would be built up at nodal points, to act as growth poles.

One of the most promising programmes of rural industrialization is Sri Lanka's network of divisional development councils, set up all over the country in 1972. They sponsor, with the help of special funds from central government, a host of small development projects in industry and agriculture. The programme involves a strong element of participation. Each council includes representatives of cooperative and rural development societies. Anyone can propose a project, but successful projects are chosen so as to make best use of locally available resources and to create a maximum number of jobs for a minimum of capital. The projects are then set up as cooperatives, with the workers owning the means of production, electing their own managers and sharing in the profits. By September 1976 some 1,882 projects were in operation all over Sri Lanka. About half of these were industrial schemes, and their products ranged from bricks, strawboard, manioc starch and textiles to fishing boats, motor spares and two-wheeled tractors. Nearly 40,000 jobs had been created and double that number were planned for 1977–8. The average investment required for each job in the industrial projects was a mere 1,300 rupees (about $100 or £50), compared with an average of more than thirty times as much for large-scale state-owned industrial corporations. A given quantity of investment in these small projects produced four times more output than the national average.

Building on tradition – village industries

Given the scattered, domestic nature of so much village industry, and the producers' lack of capital, skills and market outlets, governments have to intervene even more directly than with small-scale enterprise if they wish to help. Advice and encouragement are not enough. State institutions may have to step in to take over several of the functions carried out by middlemen, especially the provision of credit and raw materials and marketing. Producers themselves need to be organized into cooperatives and trained to run them, so that eventually they may become a new kind of dispersed small-scale industry.

The world's largest programme of rural and cottage industry is, once again, in India, where a range of measures like these have been deployed. The biggest and most important of her rural industries is handloom weaving. The country's 3·8 million handlooms employ about 10 million people directly, and as many as 10 million more indirectly; they are the greatest source of employment in rural areas after agriculture. Handlooms were hard hit in the past by competition from powerlooms and textile mills. A worker with a powerloom can produce seven times as much cloth as a handloom worker, a mill worker ten times as much. For this reason, despite lower wages, cloth produced on handlooms is often more expensive. India decided long ago that it was worth paying the extra cost of production to preserve so many livelihoods and the future of so many villages. Her sixth five-year plan aims to expand employment in the handloom sector by 60 per cent by 1983. In future, no further expansion of capacity in the powerloom and mill sector will be allowed.

State and national government in India is taking over the middleman's functions, supplying raw materials, low-cost credit and marketing. The Weavers' Service Centres do for handlooms what the Small Industries Service Institutes do for small industry. The centre at Bharatnagar, near Delhi, takes orders from government departments or commercial dealers, and places them with weavers' cooperatives which government has promoted on a large scale. It sells them raw materials and provides them with credit if they need it. It has a department developing new designs in keeping with current market tastes, and supplies these at nominal cost to the weavers. It provides sheds for co-ops to rent. One of the groups working at Bharatnagar is the Insan Handloom Cooperative Industrial Society Limited. A score of looms with hardly a space to squeeze between them are crowded into its small premises. Children play or sleep on a platform in the centre of the room, while their mothers squat by spindles, winding yarn from loose hanks on to bobbins. In the loft a worker fits dozens of bobbins on to a frame, slots their threads through an array of shafts and winds them on to a huge drum. This becomes the warp for the looms. The looms themselves are not the kind of primitive, low-productivity affair one sees in African or Andean villages, producing only thin strips of cloth, and where the shuttle has to be passed through the warp from hand to hand with a pause between each movement to firm down the threads. These are intermediate technology looms, broadlooms producing cloth up to eight feet wide. Some of the machines have six separate treadles, allowing check patterns to be woven. Others have Jacquards attached overhead: patterns controlled by hundreds of punched cards are fed into this machine, which lifts the warp threads for each new row in a different combination, producing the most complex embossed patterns for furnishing fabrics.

The Cooperative was formed in 1972, when thirteen individual weavers teamed together, chipping in 100 rupees each (£6.50 or $12). Since then the membership has grown to eighteen, and the co-op sells £30,000 ($55,000) worth of cloth each year through state and cooperative stores. All the members were once poor cottage weavers. Twenty-five-year-old Jawala Prasad, hair cropped close and naked except for a baggy pair of knickers, came from a weaving family in Uttar Pradesh. They had two looms in the house, but depended on middlemen for work and could only get enough for twenty days in the month, earning about 6 rupees a day. As they were landless, and this was not enough to live on, they left and came to Bharatnagar. Prasad alone now earns 10 to 15 rupees a day, and at the end of the year gets a share of around £10 ($19) in the profits.

Bees, seeds and handmade matches

India has valued and fostered her traditional and rural industries perhaps longer than any other country, and what began as a romantic, back-to-nature, poor relief sort of programme is now paying real dividends, and has lessons for all developing countries.

Gandhi masterminded the earliest ventures from 1920 onwards. Then, in 1953, the Khadi and Village Industries Commission was set up to stimulate employment in this field.

Under Nehru, with his concern for large-scale industrialization, it was accorded low priority, though even so it
managed to increase employment in its industries from 1
million in 1955 to 2·6 million ten years later. Unfortunately,
for at least its first decade the commission spent a lot of its
funds on supporting uneconomical activities, and did little to
adapt traditional industries so they could really compete and be
economical in the modern world. The *khadi* (coarse cloth) side
of the operation, in particular, looked like a make-work scheme,
an uneconomical drain on government resources that could
perhaps have been better spent in creating more viable workplaces in the villages. In 1965–6 grants accounted for two
thirds of the wages. Even in 1976–7 government expenditure
on *khadi* was 50 per cent more than the total value of
production.

The commission also deals with no less than twenty-two
other village industries: beekeeping, cottage matches, pottery,
soap, hides and footwear, vegetable oils, handmade paper,
coarse sugars from cane and palm, processing of cereals and
pulses, lime, shellac, fruit processing, bamboo and cane work,
blacksmithing, carpentry, fibres, aluminium utensils, gum
resins, gobar gas, and the collection of medicinal plants. Most
of these industries are viable propositions. While the government spent only half as much on them as on propping up *khadi*,
the value of their production was three times as high.

These industries fit neatly into the concept of eco-development. They use renewable resources, consume little energy and
produce useful, aesthetic and nutritious products. Hand pounding of rice, for example, loses less of the bran than milling. The
coarse cane and palm sugars, made in open pans, contain more
of the vitamins and minerals that have been completely removed from white sugar refined in vacuum pans. Vegetable oils
cold-pressed in small *ghani* presses have a much higher Vitamin E content than heat processed or chemically refined oils.
Village soap contains glycerine, which is good for the skin,

whereas soap factories usually remove the glycerine for separate sale.

Increasingly, village industries are using resources that were previously wasted. Handmade paper is made from rags, grasses and straw. The fibre industry is now experimenting with unconventional fibres extracted from pineapple leaves, banana tree stems and other neglected sources, which can be carded, twisted and woven into passable hats, mats, baskets or bags. Palm trees producing sweet sap have an immense potential – only one in four of India's 70 million tappable date and palmyra palms are exploited at present. Each palm can produce goods worth 61 rupees a year (£4 or $8) in baskets from the fibre, brushes from the bark, mats from the leaves and sweetener from the sap. Exploitation of palm sap would free much land now under cane sugar for food production. Properly farmed, palms could employ 2·5 million people, eight times more than in 1978. Hitherto unused non-edible oil seeds from trees such as *sal, mahuwa, neem, karanja* and *kusum* also have a promising future. They can be used in the making of soap, freeing edible oil seeds for use in cooking oil, which is in short supply. The residual oil cake can be used as cattle feed or for manure. Oil cake blended with urea can provide 25 to 50 per cent extra nitrogen for the soil, and save on fertilizer. Scientists at the Indian Space Research Organization have even developed a process for converting non-edible oilseeds into fuel oil. The potential for similar industries in other developing countries is immense: research on the uses of unexploited plants, trees and agricultural residues has barely begun.

Since the latter half of the sixties, the *khadi* commission has also done a great deal of research into appropriate technology to make village industries more competitive. It has developed improved spinning wheels that can wind, simultaneously, two or six spindles. The six-spindle version doubles yarn production and the wages of spinners. It has introduced an electric-powered oil press which produces 50 per cent more per day than the bullock press and enables the workers to earn a similar increase in wages.

India's rural industries programme has not yet, however, solved all the problems. The state's assumption of role of middleman does not mean that the producer will automatically be better off. Until government bodies attain the same kind of penetration of the market that the middlemen have, some outlets and sales may be lost. Moreover, the share of the cottage worker in the value of his production may not increase if the bureaucrats who replace the middlemen are overpaid, inefficient, corrupt or all three, and although India's civil service is one of the best in the Third World it has not entirely eradicated these faults. The wide dispersal of cottage producers in itself makes them difficult to help, and India's admirable schemes still have not reached a majority of workers in most sectors. Only 400,000 of the 10 million handloom workers belonged to cooperatives in 1977, for example. In the same year the *khadi* commission helped only 50,000 of India's 1·34 million potters, 31,000 of her 230,000 *ghani* oil workers, 59,000 of her 80,000 leather processors, and 21,000 of the 385,000 engaged in processing of cereals and pulses. Unless its coverage expands much faster, large numbers of the uncovered majorities may be wiped out by large-scale or modern sector competition before they can be upgraded. Indeed, they may even be wiped out by those of their fellows who were lucky enough to get government help first.

Finally, it has to be remembered that industry – even small-scale and rural industry – cannot be developed in isolation from agriculture. Industry needs an expanding market if it is to flourish. Except for the special cases of Hong Kong and Singapore – both cities artificially severed from their agricultural hinterland – every successful industrial revolution has been based on an agricultural surplus. It is no accident that some of the most rapidly industrializing areas in the Third World are situated in regions of prosperous farming: Argentina, southern Brazil, the Punjab and Haryana in India, and South Korea. Agricultural development and industrialization continue to reinforce each other for a long time. When farmers produce a surplus above their own needs, they have more money to spend on manufactures. This creates alternative employment in local towns, which leads to a shortage of labour on the land. Wages of agricultural labourers rise, and this stimulates the mechanization of farming. These processes, in turn, create greater demand again for manufactured goods and machinery. The message is clear: industry can prosper only as far as agriculture prospers and the two must grow in tandem. To try to expand industry by sacrificing investment in agriculture is a self-defeating exercise.

Industrialization: the new pattern

Slowly the outlines of a new model of industrialization have emerged. The old model, followed by most Third World governments, has been one of forced industrialization, similar to the policies pursued in Soviet Russia from the late 1920s and in Japan from the 1870s. This involves the expropriation, by government, of virtually the entire surplus of rural areas for investment in the cities and in industry. Often it may not be a real surplus at all: removing it may push the peasant below subsistence level and cause widespread suffering. The proportion of this surplus which is spent on industry – either through direct government investment or concessions to private industry – is almost entirely spent on the introduction of foreign technologies, rather than on building up indigenous technology. The result is a truncated, unbalanced form of industrialization, involving only the manufacture of consumer goods and of some basic raw materials, and with no links, or only very weak links, with agriculture. Vital aspects of industry are missing, performed in developed countries: in particular a capital-goods industry making machinery, and research and development of new technology.

The alternative model could be called endogenous industrialization. It involves building up productivity among all sectors of the population in rural areas. A much larger proportion of any surplus is left in the hands of the rural population. To satisfy their demands for consumer goods and farm inputs, small-scale industry is encouraged in rural centres, ensuring close linkage of industry and agriculture. As it does not require large or sophisticated equipment, it is easier for a small-scale local capital-goods industry to grow up to supply the tools and materials it needs. The stimulus of growing demand, coupled with intensive training and support services, will encourage the rapid development of indigenous technology. The end result, which will, of course, take several decades to achieve, will be a viable national industry in which dependence on proprietary foreign technology will be drastically reduced, and all stages of industrial production will be present.

The new model would also be juster and more humane than the old. It would avoid the tragic human costs of forced industrialization, which persist for decades even when the strategy is successful. Soviet Russia is still paying for Stalin's forcing of industrialization, which demanded centralization, hierarchical authority, repression of the peasantry and an emphasis on heavy industries rather than consumer-goods industries. Japan still bears the cost of the Meiji rulers' efforts in the late nineteenth century (also bought at the cost of immense peasant suffering) in a grossly unbalanced development which has resulted in some of the most polluted and overcrowded cities in the world. Even in those Western economies that industrialized more spontaneously, industry developed on a scale in which the individual workers are often dwarfed, depersonalized and easily dominated by managerial élites. In most Western nations industry has also developed in large conurbations, unevenly spread and leaving many areas, especially rural and peripheral ones, abandoned or neglected. As technology advanced and industrial patterns changed, many of the original centres of industry decayed in their turn, causing problems of regional blight and city poverty.

If developing countries persist with the model of forced industrialization, their development will be even more uneven and centralized than it has been in the industrialized nations. But those that choose to think again have a unique opportunity to create a new and more satisfying pattern of decentralized, even and ecologically sound industrialization.

8 Condoms, carrots and sticks: family planning programmes

The population explosion is among the most daunting of all the problems that the developing countries face. By the year 2000 the number of their inhabitants will have risen to nearly 5 billion, 2 billion more than in 1977. Most Third World nations will eventually have to support populations three, four or even five times their present size before they eventually stabilize somewhere between AD 2060 and 2170. Few have the resources to cope with this without economic and ecological disaster.

Too rapid growth affects every aspect of development and aggravates almost every problem, even where it is not itself the chief root of that problem. It accelerates land fragmentation and the exhaustion of soils. It swells the army of labourers looking for work and the legions of migrants flooding into the cities. It eats into such economic growth as poor countries manage to wring out of adverse fortune. It boosts inequality, increases landlessness, pulls wage levels down and keeps rents high. It helps to keep poor people in poverty, as the poor tend to have larger families, less food for each member, and therefore adults who cannot work well and children who fail at school because of malnutrition and disease.

Getting the population growth down to manageable levels is therefore central to removing poverty and reducing inequality. Some of the approaches I shall describe in this chapter do not fit into the small-scale, low-cost, egalitarian philosophy of the new development. But any progress in slowing population growth will contribute to realizing these goals in other spheres.

Experts and exhortations

Western models, so prevalent in the health sphere, were followed in the earliest approaches to the problem. Expensive antiseptic family planning clinics were set up in major urban centres, and their white-coated medical staff simply waited for the clients to arrive on the doorstep. In practice, such clinics served only a small section of women who happened to live nearby. The mass of poor mothers in scattered rural areas or shantytowns stayed away. A 1973 study in the Philippines revealed that the further people lived from clinics, the less likely they were to use contraceptives: 26 per cent of those who lived within one kilometre did so, but the level of use tailed off steadily with distance, until, beyond eight kilometres, it fell below 10 per cent. The reason should have been obvious: women had to give up valuable time to trek for miles, or they had to fork out bus or lorry fares they could not afford. At the clinic they might have to wait for hours to be seen. And they would have to come back every three or six months for a new supply of pills.

When it became clear that the clinics were having little impact on the situation, the fieldworker approach was tried. Trained professional staff would go out into the villages to educate, motivate and recruit new acceptors and to deliver contraceptives. This was also the great heyday of the mass media, of radio programmes and travelling films, of poster, slogans and symbols. But messages were often devised in a vacuum, without regard to the cultural attitudes of the audience, and without ensuring that there were supplies easily available for people who became interested. The audio-visual library of the International Planned Parenthood Federation, which serves family planning associations all over the world, has several museum pieces from this era. Their appeal varies from the crude threat of poverty for large families, to the call for sacrifices for the national good, or naïve promises of material benefit. A very typical poster pattern contrasts the small, two-child family, shown in stylish Western dress and surrounded with all the consumer durables a status family could aspire to, as if all this were the result of family planning, with the squawling, screaming chaos of the large brood, all of them skinny, ragged, dirty and brawling. Inevitably, the poster fails to dupe the average peasant, who knows full well he can't attain the middle-class lifestyle even if he has no children at all, and probably believes he has a better chance of attaining it if he can only beget three strong sons. A typical response to this kind of propaganda, I am told, is to say of the rich home: 'What a pity they've only got two children to enjoy it.'

Similar themes are taken up in narrative material, put across on radio or by travelling theatre groups, film shows or comic books. In *My Brother's Children*, a Nigerian film also produced as a comic, fat and prosperous Adeleke and his smart wife come down from Lagos to his home village in the bush for the naming ceremony of his brother's seventh child. Adeleke himself has only three. As soon as he steps out of his family car, his scruffy brother touches him for £2 ($4) because he can't keep up with the expenses of his swarming family. But worse is in store for Adeleke. The elder of the family, whose requests have to be respected, asks him to take all his brother's children back to Lagos with him and bring them up. He can't refuse, but he does not give in without pointing the moral: 'We should only have the number of children we can afford to support.' Adeleke explains about family planning, while his wife gets the message across to her sister-in-law, who is overworked and prematurely aged by childbearing. The brother and his wife trot off to the clinic to find out about birth control, and everything ends with a festive dance. As it happens, a study was made of the effectiveness of this particular film. Some 40 per cent of those who saw it remembered little or nothing about it when questioned later. Many of them had been more fascinated by the unfamiliar technology of projector and screen. People who had seen the film were no more favourable to family planning in their attitudes than those who had not. As the research director, Professor Okediji, remarked, 'The film show was an experience, short-lived, ephemeral, folded in the darkness of the evening and gone forever. The daylight brought pressures of urgent toil. There was no connection between the film show and the realities of life.'

It is not that the use of fieldworkers or mass media is wrong in principle. Both have an important role to play. But they lack an essential dimension for success, that of trust and face-to-face contact. They fail, in themselves, to make family planning an accepted part of everyday community life. Even if the message registers the so-called KAP gap (the gulf between Knowledge and Attitudes on the one hand, and Practice on the other) remains. That is, a majority of women even in rural areas might have heard about effective methods of contraception and might approve of them in theory, but a very much smaller proportion actually use them.

Vasectomies in the vestry: the community approach

Beginning in the late sixties, and spreading much more widely in the seventies, a new approach known as community-based distribution gained widely in popularity. It involved using the existing resources and members of the community – marketing networks, shopkeepers, traditional midwives, even housewives – to get the goods and the message across to the people. The professional staff and media operations then acquired a different role. They were no longer the front line, but provided back-up, referral, thorough training and support for a much broader front line reaching into every community.

De-professionalization was easier here than in any other sphere. The use of the condom was so straightforward that anyone could learn to explain it in five minutes flat. Provision of pills, with their sequence and possible side-effects, was a little more complex, but even here a relatively brief training course (with periodic refresher courses) would be enough to equip village distributors for their task. The use of such barefoot family planners is cheap. Their salary requirements are modest; indeed, many programmes simply pay them a commission on sales, or a bonus for each acceptor they recruit. Most important, they live in and belong to the local community and are trusted by it. The communication lines are open.

Programmes of this style have spread rapidly. Before 1970 there were only two in existence. By 1973 another eleven had been added, and in the following five years seventy more started up. In Guatemala distribution centres are staffed by satisfied users, who can reassure women with worries about the pill on the basis of their own experience. Traditional midwives give out pills in Indonesia. South Korean mothers' clubs distribute contraceptives at the same time as they teach handicrafts, cookery and home budgeting and run savings clubs. In Haiti agricultural extension workers give out condoms to the farmers' cooperatives they work with. Most daring of all, the Church of Christ in the Philippines encourages its followers to pick up pills after the Sunday service or to have a vasectomy in the vestry.

Community distribution programmes, on the evidence available so far, appear to reach fertile couples much more effectively than clinical programmes. They bring contraceptives closer to the users and save them travel time. They bring them within their budgets: condoms usually cost less than 10 cents each, pill cycles less than 75 cents, against commercial prices of up to 30 cents and $3.50 respectively. They appear to reach more of the kind of people who must begin taking contraceptives if birth rates are to come down: young couples and couples with smaller families. Continuation rates are higher than for clinical programmes. And the cost is modest – the cost of recruiting each new acceptor can be as low as $2.

Pills and priests in Colombia

One of the pioneers in the community-based distribution field was Colombia's Family Planning Association, Profamilia. Until 1965 there were no family planning programmes of any kind in Colombia and the country's population was growing at the (even by Third World standards) alarming rate of 3·4 per cent a year. Then an energetic young doctor, Fernando Tamayo, started to prescribe pills to his private patients, and soon the fashionable women of the rich élite were flocking to his surgery. They started asking if Tamayo couldn't perhaps help their maid, or their maid's sister, poor women who had five, seven, ten children. He couldn't say no, and they started queueing outside his surgery door.

Tamayo had really started something. It was as if he had opened up a valve in a boiler and all the pent-up steam came rushing out. His workload got out of hand, so he hired another doctor (who soon quit for fear it would damage his career), then another. He tried to rent a permanent base for the service, but the prospective landlady pulled out of the contract when she heard what her house was to be used for. But Tamayo soldiered on, pushed all the time from behind by the pressure of his clients' urgent need. He recalled one Saturday in the early days: 'There were just two of us – we started putting in IUDs (intra-uterine devices) at noon and worked straight through till seven, and by then we'd inserted 120 IUDs, one every seven minutes.' After the papal encyclical *Humanae Vitae* came out in 1968 against artificial means of birth control, the Colombian church hierarchy launched a series of virulent personal attacks on Tamayo, saying he was getting rich on immorality, or that he was in the pay of the CIA as an agent of Yanqui imperialism, in a genocidal conspiracy against the Colombian people. 'I knew the government wouldn't act against us,' Tamayo told me, 'because the wives of five cabinet ministers were getting their family planning services from me.' By the end of 1976, when I visited the programme, Profamilia was a booming, vigorous and respectable organization with hundreds of doctors working part time for it, and forty-seven clinics, one in every town of any size in the country. The Bogotá headquarters was thronged all day with women coming in for pills or to have IUDs put in or be sterilized.

But all the time Tamayo was uneasy about the clinical approach. He was aware that the service was not reaching the vast majority of the people who needed it most of all: the rural poor and the slum dwellers of the cities. So in 1970 he launched Profamilia's Rural Distribution Programme and followed it up in 1974 with an even bigger urban distribution programme. The idea was to take family planning out to the women in their communities, using trusted local people – nurses, dressmakers, hairdressers and housewives – as distributors. By 1977 the two programmes had nearly 1,800 distribution posts, each supervised by regional offices, with professional staff organizing supplies and educational activities.

To reach Profamilia's rural distribution post No. 9 in the hilly Sumapaz valley, we had to clamber along twisting, muddy paths between shaded groves of shiny-leaved coffee bushes, their branches lined with green berries. The post is a small, whitewashed family house hidden among banana palms and purple bougainvillea. Elbia Galbis, a neat figure in her thirties with red slacks and trim hair, trots out to meet us. Well known and trusted in the locality as a tailoress and auxiliary nurse, she made a natural choice as distributor. There are about eighty fertile women on her patch and a respectable thirty-seven of these are inscribed as acceptors in her notebook, which is ruled into columns for each month, with a cross where each woman has collected her cycle. Most of the women have safe and solid rows of crosses, but six or seven show disturbing gaps. Elbia says she will be visiting them to ask why they've lapsed. Two of her clients arrive as we are there. They ask for their 'sweets' and hand over their 6 pesos (about 9p or 17 cents), of which the distributor keeps 4 pesos as commission. One of them, Maria de Ramos, is thirty-six, and has six children aged eight to eighteen. She has been planning for seven years. Her neighbour, Elizabeth de Gonzales, is only twenty-five with three children but intends to have no more. The programme is clearly getting through to all age groups.

Our next stop was Silvania, a quiet little market town clustered round the twin towers of its red brick church. Here the post is a hardware and stationery store run by stocky Amparo de Castrillo. Above his crowded shelves of pens, sweets, envelopes and toys hangs a display board on which he has enterprisingly glued a packet of pills and an unfurled condom. Castrillo has ninety-two users on his books. Like Tamayo, he has problems with the Church. 'The padre here preaches against the pill in his sermons,' he told me. 'He says it encourages immorality and infidelity in wives and daughters. He comes out with all the old proverbs like "God sends every child with its loaf of bread under its arm," or "If two can eat, so can three and if three can, so can four." But the women here don't believe that kind of stuff any more. They say, why should we do what he tells us, he's not going to bring the extra children up for us.'

Local difficulties parallel the national obstacles. My guide for the day, Gloria de Garcia, a woman with unlimited energies who supervises the work in the valley, encountered strong resistance when she began touring her rugged patch by jeep, on horseback and on foot. Most men would hear nothing of using condoms, saying they would need a very strong willpower to put one on in the moment of passion. Many would not let their wives go on the pill either, because they were afraid this would facilitate infidelity – sexual jealousy reaches paranoid proportions in Colombia and often ends in murder. When Gloria visited one village, the local political boss pulled a gun on her and threatened to kill her if she came back. But the heaviest opposition came from priests. 'Some of them went round the homesteads warning people we were coming and telling them we wanted to poison them with pills. People would open the door to us and say "I have instructions from the padre not to talk to you." Some of the padres even asked women at confession if they were on the pill or not, and threatened excommunication if they continued. But the church opposition didn't do much harm. Every time they attacked us from the pulpit, people became curious and came looking for us.'

Because of the Church hierarchy's opposition the spread of family planning has worked a sort of miniature Reformation in Colombia, undermining the central authority of the Church and of the priests. But in other Latin American countries the Church's writ is more powerful and has succeeded in either preventing effective programmes being introduced, or frustrated their working.

Door to door delivery

Recently a more intensive form of community distribution has been tried with considerable impact. Known as household distribution, it is based on the idea of inundating an area with contraceptives, visiting every fertile woman and giving her a free 'get acquainted' supply of orals, enough for three to six months. Projects of this kind have been mounted in Egypt, Tunisia, Bangladesh, Korea and Taiwan. The canvassers chosen to make the visits are usually unqualified local people.

In Bangladesh the Cholera Research Laboratory recruited 154 village *dais* or birth attendants, and trained them for a mere day and a half before unleashing them on 140 villages in the Matlab Bazar area late in 1975. Every married woman between the ages of fifteen and forty-four was visited and handed half a year's supply of contraceptives, with a brief talk on how to use them and the benefits of so doing. Seven out of ten women accepted the pills. Two thirds of these did not use them, but showed they placed some value on them by carefully storing the packets in pots, bottles or jars hanging from the roof, where they would be protected from the perpetual danger of floods. Even so, the exercise produced results: before, less than 1 per cent of women were using contraceptives; after, 15 per cent were continuing with them on a regular basis.

Results in other countries were also significant. Between 50 and 90 per cent of women accepted the pills they were offered, and more than half of these usually started taking them within a matter of weeks. In Taiwan contraceptive users rose from 48 per cent to 60 per cent of fertile couples, and in Egypt, in an experiment in Shanawan village, usage increased from 18 per cent to 31 per cent. But indiscriminate inundation is not advisable. Distributors should be trained not to give pills to women who are breast-feeding, as they may stop lactating. Ideally, household delivery, like all CBD, should be continuous, carefully followed up, and linked to health service support to deal with side-effects.

In 1975 Bangladesh, the country with the world's worst population problem, became the first country in the world to start up a nationwide permanent household distribution scheme. As *purdah* prevented women from seeing strange men in the family compound, the visitors had to be women. By 1978 the programme had recruited 16,000 women fieldworkers, with modest education levels of five years' schooling, and given them a month-long training course. Their task was to visit every household once every two months, first getting to know the family, then offering free supplies of condoms or pills. Usually increasing wealth is the chief spur for family planning, but the deepening poverty in Bangladesh became a stimulus to limit fertility as people simply could not afford to raise children until they were old enough to work for their upkeep. The combination of pressing need and easily available supply seemed to be working. In 1977–8 the programme distributed 60 million condoms and 7·8 million pill cycles, and usage had risen from 10 per cent in 1975 to 15 per cent. There was, it is true, widespread scepticism in aid circles as to whether these were finding their way to users as intended. Tales abounded of family planning workers throwing their supplies into the river or selling them to market traders or smugglers headed for Burma, where the import of contraceptives was banned. One aid official described the government figures as 'disappearance statistics' rather than a true indication of usage. But the government set up a system of checks on fieldworkers' performance which should have prevented the worst abuses. Though there may have been leaks, the bulk of supplies probably reached the villages.

Selling happiness in small packages: social marketing

Using community distributors is not the only way of delivering contraceptives to the people who need them. Commercial companies have a long-standing expertise both in getting goods out to the remotest corners of poor countries, and in convincing people that they need them, even if they don't and have done without them for centuries. Couldn't the same approach be used with contraceptives?

The agency most closely associated with this method is Population Services International, a London- and New York-based charity. One of PSI's directors, Dr Timothy Black, noticed the uncanny effectiveness of commercial marketing while working as a general practitioner in the African bush. 'I would drive twenty miles up a dirt road to a village in the middle of nowhere, where they'd literally still be using poisoned arrows – and there would be a little Coca Cola sign on somebody's house and a few crates inside. Governments were always complaining that they didn't have the resources to distribute contraceptives, but the resources were there all the time under their noses, in the private sector. Even though there might be only one doctor to 100,000 people, there is often one retail outlet per thousand. Perhaps we ought to be thinking of contraceptives as consumer products, and the fertile couples as potential customers. It's basically a marketing problem. But the usual general posters are not good enough. It's like putting up adverts saying, "Use soap", or "Buy jeans". People need a product they can go and ask for by name.' PSI has called this approach 'social marketing'. It involves using the whole apparatus of commerce, market research, advertising and retail distribution, but for a social purpose, not for profit. It is more suited to condoms and foams than to the pill with its side effects, unless the stockists are well trained.

What was probably the first experiment of this kind was tried in the district of Comilla, Bangladesh, in 1964. But the first large-scale effort was India's Nirodh programme of condom sales, which started in 1968. The entire project involved only one government employee in the Ministry of Health. Under him came a coordinating committee of the marketing managers of six major retailing firms who sold supplies through their network of 200,000 shops all over India. In 1968, 16 million condoms were sold. By 1973, 116 millions a year were being sold.

PSI has started up several social marketing programmes. One of the biggest of these was Sri Lanka's Preethi programme which it launched in 1973 on behalf of the International Planned Parenthood Federation. Unilever market research was hired to discover what the potential market was. They found a high level of knowledge of birth control – over three-quarters of respondents were aware of effective methods. Against that, less than one in five couples were actually using any reliable method. Various names were test-marketed: Seema (meaning 'limit' in Sinhalese) and Seenasuma ('contentment'). But finally the project hit on the name Preethi, which means 'happiness' in both Sinhalese and Tamil, the island's other language. It was also, until recently, a girl's name.

The price of the condom had to be carefully planned. Since profit was not a consideration, the problem was not the usual one of finding the highest price the market could stand, but discovering what people thought the most reasonable charge would be. Strangely enough, interviewees said that free distribution would make them think the product was inferior and unreliable, which was the last thing people wanted a condom to be.

As the Sri Lankans are not the most sexually liberated of people, the advertising campaign had to be low key at first. A mail order service ran parallel, to service distant rural communities or shy town dwellers. But the main brunt of the attack was carried by 4,000 grocers' shops all over the country, from the hilly tea country to the rainforests of the south. Each one sported the red Preethi sign, and if you looked inside you would see the distinctive cardboard dispenser hanging from a shelf between the Lifebuoy soap and the canned sardines.

To back up the marketing campaign, a field educator was appointed experimentally in one region (later educators were introduced nationwide) to promote interest in family planning and provide what was probably the only sort of sex education available in Sri Lanka. Bandullah Dodampegama, who became known as Mr Preethi, would lecture anywhere, to any audience, to get the message across. And as a former advertising executive and sales rep, he had plenty of experience.

One day his audience was a village of fishermen. The day was too windy for them to put out – the big breakers crashing in over the coral reef would have swamped their flimsy canoes and wrecked the precious outboard motors. Instead, they gathered under the towering coconut palms, and the heavy monsoon clouds hung back obligingly with their load. Dodampegama had on his brightest yellow shirt and purple tie, which, he says, helps to keep people's attention. But the fishermen gave him as rough a time as the weather out on the Indian Ocean.

'We go out to sea and fight with death to catch fish,' said one, 'and when we come back we have only one recreation, that is going with our wives. Is the government trying to stop even this?' Dodampegama, who would have no trouble at all selling coals to Newcastle, had a prompt reply: 'We don't want you to stop it at all. In fact, we want you to do more of it, not less. We want you to enjoy it without the fear of having more mouths to feed.' Stretching out the condom he was holding in one hand as naturally as if it were a new brand of fishing hook, he let it go with a twang and announced: 'This can help you do that.'

Dodampegama is invariably flooded with a barrage of questions from his audiences in colleges, factories, village halls and plantations. Things like: What is the difference between castration and vasectomy? Is it good to take liquor before intercourse? Is it injurious to health to have sex more than once a month? How many times can you use one condom?

But he has encountered more serious obstacles than ignorance. The Buddhist church has frowned on the programme as an alleged spreader of immorality among the young. Buddhists believe that the birth of a child is predestined by its fate, as determined in previous incarnations, and that it may be wrong to interfere with the event. Buddhism is a potent force in Sri Lankan society and politics, and Preethi suffered a setback (though only a temporary one) when the chief priest of Sri Lanka denounced it. One of the strongest objections to Preethi is based on the Eastern idea of sexual osmosis. According to this theory, the woman's lubricating fluid is absorbed by the man in the same way as the sperm flows into the woman. This exchange of fluids is supposed to rejuvenate the man – one reason why, in the East, young girls are sexually prized. Preethi, as a physical barrier, might prevent this osmosis. These factors are the kind of thing every family planning programme in the Third World comes up against, and they have endangered the success of many a project. But the well-briefed propagandist like Dodampegama has answers for most of the objections. If destiny requires a child's birth, it will happen regardless of contraception, he tells devout Buddhists. His general policy, which all development projects in any sphere could do worse than to emulate, is to take every care not to offend ingrained prejudice, indeed to use strong traditional beliefs or values as weapons to persuade people to change their behaviour.

The success of Preethi has been resounding. Total sales of condoms in Sri Lanka were only 1·4 million in 1972. In 1977 Preethi alone sold 6 million and was being bought by two thirds of all condom users even though the government sold precisely the same product, under a different name, at one eighth of the price.

Following the success of the Sri Lankan effort, Population Services International launched a similar project in Bangladesh in 1974, in collaboration with the Bangladesh government. Sri Lanka had been a natural candidate for success with conventional marketing techniques: a small island, with a good road network, plentiful retail outlets, high literacy, wide access to newspapers and radio. Bangladesh was altogether another kettle of fish, with its scattered populations, bad communications and low literacy rate of 23 per cent. Yet by 1978 the social marketing project here was selling over 20 million condoms and a million cycles of pills a year, at the very low cost per couple protected of $2 a year (excluding a similar amount for supplies, provided free by USAID). The secret probably lay in the sheer hard-nosed professionalism of the project's marketing staff. Advertising and promotion began on a low discreet key, but soon grew far bolder than in Sri Lanka. By June 1976 the ads, run on radio, TV, in cinemas and newspapers, had reached a degree of explicitness that might startle even in a Western country: 'Raja condom is extra sensitive and has that exclusive, satiny SX 70 lubricant specially formulated for you to make the whole experience easy and natural.' Unwittingly, the admen had gone a little too far. The protests started, coming mainly from the small upper middle class of TV owners, which included top bureaucrats and political leaders. Letter-writers to newspapers complained that young boys would pipe up with embarrassing questions like 'Mother, what is a slippery condom? What is it used for?' 'In my opinion,' wrote one outraged viewer, 'such pornography-like adverts are shattering the last remnants of social values and morality.' From the very highest level, instructions came to tone things down a bit. Henceforth the offending word 'lubricated' was censored out, and condoms were no longer advertised on TV.

The salesmen were probably the most aggressive team ever assembled in Bangladesh, poached mainly from multinational firms. Marketing manager Ghulam Sarwar Khan proudly boasted of how he learned his trade with the tea company, Liptons. First he was dumped in the most godforsaken pitch in Pakistan, the Thar desert, where, as he remembers, the tracks were so slow you could leap off your camel for a pee and still catch it up further on, and the water so full of bugs that no one worked there without losing a kidney. Khan made out, and was posted to Dacca, where his boss took him on a selling mission to a brothel and told him: 'Don't scorn these people. They buy tea, don't they? Then they're your customers.' Khan's salesmen had a battery of tricks to wheedle reluctant retailers to stock the controversial new products. If they claimed to be short of cash to pay for them, they would swop a few packs for a packet of cigarettes. If they expressed fears that turnover would be slow, the reps would hire stooges to go along and buy a pack or two.

By 1978 sales of Raja and the pill Maya seemed to be levelling off. The project appeared to have saturated the market – or at least that part of the market that could be easily reached, the urban and semi-urban and the literate. The problem in reaching out further lay with bad roads, slow ferries and boats, the inaccessibility of the villages, the tiny stock of barest essentials carried by village retailers. The sheer poverty of the country, in all its aspects, was a blockage to social marketing using conventional Western methods. In future, social marketing in the poorest countries may have to learn new approaches other than conventional Western techniques, exploiting the transport and purchasing networks the poor actually use, the periodic rural markets, the traditional healers, lorries and buses and ferries.

Thus community distribution and social marketing have contrasting strengths and weaknesses. Distribution reaches wider, but may be vitiated by inefficiency and corruption unless carefully supervised and monitored. Social marketing may offer a cheap way of reaching town dwellers, yet be less capable of penetrating rural areas. Because of this complementarity, the ideal approach might be to have the best of both worlds, and run a far-reaching household distribution programme as well as nationwide social marketing, as Bangladesh is doing.

Yet even this may not be enough. It is very easy, in the family planning field, to fall into two rather condescending fallacies, both of them based on a missionary belief that the poor are benighted fools. The first of these holds that poor people want large families only out of ignorance, and a brief chat with an educated person is all they need to convince them of the error of their ways. The second is that there are, anyway, many poor people who do not want large families but have no idea of how to stop reproducing.

Poor people are not fools. Nature has provided contraceptive methods that even illiterate peasants are well acquainted with, from abstention and coitus interruptus to provoked abortion or infanticide. Even those with largish families use these methods, because few of them approach the maximum family size human beings are capable of creating. The fact is that people in many parts of the Third World do not have large families by accident. They do plan their families, and they plan large ones.

Where cultural influences are at work – as with Islam and Roman Catholicism, both of which are pro-natalist – carefully phrased campaigns of motivation and education can help. Where self-interest is involved, trying to teach people that it is bad for them to have many children will only convince them, if they firmly believe the opposite, that the teacher is an idiot. Making contraceptives available will certainly allow people to exchange unreliable and unpleasant bush methods for better ones. But it will not necessarily bring the birth rate down very much. Something more is required, in other words, beyond delivery and conventional motivation. To change people's desired family size, you have to alter the factors that make them decide that large families are in their self-interest.

Abolish Indira – and save your penis: compulsory sterilization

The bluntest way of doing this is by outright compulsion. Despite the terrifying problems facing several nations in south and south-east Asia, only one, India, has so far attempted this approach and even then not officially. It was one of the most bizarre of all dramas in a field that is never short of surprises.

Sterilization in general, and vasectomy in particular, has always played a dominant role in India's family planning effort. It started in a very small way in 1956. By 1972–3, 3.1 million people were being sterilized each year. The sterilization effort slackened off after 1973. Around this time the Indian government began to subscribe to the fashionable theory that the best way of cutting birth rates was to foster overall economic development and to integrate family planning, nutrition and health services. 'The best contraceptive is development,' health and family planning minister Dr Karan Singh told the World Population Conference in 1974. But this line did not last for long. Within two years Karan Singh was saying (quite rightly) that development might never get a chance to do its contraceptive work, because rapid population growth might prevent economic progress from ever taking place.

Only one Indian state – Maharashtra – proposed to make sterilization legally compulsory for men with three or more children, on pain of two years in jail. Karan Singh, in Easter 1976, rejected nationwide compulsion because the medical and administrative facilities to enforce it were lacking. On paper, sterilization remained voluntary. But chief ministers of Indian States, wishing to curry favour with Mrs Gandhi, vied with each other in raising targets by 100 to 200 per cent, so that in practice sterilization became more or less compulsory. Civil servants, doctors, teachers, local magistrates and mayors were expected to provide 'volunteers'. 'Targets' were set for municipalities. In the tense atmosphere of Mrs Gandhi's Emergency dictatorship of 1975–7, a target amounted to an order – jobs and heads might roll if they were not fulfilled. Only the almost hysterical fear of superiors which prevailed at that time could explain the excesses that were to follow.

The town of Barsi in Maharashtra was told it would have to sterilize 1,000 people at a camp. When hardly any volunteers showed up the town council sent along its garbage vans to round up candidates for the quick snip, and the local mill threatened to withhold its workers' wages unless they were sterilized. No official stone was left unturned to persuade people to volunteer. Professor D. Banerji, head of an inquiry into the sterilization drive, outlined the kind of pressures that were put on people to come forward or get others to do so: 'Threats to withhold: licences for guns, shops, cane crushers and vehicles; loans; registration of land; ration cards; exemption from payment of school fees or land revenue; supply of canal water; job applications, transfers, even bail.'

In many areas outright force was used. At Peepli in Haryana state a twenty-five-year-old childless widower was dragged from a bus and forcibly sterilized. He died after the operation wound became infected. When the Block Development Officer tried to round up more volunteers, untouchable women drove him off with broomsticks. Several hundred police were called in, and the rioting only died down after two people were killed and a government official threatened to bomb the village unless they cooperated. In another Moslem settlement, Muzaffarnagar, local men resisted this dog-pound approach and demanded that their seized companions be released. The district administrator allegedly replied that he would fuck their mothers first. Fifty-six people were killed in the ensuing riots. Official figures stated that 1,641 people died as a result of botched operations, and 525 bachelors were sterilized in India as a whole. Nor was the campaign carried out fairly and equitably. As always, the weakest suffered most – Moslems, untouchables, the poor. Influential people could buy their way out – or produce a scapegoat to take their place on the sacrificial altar.

More than any other single issue, the sterilization stampede lost Mrs Gandhi the elections she called in 1977. Her defeat was most complete in the states where the worst excesses had been committed: Haryana, Uttar Pradesh, Bihar. In 1971 she had won elections on the slogan *Garibi hatao* (abolish poverty). In 1977 this was turned against her in the battle cry of her popular critics: *Indira hatao, indri bachao* (abolish Indira and save your penis). What would have happened if Mrs Gandhi had continued in power, and compulsion had been maintained, is anybody's guess. But in retrospect it certainly appears to have dealt a serious blow to the entirely voluntary policies of the new Janata government under Morarji Desai. After the change of government public resistance to all forms of family planning was strong, staff were demoralized by their involvement with police excesses, and even the words 'family planning' became so emotive that the ministry had to be renamed Ministry of Health and Family Welfare. The backlash cut the total of sterilizations from 8·3 million in 1976–7 to a mere 800,000 the following year. The birth rate, which dropped by a record 1·2 points in 1977–8 because of the drive, was expected to rise in 1978–9, so that the average decline for the two years was no better than the long-term trend. It seems that suddenly applied compulsion may merely have mopped up in a single year many of the eligible men who would in any case have come forward voluntarily in subsequent years.

The Indian episode will always be borne in mind when governments are toying with the idea of compulsion. Like certain other individual liberties, choice of family size has wide repercussions on land, employment and economic growth. Any country that is faced with insuperable problems because of population pressure has the right, in theory, to circumscribe this liberty for the sake of the long-term interests of the community as a whole. The lesson of the Indian experience is that, in practice, in the context of gross inequality and administrative corruption that exists in most poor countries, it may not be possible without massive injustice, bloodshed and resentment, and these may jeopardize people's cooperation with official development efforts in all spheres.

The 'Singapore solution': incentives and disincentives

There are many less draconian ways of persuading people to want small families. The basic problem that has to be tackled is that, for poor or rural couples, the expected benefits of having many children – from child labour and marriage alliances to security in old age – exceed the costs. It is useless to ask people to 'stop at two' for the sake of national development. As long as this message, or indeed any form of population education, conflicts with the dictates of self-interest, then it is obvious that the latter will prevail. People will only start to want small families when the costs of rearing more than two or three children begin to exceed the benefits.

The overall process of development acts as a contraceptive by pushing up the costs and reducing the benefits. This works through the processes of urbanization, the housing shortage, an increase in the number of women going out to work, the breakup of the extended family, longer schooling and the decline of child labour, the spread of social security schemes. But the poor country cannot always wait for economic development to work, because the population explosion frustrates economic growth. It may have to find more direct ways of altering the relative costs and benefits.

The simplest of these is to offer incentives to people to accept family planning. A number of programmes have experimented with individual incentives. The best known of these were the circus-like Ernakulam vasectomy camps in India's Kerala state. A compound would be set up with bunting and neon lights and fifty neat white-painted booths for the operations. There were exhibitions, puppet shows, films, dance dramas, processions, floats and baby competitions – reserved, of course, for babies whose fathers were being vasectomized. Volunteers were paid 35 rupees each and given a week's free food ration and free tickets in a lottery, and came away clutching colourful bags containing three kilos of rice, one *saree* and one *dhoti*. The total value of these inducements was considerable – probably worth at least a month's wages for the average labourer. There was a sort of lugubrious absurdity about these camps. The festive air contrasted with the Freudian imagery of an authority figure carving away at people's manhood; and it seemed incongruous to apply mass production methods to the most intimate facet of humanity. But the camps served their purpose well. They got in 2,000 acceptors a day, 78,423 in just two months.

More sophisticated incentive schemes have been tried with some success. In Tamil Nadu the South India United Planters' Association started a programme in 1972, under which women on tea estates received 5 rupees a month, paid into a special savings account, for every month they avoided pregnancy. If, at age forty-five, a woman had only two children or less, she would get all the accumulated savings plus interest. If she had three or four, she would lose part of the total; if five or more, she would get nothing.

The most outstanding success story in the use of incentives and disincentives, however, comes from Singapore. Singapore certainly needed some progress in population control. Its population had risen tenfold this century, reaching the ant-like density of 3,800 people per square kilometre. In 1966 the government began its family planning drive, with a two-pronged approach – on the one hand increasing the availability of contraceptives, and on the other making sure people would want to use them. Today all couples on the marriage register are contacted to make sure they are aware of family planning methods and know how to get hold of them. In a thorough post-partum programme, every woman who has a baby or an abortion in hospital is approached and told about available supplies, and later visited at home and provided with pills if she wants them. The government made sure people would want them with a battery of carrots and sticks. The fee for having a baby in hospital, for example, was made ten times greater for the fourth child and above than for the first. Couples could claim tax relief only for their first three children. Women would get maternity leave only for their first two children. Children of a sterilized parent would get top priority in choosing their school.

The Singapore solution worked. The birth rate was slashed from 31 per 1,000 in 1965 to 18 per 1,000 in 1975. As a result, the rate of population growth slowed right down from 2·3 per cent in 1966 – around average for the Third World – to only 1·3 per cent in 1975.

In a really poor country, or in poor areas where the population is widely scattered and much less dependent on government services, taxes or subsidies, there are fewer incentives or disincentives that would work. In such places a more promising approach is to change the law of the land in ways that will tend to produce smaller families. A surprisingly wide range of laws have some direct or indirect impact on population. A country that is trying to keep its population down may find that it has some obscure clause or regulation that is quietly working in the opposite direction. Many countries, for example, have high import duties on contraceptives. Legalizing abortion or allowing the pill to be sold without prescription are changes that can help directly. Other laws can have an indirect effect. For example, raising the legal age of marriage; improving the status of women; encouraging women to go out to work. Increasing the years of compulsory schooling and regulating child labour can turn the child from an economic asset to a liability.

Birth control by social control

In most of the Third World life is a bitter, competitive struggle for survival and advantage. To many people, having more children seems a way of ensuring their survival and advancing their interests ahead of those of other people. It is a situation where individual self-interest is in conflict with the interests of the community. In the ideal model village of the new development, such an opposition between individual and community interests would not exist and personal conduct which damaged the collective good would be strongly discouraged. In an egalitarian, cooperative society, the benefits of development would be equitably shared and everyone would have an interest in increasing them. Anyone who persisted in pursuing selfish advantage at communal expense would be pressurized by social controls: disapproval, criticism, shame, loss of face and good will.

This kind of society exists in only a few places in the Third World. China is one of them, and that undoubtedly helps to explain what seems to be a considerable breakthrough. The exact dimensions of her achievement are a matter of dispute, but middle-level estimates placed her birth rate, in the mid-seventies, around twenty-five per 1,000, down ten points from a decade earlier, a very rapid fall to a low rate for an overwhelmingly rural and still quite poor society. A key element in the programme was the spread of new social attitudes through the network of the Communist Party: the idea that marriage should be deferred till the mid-twenties, that births should be spaced four or five years apart, and that two children was the best family size. Initially, there were no laws on these matters, but the social values were imposed by way of public criticism sessions. Every administrative unit down to the block of twenty dwellings, every unit of production down to the work group, had its member responsible for family planning. In some places work groups and neighbourhoods would allocate, each year, the number of pregnancies they could afford to have, and would agree on who should have them. There was an efficient delivery system backed up by the mass media.

The power of social control depends on the existence of a genuine community of interest, based on a high degree of equality and the absence of exploitation. In China this only emerged from a revolution in all economic and political relationships, which is not within view for most Third World countries. But other programmes have suggested the promise of linking family planning with broadly based institutions which the whole community belongs to and derives benefits from.

Bali, in the space of just eight years, managed to raise the proportion of fertile couples using contraceptives from almost nothing to 60 per cent, equal to many industrial nations. We have already seen, in Chapter 1, the kind of participatory grass-roots institutions that Bali enjoys. Bali's family planning programme started in 1969 with a conventional clinic approach. In 1973 it was decided to use the *banjars* (village councils) to educate and motivate villagers and to deliver the goods.

At Tampaksiring, the *banjar* meeting I opened this book with had begun its monthly deliberations with the topic of family planning. As every man becomes a *banjar* member as soon as he marries, and attendance at meetings is compulsory on pain of a fine of a kilo of rice, the *banjar* has a captive audience comprising all the potential users. The family planning fieldworker had come along to the meeting bringing a supply of condoms. The *banjar* leader's brother, Madé Ngakan, teeth bright red with betel and eyes sparkling with mischief, took over the proceedings. He snatched a condom packet, ripped it open and took one out, dangling it before his tittering audience. Squatting in lotus pose, he mimed the process of unfurling it over the penis, then leaned over and pretended to be kissing his wife and making love. The listeners fell about hysterically. Then the headman got out the bulky register in which he records, every month, what method each of the members is using. One man says he needs some condoms: 'But your wife has an IUD,' shouts Madé, irrepressible. 'Are you going with another woman?' Another man says he wants two packets. 'Aha.' It is Made again. 'So now we all know how many times you make love per week.'

On the wall of the *banjar* hall, and of every such hall in Bali, hangs a neat map of the village, with a square marking the house of every fertile couple. It is coloured in according to the contraceptive method being used. Non-users are left blank. This provides a guide for the fieldworker. He will inform, persuade, reassure, provide supplies or arrange a visit to the clinic for the women who want IUDs.

Bali is not a completely equal society even for men. There is a mild form of the caste system, and some landowners may have ten times as much land as others. But widespread landlessness has not yet emerged. There is a genuine community of interest at work – all farmers cooperate in maintaining their water supplies, and the whole village takes part in building a new market place or a temple. The tradition of mutual help means that a farmer can rely on his neighbour's aid at peak periods in the fields, and does not need to have sons for that purpose. Moreover, the *banjars*, helping the old, the sick and the widowed in times of need, provide a rudimentary form of social security, weakening yet another reason for large families.

The experience of Bali and even more of China point to the fact that not just economic growth, but growth along the lines of the new development strategies, can have great benefits for family planning. Redistribution improves incomes of the poor *before* economic growth. Participatory self-help creates a community of interest where individuals will not so readily pursue self-interest at communal expense. World Bank President Robert McNamara brought out the relation between social justice and population control when he addressed the Massachusetts Institute of Technology in 1977: 'Gains in overall national economic growth are most related to fertility declines when they are associated with a broad distribution of the fundamental elements of social advance. If the growth in national income does not result in improvements of the living conditions of the lower income groups, it will not help to reduce fertility throughout the society.' McNamara cited a forty-country survey which showed that an increase of $10 in income for the poorest 60 per cent led to a fertility decline more than twice as rapid as a $10 increase in the national *average* income, much of which might go to the rich.

Prospects

Although the new approaches still have not reached the majority of fertile couples in the Third World, it is clear that considerable progress is being made. Recently developed methods of fertility control offer ways of extending the spread of family planning and making it more effective. *Injectable progestogens* – of which the best known is Depo-Provera – can provide protection over three to six months with a single injection, without reducing breast-milk in nursing mothers. This can easily be administered by barefoot doctors as a routine part of basic health programmes. It does not involve any invasion of privacy, and cannot be forgotten or misused like the pill or condoms. Despite a controversial ban on its use in the USA, it has been pronounced safe for use in general practice by the World Health Organization's toxicology review panel. Other possibilities still at the experimental stage include *implants* made of biodegradable plastics, coated with contraceptive hormones which can be released at a constant rate over a long period. In India and the USA efforts are being made to develop an *anti-pregnancy vaccine* which could be based on a chemical known as chorionic gonadotropin, a hormone secreted by the placenta.

Even more promising developments have been made in techniques to be used after intercourse. In the first few days *steroid hormones* can be taken – oestrogen, taken within seventy-two hours of coitus, seems to be a highly effective morning-after pill, a useful method for wives of migrant labourers after conjugal visits. *Menstrual regulation* can be performed one or two weeks after the missed period. This involves evacuation of the womb contents with a plastic cannula and a hand-held vacuum syringe. It takes about five minutes, and can be performed without anaesthetic. Finally, *prostaglandins* – compounds isolated from seminal fluid – seem to offer a safe way of aborting pregnancies between one and six months advanced, with lower failure rates and fewer complications than conventional methods.

These new post-coital techniques do not require sophisticated medical training or equipment. They could easily be included in barefoot doctor programmes, providing readily available after-the-event family planning. With the majority of couples still not using contraceptives, and many of those who do using them wrongly, unwanted pregnancies are commonplace. Village women often brave dangerous traditional methods of abortion, or trek for miles to towns and pay through the nose for a backstreet abortion. Easily available, safe, cheap abortion or menstrual regulation would be a safeguard for women's health as well as a backstop method of family planning, and ought to become an essential part of basic health programmes.

But in the late seventies the well-tried methods were still providing most coverage. Worldwide, sterilization was the most widespread form of protection, used by 80 million couples. Oral pills, with 55 million users, came next, followed by condoms, used by 35 million couples, and inter-uterine devices, with 15 million users.

A massive survey of the spread of family planning was carried out in 1976 by the International Planned Parenthood Federation. In the developing countries only 24 per cent of fertile couples were currently using some modern form of contraception, against 67 per cent for Western Europe and 80 per cent in North America. Regional averages ranged from an abysmal 2·9 per cent in West Africa and 13·6 per cent in East Africa; through 20 per cent in the Indian Ocean area and the Middle East and North Africa; to 21 per cent in Latin America, 42 per cent in the Caribbean and 37 per cent in China.

By the late seventies it was apparent that in a number of countries with vigorous family planning programmes the birth rate had started to fall significantly: these included not only more advanced and urbanized developing countries such as South Korea, Colombia and Venezuela, where economic growth would have begun to affect people's desired family size, but also some of the poorest countries – India, Indonesia and Egypt – where the cost of rearing additional children had begun to exceed the benefits because of sheer poverty and pressure on land. Another group of countries with above-average success in lowering fertility were those like Cuba, Costa Rica and Sri Lanka where governments invested heavily in health and education for the rural masses.

But as with food production, the other part of the Malthus equation, unqualified optimism is out of place. In 1976 some 300 million of the Third World's 400 million women at risk were still unprotected. Continued efforts and experiments to find the best ways of delivering family planning and motivating people to use it will be essential. Wider access to effective and safe family planning is not only a right of every couple – it is one of the best ways of improving mother and child health.

9 Feeding the five thousand: better nutrition

The vast, gabled houses of Beriharjo, in central Java, are widely spaced, each standing on its owner's small patch of land. It is poor, reddish earth, dry as a bone outside the rainy season, and badly eroded on the slopes where trees have been cut down for firewood. In the rains, most of the farmers grow maize and, more and more, cassava because of its massive yield of calories per acre. In the dry season the soil is empty. I am told a man would need a hectare and a half of land in this area to support the average family of six. The village register, carefully hand-written in a big green notebook in the headman's office, shows that two thirds of the 2,500 families have half a hectare or less. Though few are completely landless, many have no more than a few hundred square yards around their house. Everyone is looking for extra work, and no one can get it. The only local industries are breaking up the volcanic boulders that litter the fields, for sale as building material, and making wooden furniture for local consumption. In the slack times of the farming calendar almost every able-bodied man leaves home to join the throngs of cycle rickshaw drivers in Jogjakarta or the snack vendors of Jakarta.

In the sixties this district, known as Gunung Kidul, was termed a nutritional disaster area by one expert. Towards the end of that decade the average food intake per person was between 1,000 and 1,200 calories per day, with less than twenty grams of protein. That is less than the human body needs to sustain and reproduce itself. The FAO recommended minimum for Indonesia is 2,300 calories a day. Infant mortality took a heavy toll and – unusual except in famines – death from starvation was not uncommon even among adults.

The situation was better, but not much better, elsewhere in overcrowded Java, and other nutritional deficiencies of the kind the poor suffer from in many developing countries were common: severe shortage of Vitamin A (found in fish, dairy produce and green, leafy vegetables), causing eye problems and, eventually, blindness; almost universal anaemia, due to lack of iron in the diet and the ravages of hookworm, and giving rise to lassitude, irritability and reduced productivity at work. Two thirds of children suffer from goitre, as iodine is lacking in the soil. Few show the familiar symptoms of neck swelling, but goitre comes in all degrees and can cause mental retardation.

When I visited Beriharjo in late 1977 a remarkable transformation had come over the place. Death from starvation had disappeared. Beriharjo had been the focus of intensive efforts to stimulate local people to improve their own nutrition and the nutritional quality of their food production. The energetic headman (formerly the village schoolmaster) showed me proudly round each of the innovations they had introduced. At our first whistle-stop a family was waiting to demonstrate goat-milking. The traditional village goats in this region are cute, petite animals but produce only half a litre of milk each day. This goat, one of thirteen donated by UNICEF, was a huge, flop-eared beast with bulging udders, and gave two litres a day, feeding on kitchen wastes and leaves collected by children. Four of the gift goats were males, and had been used as studs. Thanks to their sexual energies, Beriharjo now had forty-seven new improved animals. From here we passed on to the village fish ponds, six large tanks where fat golden carp curled through the cloudy water. This was another UNICEF gift. The carp were used to breed stock which would be transferred, in the rainy season, to the village's 271 family fishponds and fattened up for home consumption. Down the road from the fish farm was the quarter-hectare vegetable garden run by the mothers' club, where women were learning to cultivate the fresh vegetables that had been lacking in the local diet: onions, beans, tomatoes and a completely new introduction to the area, Chinese cabbage (rich in Vitamin A).

Gunung Kidul was one of seventeen areas chosen for the pilot stage of Indonesia's applied nutrition programme. At government level, food production targets now aim not just at boosting rice output, but take into account the need for a nutritional balance. The national seed breeding programme is developing varieties of rice, and also of the important supplementary foods such as legumes and vegetables. These seeds will eventually be put out through the government supplies network, and extension workers will be trained to teach farmers to grow crops that will produce a balanced diet.

At village level, a number of outside inputs are being provided. Vitamin A tablets of 200,000 international units are given to children age one to four every six months. Pregnant mothers get iron folate tablets to prevent anaemia. To combat goitre, salt will be iodized even in the thousands of tiny factories where salt water is evaporated on fires stoked with coconut husks and beanstalks. And each village will have dozens of nutrition cadres – barefoot dieticians with the task of improving family menus.

Hunger and handouts

The green revolution, the opening up of new lands, the extension of irrigation, increased use of fertilizers – all these trends have enabled food production to grow rapidly in the Third World. But because of population growth the nutrition of the average person has not improved greatly. In 1972-4, the period of the Food and Agriculture Organization's Fourth World Food Survey, the average calorie intake in developing countries was 2,210 calories a day. This was 150 calories more than in 1961-3, but still fell 4 per cent short of requirements. Meanwhile, the average resident in a developed country was consuming 3,380 calories, 32 per cent more than needed. As for protein, the typical Westerner got ninety-eight grams a day in 1972–4 (well over half of that from animal sources) while the Third Worlder got only fifty-seven grams, four fifths of which came from poorer-quality vegetable sources. During this period, the FAO calculates, there were 455 million people in the Third World who were acutely undernourished. These people were not just failing to get an adequate diet for good health, but were not eating enough to keep alive and go on working in the long run.

Hunger's impact is uneven in poor countries. Surveys show that malnutrition hits certain groups much worse than others: the poor, the landless, members of large families; children and mothers, rather than men; and the urban poor, more than the rural poor. Malnutrition aggravates the poverty that causes it. The undernourished worker cannot produce as much as the well-fed one. The undernourished child may suffer brain damage and become a failure at school, condemned to low-paid casual labour for the rest of his or her life.

Malnutrition is a disease of poverty and the best way to attack it lies in the eradication of poverty. More jobs, higher incomes for the poor, better access to the land through land reform, effective family planning – all these are essential elements. So, too, is improving health, as disease is a major cause of malnutrition. The most far-reaching strategies for improving nutrition, therefore, lie outside the scope of nutrition programmes.

Nevertheless, such programmes have an important role to play, both in making existing resources stretch further and in combating the ignorance and wrongheaded feeding practices which do cause a lot of nutritional damage. The decline of breastfeeding in favour of canned milk powder is one of the most damaging trends: canned milk is too expensive for tight family budgets, and is often let down with polluted water. Children need weaning foods that are high in protein, vitamins and minerals, yet many cultures have not developed good weaning mixes and give their babies only starchy, bulky foods. Most Third World mothers have little idea of what to give their children to cope with an attack of gastro-enteritis, which is extremely common and can kill through dehydration. Finally, there may be readily available foods which are lost through poor storage and processing, or even thrown away because the culture says they are inedible. Nutrition education can teach people simple, cheap or even cost-free ways of avoiding all these pitfalls.

Whatever advances are made in wider development fields, there are now many, and there will always be some, mothers and especially children who are acutely undernourished, and need immediate help. A good nutrition programme has to find ways of identifying these people at risk and of providing them with the supplementary food they need. In the 1960s, nutrition programmes suffered from the Western bias and paternalism we have encountered in every other sphere. Nutrition education – where there was any – was based on the kind of food recommended in those coloured charts on the walls of child health clinics in the West: milk, eggs, meat and fish for protein, lettuce, carrots, cabbages and so on for vitamins and minerals. Usually these products are either not available in developing countries, or way beyond the means of the majority. As UNICEF nutritionist Jim McDowell has commented, the standard advice was like recommending that the average Western housewife feed her family on champagne, caviare and foie gras. Those products that were available were analysed by dieticians and found wanting – the staple cereals were lacking in essential amino acids and therefore poor sources of protein. It did not occur to most of them that they could be eaten in combination with other easily available local foods, such as legumes, to provide a complete protein.

Food aid was popular, and in essence little better than a

dumping of the surpluses produced by the protectionist agricultural policies of Europe and North America. Food supplements for children were channelled through the aid agencies, and were usually based on imported dried milk. They helped, in all probability, to spread the popularity of that dangerous product. This was the soup kitchen approach. It encouraged dependence. It did nothing towards the central task, which was to help poor countries and poor communities to produce an adequate diet for their people with their own efforts and using their own resources.

Signs of a change in emphasis came with the World Food Programme, started in 1962 under the auspices of the Food and Agriculture Organization. In its first fifteen years the programme provided some $3·2 billion in food aid to 104 countries. In 1977 it shipped around a million tons of food and had, on any given day of the year, fifteen charter vessels en route with its supplies. A gigantic handout programme, you might think. But by the seventies the great bulk of WFP assistance was going to 'food for work' programmes, linked to specific self-help development projects. The food aid was distributed to workers in lieu of wages, and most projects aimed, directly or indirectly, at increasing the receiving country's ability to produce its own food. They were, in fact, food-for-work-for-food projects. Examples: rations of wheat flour, soya milk, pulses and canned fish for volunteers in Haiti building rock terraces to control soil erosion; food supplies for settlers in virgin forest in Ecuador to tide them over till they had cleared the land and it began producing; food aid for builders of rural roads in South Yemen. The biggest single country programme started in Bangladesh in 1975. By the following year, 2 million labourers were at work on WFP rations, digging new irrigation canals, desilting existing ones and building embankments to control floods. In the first seventeen months they had dug 2,500 kilometres of canals, built 3,000 kilometres of embankments and moved more earth than was shifted for the Panama canal. The wages were no giveaway: around three kilos of rice for every two cubic metres of earth (about one ton) removed.

National food self-sufficiency has been encouraged by another international programme, to develop locally produced protein-rich weaning foods. These new multimixes are based on combinations of locally available foods which are cheap and culturally acceptable to mothers. Their protein content comes from a carefully balanced mix of cereals and legumes and their calories, usually, from oilseeds. One of the earliest of these was Incaparina, developed in Guatemala by the Institute of Nutrition of Central America and Panama, made of maize flour and cottonseed flour and designed for mixing into a traditional local drink. Algeria's version, Superamine, is made of wheat flour, chick peas, lentils and dried skimmed milk. Most of these mixes are being marketed through commercial channels. But the factory-made product may still cost more than the poor mother can afford, so recent work has aimed at developing mixes which mothers themselves can be taught to make. The most promising approaches to nutrition tie in closely with the new development strategy of encouraging self-help, low-cost approaches involving maximum use of locally available resources and popular participation.

Keeping out the rats

Probably the simplest and most cost-effective way of increasing the amount of food available at village level is to improve traditional methods of food storage and processing. Rats, weevils, moulds and assorted other pests consume or spoil a great deal of the poor peasant's food before it reaches the table. It has been estimated, for example, that a third of all grain production in India is lost in storage, handling and processing. The Food and Agriculture Organization has calculated that 30 per cent of tropical Africa's crops disappear in post-harvest losses. Not just quantity, but also quality suffers – pests head preferentially for the tastiest, most nutritious bits of the stored food. FAO agronomist, H.A.B. Parpia, estimates that even if post-harvest losses in the Third World amounted to only 10 per cent, they will be costing around $17 billion in 1985. As the Third World's calorie consumption is only 4 per cent below requirements, cutting out only half these losses would meet the current food deficit.

This means, of course, improving large-scale food stores for cities and markets. But the nutrition of the average poor peasant can be considerably improved simply by teaching him to spruce up the granary next to his house. The Iteso people of Uganda, for example, store their millet in huge baskets woven from reeds or twigs. They try their best to protect their grain: the basket is plastered in mud, covered with a conical thatch roof and raised on wooden platforms above the damp earth and the floods of the rainy season. Some people even mix insect-repellent herbs with their grain, others stir in ash or sand that will scratch insects' shells and keep them out. But all these efforts fail to stop the loss or spoilage of a large part of the crop. So August, the month after the millet harvest, is called 'the month of the big stomachs', while May, when the granaries have coughed up their last reserves, is known as 'the month when the children wait for food'. UNICEF's Nairobi office has developed cheap, simple ways of making the traditional granary a more effective protection. The mouth of the granary – formerly left open to get supplies out – can be sealed with a basketwork lid plastered in mud. An insect-proof emptying spout is then put into the base, and can be made from a bamboo pipe with a wooden plug or an old tin with a press-on lid. Rat guards to go round the granaries' wooden legs can be made out of old tins beaten into a flat disc.

Throughout the Third World, vegetables are usually available only in the wet season outside irrigated areas, yet simple drying methods can preserve most of their nutrients all the year round. Another device developed at UNICEF Nairobi is a solar dryer that can dry up to sixty kilos of vegetables per day, at no energy cost, and needs only $2 worth of easily available materials to make. The dryer is a ventilated box of mud bricks, into which are set open trays of reed and wood. The vegetables are spread on the trays, covered with a polythene sheet pierced with air holes, and shaded from the direct sun with a stretched cloth. Warm air circulates through the vegetables and dries them in just two or three hours. One third of an ounce of dried cassava leaves or cowpea leaves – normally discarded or fed to animals – can provide a child's daily needs of Vitamin A. One ounce provides a third of the protein and a quarter of the iron a child needs.

Significant increases in food production can only be achieved through agriculture. But many nutrition programmes have led to worthwhile additions to local food supplies. School gardens, where pupils learn agriculture and produce food to supplement their own diets, are now commonplace. The government of Panama has encouraged the creation of large community gardens in many villages, to produce foods normally lacking in local diets. The government provides seeds, fertilizers and expert advice. A democratically elected village health committee runs the garden and distributes the produce according to the number of hours worked. The scheme is being extended to the raising of poultry, goats, pigs, fish and rabbits.

The barefoot dieticians

Increasingly nutrition programmes are creating corps of de-professionalized, village-level nutrition workers. Their task is to spread nutrition education based on locally available foods, to identify women and children in urgent need of supplementary feeding, and to provide nutritional first aid in gastro-enteritis cases. Often these functions may be combined with health work.

Kasa block is a hilly, forested rural area of seventy villages north of Bombay, on the Indian coast. A single doctor looked after the health and nutrition problems of the 75,000 illiterate tribals who lived here. Kasa was chosen for a pilot health and nutrition project which began in December 1974. The villagers themselves were asked to elect mothers with a minimum of schooling to become part-time social workers covering the health and nutrition needs of about 2,000 people each. They were given a four-week training course and launched into the field. Their duties involved visiting all married women in their patch once a month. The project's technical director, Professor P.M. Shah of the Institute of Child Health, Bombay, describes a typical day's work: 'The worker collects all the children and mothers in someone's house, or beneath a tree. She weighs all the children, identifies the grade of nutrition, decides whether nutrition supplements are needed, inquires about illness, administers medicines, talks to mothers about feeding, hygiene and child care. She inquires about the menstrual history of the woman, records abortions, stillbirths and the state of pregnancy. She chlorinates the water in drinking wells in her area once a month.' The children and mothers at risk get food supplements of protein-rich roasted chick-peas and groundnuts plus jaggery, a coarse brown sugar, for extra calories – all locally available and acceptable foods.

One of the most comprehensive of the nutrition programmes involving local participation is Indonesia's Applied Nutrition Programme. The lynch-pin is the nutrition cadre, a sort of dietician, cookery teacher and baby nurse rolled into one. The cadres are literate villagers, most of them women, who volunteer for the job and do it without pay. Their training course lasts only a couple of days and is held in the village itself by travelling instructors. The course covers the principles of nutrition, how to devise balanced meals for children and adults from cheap local foods, how to weigh children and fill in their growth charts.

In Beriharjo the headman's wife supervises dozens of cadres, each of whom looks after only five or ten families. Cadres like Ngatini, a thirty-six-year-old farmer's wife, who volunteered for the job for no other reason than that she wanted to help her neighbours. Ngatini's job is a complex one. She gives out the supplementary Vitamin A and iron pills. When a child has gastro-enteritis, she provides nutritional first aid. As a child can quickly become dehydrated and lose essential body salts in this condition, UNICEF and the World Health Organization have developed a compound known as Oralite, now in use all over the world. This is a compound of salt, bicarbonate of soda, potassium chloride and glucose, which is mixed with boiled water and restores the sugar, salts and liquid that the child is losing. Ngatini will be teaching mothers to make their own rehydration drink with kitchen salt, sugar and bicarbonate. Education is perhaps her most important function: teaching people to look after their own nutrition. She has to persuade fathers to grow more green, leafy vegetables in their home gardens, and more legumes for protein. She holds cookery sessions with the mothers, at which they try out new recipes based on locally available foods. Devising weaning foods that small children will actually like is no easy matter – most Beriharjo mothers, to avoid problems, would give their children mashed white rice mixed with sugar. Ngatini has been teaching them ways of cooking greens and legumes to mix in.

Often menu planning is a question, not of imposing alien diet patterns, but of tapping what the Indonesians call 'the wisdom of village motherhood' – the collective experience of local mothers, passed on from generation to generation, on how to make the tastiest meals out of scarce resources, how to cook foods so that tender and finicky young stomachs will accept them. The joint cooking sessions are also opportunities to educate mothers on the basic principles of nutrition such as the importance of breast-feeding, or the need to give pregnant mothers more food, not less, as traditionally happens.

The applied nutrition programme has a central ritual which

both discovers the nutritional status of the child (thus identifying cases for emergency feeding) and motivates the mother to improve it. Once a month, all the mothers of each sub-village in Beriharjo gather in one of the bigger houses to weigh their children. At the session I attended, an easy-to-read vertical market scale was slung from a roof beam, and a pair of denim shorts attached to the hook. Cadres are trained to call the brave children first so the others gain confidence, but that day there didn't seem to be any brave children, and kiddies bawled, screamed, writhed or sobbed quietly as they dangled helplessly in mid-air while their weight was read off. This was then recorded on a special card, based on the Road to Health Card developed by Dr David Morley of London's Institute of Child Health. The vertical scale of the card covers the weight, the horizontal scale the child's age. The card is marked with curving, coloured bands which show the progress a healthy child ought to be making. As there are several bands, the chart allows for genetic differences between children. If the child's weight grows with age along the same colour band, or higher one, everything is okay. If the line of weight growth drops on to a lower band, that is a danger signal indicating that he or she is suffering from some degree of malnutrition.

In many mother-and-child health programmes, the weighing is done at clinics, and after queueing up for hours the mother may be told that her child is fine. After a few such visits, the mother soon loses interest and stays away, so most of the problem cases never get discovered. It was the mothers' own complaints about the clinic system that led to a new approach in the Indonesian programme. One of the men who helped to develop it, Dr Jon Rohde, an ebullient American from the Rockefeller Foundation, explained: 'The mothers told us, "Come on, we're tired of hearing crap like eggs are good for you. How do we know if our child needs extra food or not? How can we tell if it's worth a visit to the clinic? What can we ourselves do about it, here in the village?" ' Weighing close to the mother's home, organized and conducted by trusted neighbours, had none of the cost, lost time or communications problem of the clinics and experts. If a child's weight falls for one month, the cadre checks with the mother what food she has been providing, how the child's appetite has been, if he or she has had any illnesses. The cadre may suggest changes in the diet, or refer the case to the local health cadre if disease is involved. Often the concern of a better-informed neighbour is enough to motivate a mother to pay extra attention to the child at risk. If a child's weight falls for two months running, he or she is referred to the health centre.

This regular monitoring of all local children enables cadres to pick those in need of supplementary feeding. These children get an extra 150 calories and fifteen grams of protein a day for 120 days, at group meals which the mothers themselves cook under the supervision of cadres. In this way they learn practical nutrition at the same time as their child recovers. After the weighing I attended, there was a meal for the malnourished children, which was quite delicious. First came a broth of greens, tomatoes and carrots, then rice, with small cakes of spinach omelette and soya curds, followed by a banana. The cost was met by the government. The idea is, eventually, that villages will organize and finance this themselves, setting up village nutrition committees and raising a levy on inhabitants to set by a store of food for supplementary feeding.

The final element in this highly complex and comprehensive programme is that it is linked with a basic health delivery scheme, similar to those described in the next chapter, and provision of clean water supplies, both of which are essential to eliminating disease-related malnutrition.

Nutrition programmes of this kind mobilize the people themselves and educate them, so they become the major forces for their own self-improvement. They help to eradicate nutritional deficiencies such as anaemia, xeropthalmia (which can cause night-blindness) and goitre, prevent avoidable deaths from gastro-enteritis and make better use of whatever nutritional resources a village has.

Villagers can be taught to combine traditional staples to get a balanced protein: rice with soya beans, maize bread with beans, millet plus peanuts. These cereal-legume combinations are as good for the soil as for the human body. The cereal can be rotated or grown together with the legume, which fixes nitrogen to enrich the soil. Home food processing can be improved so as to reduce nutrient loss. Traditional methods usually keep more of the food value (see page 174). The spread of over-refined white flour, white rice, white sugar, is damaging nutrition in the Third World as it has done in the West. Urban areas can be helped in similar ways. Allotment gardens can be promoted and food co-ops set up to buy in bulk and cut costs. These approaches, combined with nutrition education, surveillance, and scientific advances to improve yields and protein content, can achieve much.

But they may not greatly alter the central problem of insufficient calories. When all possible has been done to boost national production and improve the balance of consumption, the problem of distribution of food will remain. The landless and near landless and the poor simply cannot afford enough food. In the last analysis only a frontal attack on poverty can eliminate hunger from the world.

10 Heal thyself: new approaches to health care

If you look carefully, in any western Nigerian market, in among the dried stockfish, the cassava flour, the tie-dye cloth and the brashly painted enamel pots and pans, you will find a section selling rather unorthodox merchandise. Here old women, their breasts hanging like empty leather pouches, sit by their motley collection of wares: bright parrot feathers, coloured stones and pungent powders, seeds, severed and mummified monkeys' paws and eyeless, shrunken heads, ram horns, brimming baskets of birds' beaks and claws, rattling piles of dead, desiccated lizards, and wire cages with live green chameleons rolling their staring, conical eyes.

These stalls are the traditional equivalent of a pharmacist's shop. Western medicine is still unavailable to perhaps as many as 2 billion people in the developing countries. That does not mean they simply wait for illness to pass or kill them. Their own traditional forms of medical care were in evidence long before the Europeans arrived, and these same systems still cater, often with greater effect than might be supposed, for the health needs of the poor majority.

In western Nigeria there is a whole range of traditional practitioners. There are barber surgeons who will do you a quick tonsillectomy with a lancet forged from the steel band round a packing case, or give you a tonic bloodletting with vacuum cups made of cattle horns. There are faith healers from the revivalist Christian cults and apostolic churches. There are quack doctors selling patent cure-alls. And there are herbal healers and diviners dealing with any complaints from malaria to mental illness. British social psychiatrist, Una MacLean, in a survey of health habits in western Nigeria, found that use of traditional healers and medicines was widespread. In part of Ibadan, nearly three-quarters of the population sometimes used traditional remedies, two thirds of the men had themselves made up such remedies using their own or the healer's formula, and half the families consulted traditional healers. Traditional medicine's coverage and reach far exceeded that of modern medicine: the quarter of Ibadan studied had twelve healers for a population of under 6,000, rivalling the very best doctor/patient ratios in Europe.

Each of the major culture areas has its own brand of traditional healer, its own system of ideas about the origin of disease and the right kind of treatments. Rural Latin America has its *curanderos*. In the Mexican village of Tepotztlan, studied by American anthropologist Oscar Lewis, the *curanderos* were usually women charging modest fees of 25 to 50 centavos per herbal cure. Those with more money to spare, or more terrible afflictions, could consult the more powerful and prestigious *magicos* who cost two to twenty times more. Showmanship was an essential part of the *magicos*' performance. Tepotztlan's Don Rosas would take patients to a chapel-like room, retire behind a curtain and go into a trance in which he would pronounce the illness his client was suffering from and prescribe treatment. Is there really much difference between the awe thus inspired and the blind trust which Western patients place in their own medical showmen? The placebo effect is powerful worldwide. The Mexican villagers believed (in an analysis that is common to most rural areas in Latin America) that diseases originated in 'hot' or 'cold' causes such as draughts (cold) or rich foods (hot). The *curanderos* and *magicos* shared this conception, and their expertise in these matters was unquestioned. If they failed to cure a complaint, this was put down not to their incompetence but to the disease being too strong for any remedy to work. And when cures came about (as they very often do) by the natural process of the disease running its course, the healer would be credited with curing it. But the villagers' attitude to Western doctors was quite different. If a doctor failed to effect a cure, he would permanently lose their confidence, because they would consider it due to his failure to understand the 'hot' or 'cold' nature of the disease involved.

South Asia has perhaps the most complex system of indigenous medicine in the world. It has its magicians, exorcists, bone-setters, cuppers, cultists, surgeons and thorn-pullers, as well as healers trained in the highly developed ancient medical systems of Ayurveda, Unam and Siddha. Ayurveda, which means 'the science of life', may predate Hippocrates by a millennium or so. There are references to it in the Vedic literature, though the earliest extant authorities, *Sushruta Samhita* and *Charaka Samhita*, date from the fifth century before Christ. Ayurvedic doctors pay much attention, in their diagnosis, to important social, psychological and nutritional factors ignored by most Western practitioners. In Indian medical philosophies mind and body are treated as one. Illness is often seen as the result of moral weakness requiring some kind of ritual atonement. Treatment is a social affair involving not just the patient, but the whole family, and the most powerful members of the family have a large say in what treatment should be used. Western-style doctors often fail in Indian rural settings because they ignore these important local beliefs and social structures.

Just as spontaneous settlements have many lessons for open-minded city planners, so modern health care for the Third World can learn a great deal from traditional medical systems. Trust is an essential element in medical treatment, because of the placebo effect, and rural people trust the traditional healers because they have an assigned place in the social structure and analyse illness in the same terms the patients themselves perceive it. They also share the same culture and speak the local language, which outside doctors often do not. Traditional medicine is an example of appropriate technology: it is labour-intensive, uses local materials, respects the local social system, has wide coverage and costs little. Geographically, economically and culturally, it is highly accessible to the majority. Western medicine may, for certain types of condition, be more effective, but it is being increasingly recognized that some traditional cures often 'work' for many ailments, especially for mental illness, and may be more cost-effective than expensive Western treatment. Western medicine in Tepotztlan cost ten times more than the very best and most expensive traditional treatment, and two hundred times the cheapest. Since it is almost certainly not even ten times more efficacious, on average, it makes economic sense for people to use their local healer. They are actually getting more cure for their money.

A revolution in health care

Until recently, the Western-modelled health services of most developing countries had nothing but scorn for the traditional medical systems. Yet they themselves were doing far less to combat illness among the poor majority of their populations.

The dominant diseases in the Third World are infectious, parasitic and respiratory diseases long conquered in the West. Their incidence is heavy – the average person may turn out to have one or two worm infestations, and get stomach complaints once every month or two. Life expectancy ranged, in the mid-seventies, from forty-six years in Africa to sixty-two in Latin America. Infant mortality carries off between 4 and 20 per cent of children before they reach the age of one. As poor health cuts a man's ability to work and, via malnutrition, his children's success at school, it contributes to keeping poor people in poverty just as much as undernourishment. Yet so much of it is easily and cheaply avoidable. The prevalent diseases are almost all environmental in origin, transmitted by dirty hands, polluted water, by way of water holes, mud floors, bare feet, or injected by mosquitoes, blackfly or tsetse. Simple environmental improvements – the most important of which is a clean and ample water supply – could clear most of them up while immunization could protect against most of the rest.

Yet in most developing countries less than one fifth of health expenditure goes on health prevention. The rest is spent on expensive cures: doctors trained along Western lines and equipped to deal with Western diseases; hospitals; imported drugs. The cost of this kind of service is so prohibitive, for a poor country, that it can only be provided for a small minority in the towns. Rural doctors may typically have to serve 50,000 or 100,000 patients, most of whom they never see. The World Health Organization has estimated that 60 to 80 per cent of the people in the Third World have, for all practical purposes, no access to modern medical services.

During the 1970s it dawned on a large number of developing countries that they would not be able to provide health care for the majority of their people until the end of the twenty-first century if they continued along the old lines. A revolution in health care was required. The lines such a revolution could take were sketched out in pioneering health programmes in Russia, Venezuela, Cuba and China and in voluntary projects in Bangladesh and Indonesia. The new thinking was systemized in the two United Nations organizations in this field, the children's fund, UNICEF, and the World Health Organization. Its goal is what WHO's Director-General, Halfdan Mahler, has called 'justice in health'. 'Health care has to be equitably spread,' Mahler wrote in 1978. 'Planners should not be asking, "To how many people can we provide good health care?" but "Given these resources, how do we use them to provide health care to everyone?" ' In the new approach the emphasis in health care has to be shifted from cure to prevention, from provision at Western standards to the urban privileged to satisfaction of the basic health needs of the underprivileged. Or, again as Mahler put it in his address to the thirty-first World Health Assembly in 1978: 'The just distribution of health resources is as important as their quantity and quality. To reach a more equitable distribution it is necessary to pay greater attention to those least served, the social periphery, the disease-ridden majority. Our guiding principle should be the greatest health benefit to the greatest number of people at the lowest cost.'

The new approach in health is known as primary health care. A joint paper published in 1978 by the World Health Organization and UNICEF defined this as 'a practical approach to making essential health care universally accessible to individuals and families in an acceptable, affordable way with their full participation'. In September 1978 an international conference at Alma Ata in the USSR helped to develop the concept and diffuse it further. The conference declared that primary health care should include delivery of the following services: health education; promotion of better nutrition, clean water and sanitation; mother-and-child care and family planning; immunization; prevention and control of infectious diseases; appropriate treatment of common diseases and injuries; provision of essential drugs; and promotion of mental health. Popular participation is an essential component. With the help of health education and motivation, people will come to assume a much greater degree of responsibility for their own health, through preventive measures at family and community level. They will become agents of their own development, instead of passive beneficiaries of programmes directed from on high. But they will also participate in running the health service at primary level, helping to define what are the local health priorities, providing free labour when needed and staffing committees that will ensure that the health system meets their needs.

The science of medicine itself has to be decolonized, demystified, de-professionalized. A new appropriate technology of simplified medicine has to be developed: low in cost, easily mastered by ordinary people, using local resources wherever possible and drawing on those traditional methods that are known to work. To quote Halfdan Mahler again: 'We must break the chain of dependence on unproved, oversophisticated and overcostly health technology,' and evolve an 'essential health technology, a technology which people can understand and which the non-expert can apply.'

Part of that new appropriate technology will be a more simplified set of medicines. The cost of many proprietary Western drugs makes them unsuitable for the task of providing remedies for the poor majority. Yet most Third World countries continue to import them in great variety and quantity, so that they may often account for 40 per cent of the health budget. An increasing number of governments are now cutting back their purchases to a smaller number of drugs, and wherever possible buying generic drugs free from patent restrictions, rather than more expensive brand-named products. Some have set up small-scale manufacturing units nationally. For the guidance of national health services the World Health Organization has produced a list of just 200 essential drugs – chosen for their cost-effectiveness and safety – which could cover the bulk of health requirements in tropical countries, though naturally each government would adapt this list to local circumstances. The reduced list allows bulk purchasing to cut costs, and also makes the task of monitoring drug performance easier.

Another element of primary health care which is beginning to emerge is the 'risk' approach, which we have already seen at work in the field of nutrition. This involves giving special attention to those groups of people who are most at risk, first of all, mothers and children in general. It is now known that many diseases of adulthood have their origins in infancy – the child is father to the man. Attention to mother-and-child health means healthier adults. More specifically, it means that village-level health and nutrition workers will pick out, from regular checks of the whole community, those individual cases where there is a greater risk of illness or death, and give them continuous surveillance and extra care. So children at risk may be sifted out by weighing, and given priority for scarce medicines or food supplements. Mothers at risk of pregnancy complications can be picked out by recording their previous history or checking for signs of gross underweight or pre-eclampsia which will jeopardize the birth. These mothers can be given special nutrition, relieved of heavy work in the last, critical three months of the pregnancy, and guaranteed a trained attendant at the birth. The risk approach cuts costs by ensuring that resources are concentrated where they are most needed and will have the greatest impact.

To meet health needs at village and shantytown level a new front line of primary health care workers is needed, chosen by the people from among the people, simply trained and simply equipped, supported by the community and backed by the expertise of the professionals. Coming from among the people, such a worker is better placed to know the people's needs and to communicate with and be accepted by the people than the over- and mistrained doctor who serves time in the bush reluctantly, all the while dreaming of transfer to the city. This new approach to health care is made possible by the realization that the poor suffer predominantly from a small number of complaints, most of which are amenable to simple treatment and are preventable by a few low-cost measures. You don't need a brain surgeon to deal with a headache.

The most influential model for the new approach to health care was China's medical system, which was remodelled in the mid-sixties. In a directive of 26 June 1965 Mao ordered: 'In medical and health work, put the stress on the rural areas.' Medical research was refocused, from the preoccupation with academic prestige to the treatment of common illnesses. Periods of training for health professionals were shortened, so more of them could be turned out faster. Urban health workers were drafted into mobile teams to serve rural areas and to train health auxiliaries. The barefoot doctor was born: these were peasants selected by their fellows for a short, three-month training course. Their tasks were largely preventive – they were expected to give health education, perform vaccinations and organize sanitation programmes and other campaigns. They would also give medical care for simple ailments and first aid for injuries and emergencies. They were only part-time health workers – the rest of the time they would be in the paddy fields, doing agricultural work along with everyone else, barefoot. Hence their name.

Traditional medicine was harnessed into service. Acupuncture and herbal remedies took their natural place in broadening the range of treatments that could be offered. Barefoot doctors and pharmacists were encouraged to go out looking for medicinal herbs, or to cultivate them in their gardens.

Mass participation was another major emphasis. It was based on Mao's principle of following the 'mass line', trusting the wisdom and energy of the people themselves, which can accomplish miracles. The masses were mobilized in sanitation work and in the Great Patriotic Health Campaigns, which successfully wiped out flies, mosquitoes and rats. Schistosomiasis or bilharzia was once endemic in eleven of China's thirty-three provinces and plagued some 33 million victims each year. It is caused by a single-celled fluke which passes out in human urine or faeces and spends part of its life-cycle in a particular species of water snail living in the paddy fields, before boring its way back into humans again through the skin of the feet. The incidence of this disease has been cut by two thirds by a gigantic mass effort. Students and health workers educated people about how the disease was passed on. Then the ponds and paddy fields where the water snail lived were drained and the banks plastered in mud to suffocate the snails. Finally, safe methods of excreta disposal were introduced so the parasite's eggs could not pass into water with human faeces, which is used extensively as fertilizer in China.

The Third World Tomorrow

Cool, clear water

One of the first spheres where the new approach was applied was in improving sanitation and water supply. Water is involved in some way in many endemic diseases in the Third World. It transmits cholera, typhoid, gastro-enteritis, guinea worm and bilharzia. The need to live close to rivers exposes people to insects transmitting yellow fever, malaria and sleeping sickness. Lack of water for washing aggravates scabies, leprosy and trachoma. Provision of clean water helps to cut most of these diseases by at least a half and is the cheapest possible way of doing so. Average provision costs vary between $6 and $24 per head. Sophisticated facilities of the kind Westerners are used to – complex treatment plants, four-gallon flush toilets – are quite unnecessary. Groundwater is usually pure enough to need no treatment. Chlorination or simple filters of sand and other local materials can deal with most pollution problems. Rainwater can be collected where groundwater is inaccessible: in Mali the Dogon tribe have converted some of their clay granaries into plastic or cement-lined storage tanks for water gathered from flat house roofs.

Costs can be further cut if local people participate in providing their own water supply. Most water programmes now include a strong component of community involvement. Local people are consulted as to their needs, they contribute their labour and cash and often maintain the installation after it has been built. This participation serves as an education in health principles, and is often a community's first experience of collective action to improve their lot. Frequently it leads on to other efforts of self-development.

Composting latrines may be the ideal long-term solution for rural areas – providing sanitation and organic fertilizer at the same time. But water supply seems to be a field where the Western solution, a tap in every home, does produce the best results for health. The reason is that distance from the source appears to make a great difference to the extent people use safe water. A survey in Bangladesh found that nearly 100 per cent of families used a tubewell for drinking water if it was within 100 yards of the house, but only one in three did so if it was 300 yards away. Beyond 1,000 yards usage dropped to 10 per cent.

Thanks to a massive well-sinking programme backed by UNICEF, three quarters of Bangladesh's families were within 250 yards of a safe well by 1977 and, very unusually for the Third World, the rural areas were much better supplied than the urban. But problems persisted. Even when they lived close to the well, most people continued to use river and pond water for washing their clothes, their bodies, their pots and pans, and even for cooking with. In parts of Africa families who have no choice but to use the tubewell in the dry season go back to the stream when the rains fill it again. Continued use of waterholes maintains the risk of bilharzia, guinea worm, sleeping sickness and yellow fever. Supply points for safe water have to be closer and more convenient than alternative dirty sources before they will be used for all purposes. Poor people may even use dirty water sources from further away if they cannot afford the charge levied for clean water. But any improvement on the dirty waterhole is worthwhile. There are many steps from there to the tap in the kitchen, and this goal can be approached gradually, as and when funds permit.

The impact of clean water on health will be immensely greater if it is coupled with advances in hygiene. Dirty hands can transmit most of the faecally borne diseases, while messy homes and compounds breed illness. Household latrines may spread some diseases even faster than going in the bushes, if they are not kept clean. More water does help to keep the house and toilet cleaner. But habits of hygiene are frankly appalling in many parts of the Third World. Educational efforts here would pay off handsomely at little or no cost.

Water itself can be used as a bait to improve hygiene. Sanitation in Sarawak's *kampongs* or longhouses used to be appalling. Yards were fouled by human and animal faeces and accumulated refuse. Water would be obtained from polluted rivers and streams, and fetching it would take up a great deal of women's time. Sarawak's Rural Health Improvement Scheme started in the early sixties to try and improve this situation. At first it concentrated on education and exhortation, but this had little impact. In 1967 the approach changed: it was decided to use the offer of clean, accessible water (which everyone wanted) as an incentive for self-help sanitary improvements (which few saw the need for). Water-taps would be provided for each household if they agreed to contribute free labour to build and maintain the water system – and to build sanitary toilets for themselves, clean up their longhouses, dig drainage ditches and fence in their pigs. The scheme proved immensely popular, and by 1980 half of Sarawak's 2,800 *kampongs* will have been sanitized.

Barefoot doctors of the Andes

By the late seventies one kind or another of primary health care or barefoot doctor programme had been introduced in many countries: in Latin America, Cuba, Colombia, Peru, Venezuela, Honduras, Costa Rica and Guatemala had such programmes; in Africa, Tanzania, Niger, Cameroon, Sudan and Guinea Bissau; in Asia, India, Bangladesh, Indonesia, Iran, Thailand, Mongolia, Afghanistan and Nepal. And new countries were starting up similar programmes each year. The front-line workers in these programmes vary considerably in their responsibilities and degree of expertise. In Indonesia and Tanzania they are part-time unpaid volunteers. Afghanistan's 'friends of health', chosen by village elders, get only three weeks' training, while Mongolia's *feldshers* are almost general practitioners. The form and degree of local participation also varies: in some programmes local villagers propose or elect their health worker, in others they do not. The degree of community contribution, through health committees, free labour, premises, transport and payment of fees or wages, ranges from nil to almost complete carrying of costs.

The basic health delivery programme set up in south Peru by the government in conjunction with the World Health Organization and UNICEF is typical. The high, treeless *altiplano* generates its own characteristic set of health problems. Scorching hot days are followed by icy winds and freezing nights. The hardy Aymara and Quechua Indians who live here have little pity on themselves. Women and children are out before dawn, pasturing the family herds, more concerned about the animals' health than their own. If the animals die or are stolen, they will die too – in their calculus it is worth risking illness so as to ensure survival. Here in the high Andes, respiratory illnesses – tuberculosis, whooping cough, pneumonia – cause three times more deaths than the killers of the hot lowlands, stomach complaints. Infant mortality, like that of llamas and alpacas, rises and falls with the harshness of the weather. In the rural areas local health officials believe that in bad years as many as 500 children per 1,000 may die before their first birthday.

Health services were reaching only a small minority here. The population is extremely sparse except on the shores of Lake Titicaca, the state of the roads is appalling, and lorries pass through rarely. With average incomes of only $44 per head (in 1976), people cannot afford doctor's fees or fares. Two thirds of them cannot speak Spanish, the language of doctors. There is, on average, only one doctor per 22,000 inhabitants, but three quarters of the doctors are concentrated in the three main towns, along with all the nurses and dentists. So people's teeth rot, and they resort to the *curanderos* (healers) for herbal remedies and incantations and chew coca to deaden pain. The *parteras* (traditional midwives) worry more about such rituals as burning rubbish on the threshold, or putting crosses of straw on the mother's stomach, than with cleanliness. More than a third of them use broken glass, stones or ordinary knives to cut the placenta.

UNICEF, the WHO and the Peruvian government drew up a comprehensive plan to improve the region's health services. The lynch-pin of the plan is the barefoot doctor, termed here the *promotor de salud* (health promoter). Victor Charca had been doing the job in the lakeside village of Machajmarca for just two months when I met him. Only twenty-four, his usual occupation was helping his father on their scattered family plots. He had the quiet, pensive reserve of the *altiplano* Indian, but he had seven years' schooling behind him and was literate in Spanish (the only formal qualifications required). Charca was elected at a village meeting of the ninety-two families of Machajmarca. He spends about two hours a day on health work, but receives no salary. Instead, his services are paid for by his patients. The community itself met to decide an appropriate scale of fees and charges for drugs, and built with its own hands the smart, mauve-painted, tin-roofed building on a hill that serves as Charca's health post. Inside the long, one-roomed building, wooden benches line the walls for patients to wait on.

Charca has made a handwritten poster for his patients' guidance, which lists the services offered by the health auxiliary: 'Sanitary education, home visits, first aid, tuberculosis examinations, vaccinations, attendance at births, supply of medicines, personal medical attention, coordination with local authorities and institutions, daily and monthly reports on activities.' In fact, his functions are broader than the brief catalogue suggests. He provides attention to mother and child, with pre- and post-natal care and advice, as well as acting as the midwife at the birth. He gives vaccinations against tuberculosis, measles, polio, smallpox, yellow fever and rabies, and a triple dose against whooping cough, tetanus and diphtheria. It is his responsibility, also, to organize vaccination campaigns to inform and convince people of the need for immunization. He promotes sanitary improvements such as latrines or water filters, and tries to teach his community, through meetings and talks, to prevent disease by good hygienic practices. As he goes along, he keeps a continuous census of births, illnesses and deaths with their causes. And he is, of course, trained and equipped to deal with the most common and straightforward ailments such as diarrhoea, pneumonia, aches and sprains, wounds, eye infections, stomach pains, anaemia and skin complaints.

Charca's technology is basic, boiled down to the bare essentials needed to do the job. His transport is a bike, provided by UNICEF. His auxiliary's kit prepares him for most eventualities, consisting of a limited number of basic drugs such as analgesics (in pill-syrup and injectable form), a few antibiotics and sulpha drugs, eye ointment, chest rubs, de-worming pills and powders, along with cotton, gauze, bandages, hypodermic syringes and needles, scissors, thermometers, a sterilizing dish and two planks of wood to make a stretcher. It is up to him to keep the kit fully stocked, covering costs with the fees charged, and he is free to add extra medicines if he finds them useful.

One of the most important items of his equipment is his *Health Promoter's Manual*. Its 110 cyclostyled pages sandwiched between a green cardboard cover contain, in simple everyday language and illustrated with graphic cartoons, a complete guide to all the subjects Charca covered in his basic course: basic anatomy, prevention and sanitation, first aid, hints on diagnosis, recommended treatment for the most common diseases and dosages for the drugs. The section on the transmission of gastro-intestinal diseases is worth quoting as an example of the down-to-earth simplified style: 'A man with diarrhoea goes to the riverside. A pig eats his faeces and tramples it with his feet. Then the pig goes into a house. A child is playing on the floor where the pig is walking, so the child dirties itself with the crap [*sic*] of the sick man. The child cries, so the mother picks him up. Then she peels potatoes, forgetting to wash her hands. All the family eats the potatoes. Then all the family catches diarrhoea.' The process is illustrated by a cartoon strip, the parting illustration of which shows a row of defecating people with the runs. It is an object lesson to contrast this and similar barefoot doctor manuals with the huge textbooks of conventional medical education, and it shows how relatively little specialized knowledge is required to cope with 90 per cent of health problems.

It would be very easy for a barefoot doctor in a far-flung rural area to make errors of practice and diagnosis, perhaps even grave or fatal ones. The possibility of such mistakes is the main argument opponents (usually medics with a vested interest in maintaining their monopoly) raise against barefoot doctors. It is a real possibility, so schemes must contain provision for thorough and ongoing supervision. The Peru programme covers this problem well. The promoter has to keep a diary of patients seen and action taken, and show it regularly to his supervisor at the health centre. Every three or four months he must attend refresher courses and sit exams to test his knowledge and keep it active. If he does not do his work to the satisfaction of his supervisors on professional skills, and of his community on service, his official card can be revoked and someone else can be given his job. Of course mistakes will be made, just as they are made by young general practitioners and hospital doctors, but like these, the barefoot doctors develop their skills and expertise with experience.

Paramedics as surgeons and pathologists

The farmer staggers along the village path under the burden. His wife's emaciated body, draped in a coarse blue saree, is arched backwards in the rigor of tetanus. He is heading for Gonoshashthaya Kendra, the People's Health Centre at Savar in Bangladesh. On the bed at the clinic, the woman's face grimaces in the familiar *risus sardonicus* of lockjaw. She says she did not cut herself: but on the calloused, grimy sole of her foot, sure enough, is the telltale nick where the germ penetrated. She will have the benefit of a new treatment. Instead of pumping over 100 ampoules of tetanus toxoid into the veins, just two ampoules will be injected directly into the spinal column, so it can reach the nervous system more quickly. A female staff member makes the delicate lumbar puncture required: a few drops of spinal fluid oozing out confirm her success. That staff member, astonishingly, is a paramedic, working under the supervision of a doctor.

The People's Health Centre, one of the first projects outside China to make wide use of paramedics, remains today one of the boldest experiments in bringing health care to the rural poor of the Third World. Few barefoot doctor programmes have dared to entrust to modestly educated, briefly trained workers the range of functions routinely performed by the paramedics of Savar, from clinical pathology to minor surgery and tubectomy. Gonoshashthaya Kendra was founded in 1972 by a radical young Bangladeshi doctor, Zafrullah Chowdhury, now aged thirty-seven. After taking a medical degree from Dacca University, Chowdhury spent five years in Britain and was within a month of taking his final exams for the Royal College of Surgeons when, in March 1971, civil war broke out in what was then East Pakistan. Chowdhury dropped everything and rushed back to set up a field hospital to treat wounded freedom fighters. Trained doctors and nurses were in short supply. Forced to rely on girl volunteers with no previous medical training, Chowdhury soon discovered the potentialities of the paramedic. After a couple of months learning on the job, the girls were soon at home with all duties from injections to assisting in the operating threatre.

The health situation in the new nation of Bangladesh was in some respects reminiscent of wartime scarcity. Doctors and nurses were in short supply – even today the country has only around 8,000 doctors for its 80 million inhabitants. Three quarters of the doctors work in the towns, but nine out of ten people live in the rural areas. The use of cheaply and rapidly trained paramedics was quite simply the only way to bring health care to the villages. Chowdhury established GK, as its workers call it, on land donated by a friend's father, twenty-two miles north of the capital, Dacca, to prove the concept could work.

Today Savar's full-time staff of 114 provide a comprehensive health service to a population of 100,000 and expanding, in a three-tiered system in which each level offers increasingly sophisticated expertise and equipment. At the centre is the health complex at Savar, with a fifteen-bed hospital, operating theatre, full-scale pathology lab, large pharmacy and a small staff of trained doctors. Below that come four subcentres, each one serving about fifteen villages with a population of 15,000 to 20,000. Each subcentre also has a small operating theatre for minor surgery and tubectomy, the basic equipment to do its own pathology examinations, a small pharmacy and two inpatient beds. Working out of each subcentre are five or six paramedics, the solid base of the pyramid. Each one spends most of his or her week in two or three villages, with a total population of around 3,000 and a radius of about five miles, easily covered on foot or by bicycle. Each paramedic works together with a trainee, who looks, practises and learns from the experienced partner.

To get an idea of the range of village work, I followed on a day's rounds with Joseph Das, a twenty-three-year-old paramedic with nine months' experience and twelve years of education behind him, and his 'apprentice', Rafiq-ul-Islam, nineteen, a local village boy who failed his matriculation and was previously unemployed. Our first stop was to visit a thirty-five-year-old mother of seven children who had been getting three-monthly shots of the injectable contraceptive Depo-Provera for the past two years. She was suffering menstrual irregularities and spotting that were interfering with her marital life. Das gave her an iron supplement. On to a compound where the daughter was to be married the following week – all potential mothers in the area get an anti-tetanus injection. Islam administered it in a businesslike fashion.

At the next house one of the boys had diarrhoea. Das took time to show the mother how to make Savar's patent village formula for rehydration, devised for maximum cheapness and ease of preparation: just as much salt as can be picked up between two fingers and a thumb, enough *gur* or raw sugar to fill four cupped fingers, thoroughly mixed in a glass of water. He mixed the formula on the spot and gave it to the boy to drink: 'If I tell them, they will not do it. If I show them, they will do it.' Finally, we checked on the progress of a mother-to-be – Das measured the girth of her calf two inches above the ankle. He was looking for signs of the watery swelling that indicates pre-eclampsia – a condition of high blood pressure and loss of protein in the urine that can lead to premature labour and unnecessary perinatal deaths. The calf measured nine inches – well above the safety level of six to seven inches. Das told her to stop taking salt (to bring down the blood pressure) and to eat more bread (for protein). On her record card he noted her expected day of delivery so he could visit once a week in the last month, and attend the birth if need be.

Savar's paramedics are also trained to make routine pathology examination of blood, urine, stool and sputum samples – this is essential so that the subcentres can screen out serious cases which need referring to the health complex at Savar. Many of the paramedics are also adept at tubectomy, menstrual regulation and even abortion. Tubectomy is usually performed by female paramedics, who are preferred to male doctors in *purdah*-conscious Bangladesh. Savar's paramedics carry out nearly 1,000 tubectomies a year. They learn about sterilization, assist in the operating theatre, and perform ten to fifteen operations under the eye of a doctor before being trusted on their own – though a doctor always has to be available just in case.

The infection rate in operations done by paramedics, at just over 5 per cent, is a good deal lower than that of doctors, at 8·7 per cent.

X-ray technology will soon be added to the list of skills the paramedics will acquire. The idea is that there will be at least one auxiliary at each subcentre practised in each specialist skill. As there are not enough doctors and other specialists to go around, teaching paramedics to do these things is quite simply the only way to ensure they are available within reach of the village.

Yet most of the paramedics have at most ten years' education – indeed, Savar has now reduced the requirement to six years, or effective literacy in Bengali, because it proved impossible to find enough local people with ten years' schooling. So how does the People's Health Centre work the transformation, with a basic training period of only six months? The secret seems to lie in the no-nonsense approach of learning by doing. The new recruit spends his or her day tailing an old hand, first watching what the latter does as it is explained, then practising it under supervision, until he or she is finally skilled enough to do it alone – and teach others. Perhaps the major problem in training, Savar has found, lies not with the trainee but with the 'expert'. The doctor, who has been reared on high jargon with little understanding of the health needs of the majority, has to re-educate himself so he can make ideas and procedures understandable to his less sophisticated pupils.

One of Savar's most interesting experiments is its village health insurance scheme. While many preventive services such as immunization or family planning are free to all, curative services, medicines and use of clinics are available only to members of the insurance scheme. The subscription most people pay is two *taka* per month (about 7p or 14 US cents), equal to one fifth of the daily agricultural wage. In exchange they get free treatment, including drugs, whenever they need it. But despite the low cost many poor families have fallen behind with payments and dropped out of the scheme. So Savar is now planning to introduce a scale of subs in which the poor will pay very much less than the rich. The danger is that the rich may opt out, thus jeopardizing the whole idea.

Village health insurance schemes could make a useful contribution in the Third World. Without insurance, the cost of sickness – whether in payment for treatment or lost income if there is no treatment – can cripple a poor family, and the poor fall ill far more often than the rich. A scheme with contributions calculated according to income could be a big step towards justice in health.

Because of its radical approach, Gonoshashthaya Kendra has not always had a smooth run. Local *imams* have railed against the emancipation of women, landlords against cut-price loans, quacks and doctors against paramedics and preventive medicine. One Savar worker, Nizamuddin, was brutally murdered in November 1976 in the village of Shimulia, at the instigation, Chowdhury is convinced, of a coalition of powerful local vested interests. But patient work and effectiveness have clearly won the allegiance of the vast majority. Maternal deaths and diarrhoeal diseases are now extremely uncommon in the catchment area. The proportion accepting family planning is double the national average of 15 per cent. Death rates, birth rates and population growth rates are all appreciably lower.

New careers for witch-doctors

With its low cost, high coverage and instant acceptability, traditional medicine fills several of the requirements of the new approach to health care. Increasingly, programmes are beginning to incorporate the best of their local medical traditions and structures, both the herbs and the healers that use them. Since 1974 both the World Health Organization and UNICEF have officially favoured the mobilization and training of healers in elements of modern medicine. And in June

1976, WHO set up a working group with the brief of promoting the contribution of traditional medicine to health care and of stimulating scientific research into its remedies, both their chemical make-up and their effectiveness.

What little research has been done so far in this field has come up with promising results. For example, the flesh of the pawpaw (sometimes called medicine fruit) seems to be able to heal recalcitrant wounds. Extracts of the root of Indian rauwolfia, widely used in Asian pharmacopoeias, reduces blood pressure. In Ghana the Centre for Scientific Research into Plant Medicine, working together with traditional healers who indicate how herbs are used, has discovered remedies for several conditions for which Western medicaments are of little use. The hard-to-treat guinea worm normally has to be painfully pulled head first out of the blisters it raises on the leg of victims, by winding it round a stick. The worm was spontaneously expelled by forty-three out of forty-four patients given a decoction of the root of *Combretum mucronatum*, a herbalist's remedy. Shingles cleared up within a week when the root bark of *Balanites aegyptiaca*, ground into powder and mixed with water into a paste, was applied day and night. Moreover, as the ingredients of traditional remedies are available locally and not subject to patents or licences, they can form the basis of a drug manufacturing industry in developing countries and help cut the staggering cost of imported drugs.

The personnel, as well as the plants, of traditional medicine are being drafted in the war against disease. India was one of the first countries to recognize and exploit this potential contribution. As early as 1920 it became the policy of the Indian National Congress to make full use of the network of ayurvedic doctors. Today, when there are perhaps 150,000 Western-style doctors in India, there are no less than 200,000 qualified ayurvedic practitioners and another 200,000 who have learned ayurvedic medicine on the job. There are almost as many recognized ayurvedic medical colleges as modern ones, and state and national governments in India support 15,000 dispensaries and 239 hospitals offering ayurvedic treatment. These two complementary approaches to human health problems would both benefit if they could be integrated, both conceptually and in personnel, but little progress has been made in this direction.

Other programmes have successfully retrained traditional practitioners in modern skills. Not everything the healers and birth attendants do is unequivocally good, indeed some of their practices are downright dangerous. Retraining programmes have to discourage harmful habits. Afghanistan's village midwives or *dais* have been retrained in modern methods, as have Senegal's *sage-femmes* and the Philippines' *hilots*. In many countries, as we have seen, midwives have been recruited as distributors of contraceptives, for example, Indonesia's *dukuns*, India's *dais* and Malaysia's *bidans*.

Some of the most effective community health workers turn out to be adaptable traditional healers retrained in modern techniques. Where communities are allowed to elect their new barefoot doctor, the healer – if he is willing – is often a natural choice, and programmes ought to bend their education and literacy requirements to accept them. This combination is the ideal solution, avoids the damaging conflict of medical systems and the persistence of dual health care, and allows the gradual infusion of modern health concepts such as all-important knowledge on how diseases are transmitted. In Thailand's primary health care programme some of the local health communicators and village health volunteers were formerly, and still are, also medicine men.

Restructuring the system

Basic health care programmes are not without their pitfalls. There is a real danger that the barefoot doctor, paid for by community contributions, may become, for some countries, simply a makeshift way of getting the underprivileged to provide cheap, low-grade health care for themselves, while the high-technology Western medical sector in the cities jogs along just as before, sucking up the lion's share of the health resources to service the urban middle class and line the doctors' pockets.

It may be right that the people should pay some nominal contribution to the cost of their health care. But the level of charges must be carefully calculated or they might deter the poor from using the scheme. Disease is an all-too-familiar part of life for the poor. They often accept known health risks at work and at home, to earn a living or to reduce their expenditure. As their funds are so limited, they usually prefer to sweat out diseases rather than pay for expensive treatment or bear the cost of preventive measures like water filters or cement floors.

Therefore the early stages in primary health care ought to be financed much more by redistribution of health budgets than by contributions from villagers. If primary health care is to mean real justice in health, it must involve a transfer of resources away from the high-technology, prestige sector. It must mean that poor countries cancel orders for body scanners for their top teaching hospitals until such time as the villager has been provided with accessible first aid. It has to involve not only the provision of grassroots workers, but the complete restructuring of every level of the health service, so the whole system is geared to providing for the needs of the majority. This means – as happened in Colombia's rural health plan – that the higher levels of the system take on the function of servicing the lower. The role of the professionals changes. In the new system, their job is to train the primary workers (as well as to learn from their experience of dealing with day-to-day health problems), retraining and upgrading them on a continuous basis, and to supervise their field work, provide them with supplies and act as a place of referral for more complicated or serious cases that the primary worker has not got the equipment or knowledge to deal with.

Health education, too, has to be reshaped, so it can turn out the new kind of health professional required: excellent not only as clinical specialists, but as the WHO's Director-General Halfdan Mahler put it, 'as health leaders, community educators, guides and generators of simpler and socially acceptable technologies'. Education needs to be more community-oriented instead of hospital-oriented, more concerned with prevention rather than cure and with service to the people rather than professional 'excellence' and self-advancement.

Biomedical research also has to undergo a sea change. It has been estimated that only around $30 million is spent each year on research into tropical diseases, less than the United States spends on cancer research alone. According to WHO experts, practically no major new treatment has emerged in this field for thirty years. To remedy the situation the World Health Organization launched, in 1977, its Special Programme for Research and Training in Tropical Diseases, covering malaria, schistosomiasis, filariasis, sleeping sickness, leishmaniasis and leprosy.

In the country of the blind

There are some health problems, however, where popular participation and primary health care are not enough, and the full panoply of modern technology and organization has to be brought to bear in a military-style operation. This is often necessary where the target is the complete eradication of a disease, or an insect carrier of disease which cannot be eliminated by improvements in water supply or sanitation, better nutrition or other community measures. Such operations may not use the methods of the new-style development programmes, but they are important to the goals of eliminating poverty and improving the productivity of poor people and poor countries. One of the most dramatic battles in the war against disease has been the campaign against riverblindness in West Africa, in which seven governments and four international agencies are collaborating.

Bayure Nakulema's white pupils stare out wildly from a ground of blood red. Though he is forty-five, he still has a young face and vigorous gestures. In his late twenties Bayure was a power to be reckoned with in Wayen. Son of a former chief of this Mossi village in Upper Volta, he was a favourite to succeed the ageing incumbent, and was wealthy enough to afford two wives. Ten years ago riverblindness took away his sight. Today Bayure wears tattered trousers. He can no longer work his own fields, though for a while, when he could still make out light and dark shapes, he did try to plant, weed and harvest by feel and grope. His compound is small and bare. His granary, a giant clay pitcher perched on logs, is empty save for a few desiccated maize cobs. Bayure is angered, agitated, rebellious about his affliction, and understandably so. His first wife left him. His second, Kayaba, is pretty but her eyes, half closed, move rapidly from side to side. She too is blind.

Riverblindness afflicts perhaps one in ten of the population of Wayen, and one in four of its most productive group, the adult males. The village is a sad testimony to the misery disease can add to an already poor economy. There are no bicycles or radios here. The men are dressed in the most motley assortment of European jumble, imported in bales and sold on local markets. Riverblindness ages its victims prematurely: they have tough, wrinkled skin which they are forever scratching. Many have large cysts on the knees and about the head. All day long they sit staring at the floor, or they are led about by children.

Riverblindness is caused by the worm *Onchocerca volvulus*, whose larvae are transmitted by the bite of the blackfly which breeds in fast-flowing rivers. Wayen, like the other villages that are similarly crippled, is the nearest settlement to the river, the first reservoir of human blood which the blackfly must taste before it can breed.

There are perhaps 20 million riverblindness victims across the world, but the disease takes its heaviest toll among the inhabitants of the Volta basin, where one in ten people have some degree of infection. Some 65,000 square kilometres of fertile river valley land are left vacant in fear of the disease. In 1972 a consortium of development agencies came together under the aegis of the World Bank to fight the disease, with the World Health Organization holding the front line. For nearly three years a preparatory mission searched for the most effective way of eradicating riverblindness. Every human affliction has its own unique ecology: the task of the mass campaigns is to find the weak link in the chain and break it.

The adult *Onchocerca* worm spends its fifteen-year lifespan in human hosts, and continually breeds embryos known as *microfilariae*, which migrate to the skin and eyes, causing the external symptoms. No satisfactory treatment existed to cure the disease: hence it had to be attacked through its other host, the blackfly, a tiny insect like a fruitfly, which picks up *microfilariae* when it bites humans. By one of those curious specializations that abound in nature, the female blackfly will lay her eggs only at rapids in fast-flowing streams, on rocks or branches. When they hatch, the infant larvae crawl down just under the surface. Here they live from suspended organic material and dissolved oxygen. The chosen strategy was to locate all the breeding sites and kill off the larvae with a biodegradable insecticide harmless to most other forms of life.

The war on the blackfly began in December 1974. Operations are planned and executed like a military campaign, with a continual flow of information about the enemy and the terrain. Helicopters locate and map the breeding sites, teams of fieldworkers plot the concentration of blackfly, hydrologists measure the flow of water in the rivers. At the headquarters of the vector control unit in Bobo Dioulasso, each site to be sprayed is marked on the map with the exact amount of insecticide to be dropped. The actual spraying is being done by an American private firm, Evergreen Helicopters.

As we take off at dawn from a corner of Bobo's tiny airport, only a veil of smoke over the scattered villages breaks the monotony of the savannah landscape. We follow a spraying copter up the Black Volta, a winding thread of greenery over the dry scrub. The copter twists and turns along the bends of the river, looking out for the white water of rapids – the telltale sign of a breeding site. We put down in a field and clamber down the steep river bank to where a reef of freshwater oysters cuts the stream in two, speeding up the flow. On the far bank a dead tree has fallen head first and its trailing fingers cleave the water and catch leaves. My entomologist companion, Dutchman Jeff Henderieckx, wades over waist deep and examines the leaves. Sure enough, there are the blackfly larvae, an ugly cross between a maggot and a shrimp. We move on to a bridge where the spraying ship will soon pass. Women are washing clothes by the bank, and a herdsman arrives with a dozen long-horned cattle who drink long, greedy draughts. Suddenly the copter buzzes over, weaving into position for the drop. A burst of white shoots out in a brief ejaculation, spreads downstream and hits the breeding site with precision. The villagers gape, and the cattle break into a panic-stricken stampede.

The whole massive programme has given frequent headaches to Pierre Ziegler, the tall crew-cut Frenchman who is in overall charge of the $11 million a year budget. Three weeks after the start of spraying, a plane and one of the helicopters crashed. Since then there have been repeated hold-ups due to spare part delays and delicate political problems. Two separate frontier disputes among the seven participant countries have meant long detours for the helicopters. And there are accidents almost daily, some of them fatal; all in the routine of a large-scale development project.

The results of the *oncho* programme are encouraging. One area, where a pilot project was tried, was treated continuously for four years. Children under three years of age here had no trace of *microfilariae* in their skin samples. Counts of blackfly numbers from the fieldworkers catching flies by the rivers have fallen dramatically, often to single figures where before there were hundreds. Only one worrying note intrudes. One section in the south of the project area that had been cleared of blackfly has been reinvaded. No one knows from where exactly, but the nearest possible source is a couple of hundred miles away, suggesting that the agile *Simulium* is capable of flying twice as far as was previously thought possible. The programme will push on until all the larvae have disappeared, but it will not end then. It is scheduled to continue for another fifteen years after that. This is the lifespan of the adult *Onchocerca volvulus* worm. As long as these are still present in humans, blackfly could become reinfected and start spreading the disease once again.

Report from other war zones

The greatest success story among the mass campaigns was the eradication of smallpox. For the first time in history a disease that had been among the world's worst killers was wiped off the face of the earth by a massive international effort.

Jenner discovered the smallpox vaccine in 1796, and its widespread use drove the disease from the advanced countries. But in the mid-1960s it was still endemic in thirty countries and cases were reported in twelve others. There were around $2\frac{1}{2}$ million cases a year, and one in five of these died, while many of the rest carried visible marks of its ravages on their faces, disfigured by holes and blotches. This was one disease for which Western medicine could offer no cure for the victims once they had been infected.

In 1967 the World Health Organization initiated a worldwide campaign to stamp out the disease. Given the shortage of funds and the poor coverage of health personnel in developing countries, it was useless to try to vaccinate everyone – this would inevitably have left gaps from which new epidemics could begin, and would have been prohibitively expensive. The strategy the campaign chose, therefore, was to concentrate resources where they were most needed. Every new case of smallpox was located and tracked down by travelling teams who would ask around in schools, markets and community institutions. Everyone who had come into contact with the reported case would be vaccinated, creating a human barrier against further transmission.

The strategy produced fast results. Smallpox was eradicated from Brazil – the last Latin American country to harbour cases – in 1971, and from Indonesia in 1972. In Nigeria 50 million people had been inoculated by 1969, and the disease seemed to have disappeared. But in March 1970 a young girl came into Kaduna hospital with smallpox. The surveillance teams traced her movements back to the village of Amayo 500 kilometres away. Here more cases were found, and a vaccination drive was staged. The team discovered that the disease had been brought into Amayo by a boy from another village. So this village was searched and all villages within a fifty-mile radius. No other cases were found. Smallpox had been stamped out in Nigeria.

By 1977, the disease had been wiped out everywhere except for suspected pockets in Ethiopia and Somalia, where desert nomads could harbour the disease unnoticed, and pass it on to town and village dwellers as they moved through. What was believed to be the last natural case of smallpox in the world was recorded on 26 October 1977, at Merka town, Somalia. Two years of surveillance were to follow, in case the disease should reappear, and a stock of vaccine enough to protect 300 or 400 million people will be preserved in case of unforeseen emergencies. The whole eradication campaign had cost around $300 million and involved more than 150,000 staff and half a billion doses of vaccine. It saved, in the cost of vaccination, control of outbreaks and economic losses due to the disease, perhaps $2,000 million a year.

The oldest of all the mass campaigns is the fight against malaria, one of the most pernicious contributors to poverty because of its impact on performance and absenteeism at work and school. In 1955 the World Health Assembly passed a resolution requiring WHO to mount a worldwide campaign against the disease. Sprayers armed with DDT to kill the host mosquitoes moved into action all over the globe, carrying their sprays by jeep across the Sahel, on horseback in the Andes, backpacking them over mountain streams in Nepal.

The campaign was not without successes. Of the 2 billion people who live in areas once affected by the disease, more than 800 million have been freed from the malaria threat. But it still exists in 107 countries and is a serious problem in sixty of these, with a total population of some 600 million. Mosquito resistance to insecticides has been reported in sixty-two countries. In twenty countries the malaria parasite itself, *plasmodium*, has evolved strains that could resist the main chloroquine treatment drugs. Oil price rises forced many countries to go slow on their programmes. As a result of these setbacks, reported cases rose from a low of 1·4 million to 5·3 million in 1975. The World Health Organization in 1976 abandoned its previous goal of worldwide eradication within a decade. The failure of nationwide eradication programmes meant that, for this disease, new strategies would have to involve the community itself. Anti-malarial drugs may have to become a standard part of the primary health worker's kit in endemic areas, while community energies and contributions can be mobilized in environmental projects aimed at eliminating mosquito breeding sites in swamps and ponds, through soil drainage, tree planting and the introduction into rivers and canals of fish that feed on mosquito larvae. But the fight will be a long one. Mosquitoes can breed even in a cow's hoofprint filled with water.

Prospects

Health is one sphere where hopes for progress are not entirely pious or pie in the sky. In 1977 the World Health Assembly set the goal of health for all, sufficient for social and economic productivity, by the year 2000, and immunization for all by 1990. In the same year the World Water Conference set the target of clean water for all by 1990. If the new approaches to health care are universally adopted, and community participation is mobilized, these targets stand perhaps a better chance of realization than many others in the development sphere.

As with all radical reforms, there will be powerful resistance from vested interests, including the socio-economic élites, the medical establishment and the bureaucracy. The fact is that the well-fed élite of the modern sector, with their sanitized urban environments, do not suffer much from the common run of tropical ailments. Often their morbidity patterns are quite similar to those of the inhabitants of Western countries, with heart disease and cancer among the main killers. However inappropriate for the rural majority, Westernized medical care is more appropriate for the élite. It can be expected that they will use their political muscle to fight for continued provision for their needs, at public expense if possible. Bureaucrats, for their part, are unlikely to welcome or cooperate with participatory schemes that reduce their power or increase their answerability to the people. Inappropriate health care, in other words, is another expression of social and political inequality. Success in introducing the primary health care approach will be more likely if combined with attacks on other forms of inequality.

But health care alone cannot ensure better health for the majority. To begin with, it must be combined with vigorous family planning programmes. Otherwise it may increase the rate of population growth, at least for some years or decades until women adjust their fertility to the fact that more of their children are surviving. Family planning in itself has a major contribution to make to improving the health of mothers and children. Wider spacing of births reduces the drain on the mother's organism and enables her to breast-feed each new baby for longer. Nor is health likely to improve dramatically unless people are better nourished. For that, and for healthier housing and sanitation, they need more money and more productive employment. In the final analysis, good health depends on progress in all the other fields of development.

11 Learning to develop: basic education

Barefoot and gracile in a scanty purple vest and gathered knickers, twelve-year-old Janif, like most poor Bangladeshi children, has a full day. She gets up before sunrise, fetches water from the well and waters the vegetables in the tiny garden that represents the family's landholding. She takes a midday meal of plain boiled rice to her father working in this or that man's fields. In the afternoon she collects fallen branches and cuts woody shrubs for fuel, grazes and washes the three family goats, and may help her mother to clean the house. Surprisingly, she found time to attend government school for a brief period of three months, but she had to leave when her elder brother took a job away from home and some of his work duties fell on her.

There are few Asian countries where the labour of children is more intensely exploited than in Bangladesh. From the age of four onwards you see them carrying produce to market or with their heads buried deep inside a load of firewood. From the age of eight some of the boys may be holding down full-time jobs guarding cattle. The heavy demands of work are one of the prime reasons why poor children drop out of school or stay away altogether, why Bangladesh's primary enrolment rate in 1973 was only 56 per cent, and why its literacy rate, at 22 per cent, is one of the lowest in Asia.

Throughout the Third World formal education expanded with amazing rapidity in the fifties and sixties. The number of pupils at primary and secondary level rose from 135 million in 1960 to 247 million in 1970, representing a gigantic effort in mobilizing funds, institutions and teachers. But in the mid-seventies it became apparent that the big boom was over, and that education was failing in its potential role as a prime agent of national development. As budgets grew more constrained by the debt problem, the growth in enrolments levelled out, so that in 1975 still only 62 per cent of primary-age and 35 per cent of secondary-age children were attending school. The number of children out of school was expected to rise from 300 million in 1975 to 400 million in 1985. The number of illiterates in the world was also rising, and in 1980 stood at 800 million (two thirds of them women), or 29 per cent of all adults.

Schools were failing to shift the great, inertial mass of ignorance. They were failing, too, to provide equal opportunities for poor and rural children. Schools were sparse in rural areas, while fees and other costs deterred the poor. Their children, in any case, were educationally handicapped from the start because early malnutrition and lack of stimulation had prevented their brains from developing fully. And so enrolments in poor areas were lower and the drop-out rate among those who did enrol much higher. Sometimes less than 10 per cent of rural pupils who started school would stay the course even till the end of primary school.

Without education, and in particular the paper certificates which seemed to be its prime purpose, the children of the poor were condemned to low-paid jobs. Even for many of those who did persevere at school, often repeating one, two or three of the years, the payoff was unemployment at the other end, as there were not enough jobs commensurate with their exaggerated expectations of salary and status. So the education system became a mechanism for ensuring high rewards for the few and failure plus continued poverty for the many.

Nor did it help countries to develop. The curriculum, often taken over without modification from the colonial powers, was academic and irrelevant, often in a foreign language. It provided pupils with none of the skills needed for survival and community improvement in the villages or shantytowns where most of them would live their adult lives. Instead, it alienated them from their own culture, filled their heads with urban values and urban dreams, gave them only the ambition to head for the cities and abandon their villages in poverty, ignorance and stagnation. It became little more, as educationist Philip Coombs has written, than 'a transmission belt for moving talent to the cities'. If it was to serve its purpose as an engine for real, grassroots development, it desperately needed reform: to even up the chances of the poor and of rural areas, to cut costs, and to deliver the kind of learning everyone needed for community and national development.

The school for ragamuffins

Janif, the girl we began with, does go to school again now, but the school she attends was purpose-designed to avoid all the many pitfalls that make the children of the poor educational failures almost from birth. Gono Pathshala, the People's School at Savar, Bangladesh, is one of the boldest experiments in preventing educational failure among the poor in the Third World, indeed in the world. The school grew out of the barefoot doctor programme at the People's Health Centre (see page 238). Zafrullah Chowdhury's medical work in the village convinced him that the educational needs of the poor were as pressing, and as little provided for by existing services, as their health requirements.

Rather than start up a school on worthy *a priori* principles, Chowdhury got a young graduate, Shoba Nurun Nahar, to conduct surveys in several villages to find out why government schools were failing the poor. She discovered that only one local boy in three and only one girl in seven ever completed the primary course, and they were almost exclusively the children of rich and middle peasants. Schools, as constituted, were an institution for advancing these classes, and deterred the poor and landless through a combination of economic and social pressures. Poor families could not afford school books, and needed every penny their children's labour might earn or save. Poor children were victimized by teachers' middle-class expectations: they had only rags to wear, but were expected to come to school neatly dressed in shirt and pants, or dress, and shoes. They were often asked, in front of the class, why they came to school so dirty. The curriculum, too, was alien, urban, middle class, irrelevant to the needs of rural life. There was no incentive to learn. But if children answered questions wrongly, or didn't turn up for school for a day or two, they would often get a beating.

The People's School, of which Shoba became head, set out systematically to eliminate all the deterrents that alienated the poor from education, and to provide them with the practical knowledge they needed to improve their lives. In order to reverse the bias of official schools, only the children of poor peasants owning less than one acre of land are admitted. There are no fees and all books, slates, pens and chalks are free. No action is taken if the child is off school for a good reason, such as family responsibilities. Indeed, everything possible is done to help the children combine school with work. Some pupils even bring to school goats and cattle or younger children they have to look after. The school is closed on the main market days and during the harvest season, when children's duties at home are heaviest. No comment is ever made about the children's clothing. At the morning line-up, when they do exercises, they look like a brigade of ragamuffins, in a motley assortment of patched and baggy knickers, vests, crumpled shirts, grubby *lungis* or outgrown dresses bursting at the seams.

The school itself is built of simple village materials to make it seem homely: walls of bamboo and woven palm leaf panels, thatched roof, floors of mud, and no chairs – total cost a mere $1,000 or £500. The curriculum is intensely practical. Part of every day is spent farming, learning to grow nutritious foods like beans and green vegetables, neglected in the habitual diet.

259

Older children, girls included, learn carpentry. Health education is emphasized. Children are taught the importance of washing, with a daily bath, as scabies is endemic. Reading and writing are taught by the 'look and say' method – starting with the recognition of short whole words taken from daily village life. Wherever local dialect diverges from standard Bengali, the dialect word is used – the opposite of what happens in government schools.

More adventurous than the content of the schooling is the way things are taught at Gono Pathshala. The monitor system – children teaching other children – is used extensively. Whereas in official schools the brightest are encouraged to surge ahead and the rest tend to be neglected, here the most advanced older pupils help the other children to practise what the teacher has taught them. Cooperation is emphasized, not competition. Surprisingly, the children take naturally to this system and sit round blackboards with rapt attention listening to their child mentors. Children work in self-chosen groups of about ten. Promotion to the next higher class is not automatic, but has to be earned by the group as a whole. So if there are one or two laggards, everyone concentrates on helping them to reach the required standard. Results are promising. After only eighteen months at the school, the oldest pupils have made as much progress in reading as they would in three years of formal school.

Even the People's School does not reach all, or even a majority, of poor children. Perhaps the most revolutionary aspect of the whole enterprise, put forward, the teachers insist, by the children themselves, aims to remedy that. One day a week the top class spends in the villages and fields, teaching their brothers, sisters and friends who don't come to school. So little classes gather on family verandahs with their pencils and exercise books and listen to their diminutive professors. One girl, Komola, aged eleven, recruited a class of full-time cowherds. Once a week she gathers them under the shade of a mango tree and teaches them to read and write. Dulal, a slim twelve-year-old with his meagre lunch of pop rice in a twisted rag, had been coming for only three weeks, but already he could read and write his own name and those of his father and his village. Dulal's father owns no more than the land his house stands on, and the boy has been working as a cowherd since the age of eight in the employ of a local government official. Because the job is far from home, he sleeps at an uncle's house. His employer has now asked him to do extra jobs, as he recently raised his pay to £1.30 per month plus food. Dulal has no choice but to comply. In future he will not have enough time to come to Komola's weekly lessons, and will probably remain illiterate. Reforms far wider than just in education will be needed to help the many like him in Bangladesh.

Rethinking education from scratch: the Ivory Coast

Though it has valid lessons for all educational reformers, the People's School is an isolated experiment, a pilot project. If educational reform is to benefit the majority of children, it must be introduced on a nationwide basis, and that can only be done by governments. The Ivory Coast has tried to provide a national curriculum that would be relevant to practical development needs – and to equalize the quality of education right across the country.

Koussabliéko primary school, near Bouaké in the Ivory Coast, looks just like any other. One-storey classrooms range off a long verandah shaded with louvres from the hot sun. Inside there are lines of lift-up desks, slates and chalk. At 7.50 a.m. children in khaki shirts, shorts and skirts are running towards the school from all directions, schoolbooks on their heads, to be in time for the bell. They form into lines, shuffle and space out an exact arm's length apart, and stand quietly awaiting the order to file into their classrooms.

An array of high aerials and solar batteries in the playground is the first indication that all is not as conventional as it seems. Inside the classroom the teacher starts the day with a few questions for the children ('Is there someone at the blackboard?' 'No, there is not someone at the blackboard,' answers one child whose grammar is still a little shaky.) Then he bangs his stick for silence and turns on the television set that has been sitting quietly in the corner. 'Bonjour les enfants,' says the friendly announcer. 'Bouzou moseu,' say the children, as if he can hear them. There follows a film, designed to introduce some new French words, about a young boy being shown round the capital city, Abidjan. The children watch, head in hands, totally enthralled by their solar-powered set.

In every one of the Ivory Coast's 800 primary schools television programmes like this one provide the entire framework for the day's teaching. There are transmissions for each age group, and each one is followed by a gap of forty or fifty minutes, during which time the class teacher expands on and reinforces the main points the programme was trying to get across. He follows almost slavishly the suggested scheme in his teacher's guide book. It may seem somewhat regimented and centralized – from the chic suburbs of Abidjan to the subsistence villages of the dry north, each class will be doing exactly the same thing at the same time (just as they might be in France, incidentally). But this very uniformity creates something that never existed before, and which is rare in Third World education: equality of provision. For the first time the isolated bush school is not at a disadvantage compared with its urban counterparts.

Formulation of the Ivory Coast's reform began towards the end of the sixties when the country's political leaders felt the need to escape from the traditional academic curriculum, which had been dominated by textbooks imported from France, full of French culture, French history, French geography. They wanted an education system that would be more practically oriented, more closely geared to the country's real development needs, encouraging creativity and adaptability rather than mechanical rote learning. They wanted each level of education to be self-sufficient rather than, as before, merely a preparation for the next higher stage, ignoring the needs of the majority who would leave school before ever getting that far. The idea was that a pupil who left school after the primary course would be equipped for the life that awaited him or her as a worker, farmer, citizen and parent.

These aims involved the total rethinking of the curriculum from first principles – an upheaval that many developing countries were undergoing in the seventies. Curriculum reform is an immense enterprise, and not the least of its problems is putting it into effect: books have to be written, illustrated, printed and distributed, teachers have to be retrained. Using normal methods, it could have taken ten years to put all the country's primary teachers through a reorientation course. Television allowed the change to be made overnight. The teachers are retrained on the job, through special broadcasts out of school hours. The extensive back-up materials and guidance notes make sure they can cope. Textbooks are distributed by a fleet of vans, whose drivers are also trained in TV repair. Television might seem an inappropriate technology for education in a developing country, but the appropriate technology sometimes turns out to be the most advanced available. In this case TV proved to be the cheapest way of achieving the objectives. The World Bank estimated that to maintain the traditional system, with its high wastage rates, would cost 44 per cent more per pupil who graduated.

The content of lessons is down to earth. History, geography and science have been fused into a single subject, environmental studies, in which children learn about their country, their region and their village. In the north there are lessons about millet and cotton, the dominant crops – in the south yams and bananas get more attention. City life is deliberately demystified and de-glamorized. In one story, *Moussa's*

The Third World Tomorrow

Return, a youth comes back home after five years in Abidjan, and finds that his parents have changed their old mud hut into a nice, whitewashed, concrete-floored, tin-roofed house. At first Moussa is reticent about why he came back, but finally admits that he got the sack from his garage mechanic's job. He got fed up with the crowds, the traffic jams and the unemployment, so he came back home, and now he hopes to set up a business in the village repairing cars. Perhaps the tale would not put every aspiring city migrant off, but at least it tries to set the record straight. In contrast, most educational material in the Third World carries what educationists term a 'hidden curriculum' favouring Westernization, city life and non-manual work.

The Ivory Coast's programme is using the most modern technology and teaching methods to offer a curriculum that relates to the real needs of the nation and the village. Relevance to real life will, of itself, help to cut down the drop-out rate, while a better standard of teaching will reduce the numbers who repeat years. As most drop-outs and repeaters are the children of the poor and the underprivileged, any reduction in wastage can only help these groups.

Other reforms have been tried to make education systems fairer. Some countries have located all new schools in under-provided areas, to even out the availability of education across the country. Others have provided universal free primary education, hence removing the cost deterrent to poor families. Several countries have eliminated repeaters by making promotion from one class to another automatic. But however fair the country succeeds in making its schools, the child from the poor home is still much more likely to fail than his wealthier counterpart, because his brain may have been permanently damaged by malnutrition and the absence of stimulation in his earliest years. Efforts to remove educational handicaps of the poor have to start long before school age. Promoting early stimulation by parents is one of the cheapest and best approaches.

Educating the little shepherds

The Quechua and Aymara children of the Peruvian mountains are sad, almost angelic creatures. From the age of four they are already working from dawn till dusk, pasturing the family herd of cattle, sheep and llamas. The climate is hard – children often have their lovely moon-shaped faces scarred with chilblains from the mountain cold. Only two thirds of primary-age children attend school, and the drop-out rate is catastrophic: three quarters of those who start the primary cycle do not finish it. Malnutrition affects 90 per cent of the children in some provinces, and children get little of the stimulation that could compensate for malnutrition and help to develop their brains. Parents seem stinting with their affection – you rarely see them laughing or playing with children. Discipline is harsh, often arbitrary and brutal. But the school, until recently, made no compromises either. Children were plunged straight from their Quechua- or Aymara-speaking world into the totally alien Spanish world of formal school. Naturally they usually performed badly, so their parents would see little point in prolonging the agony and often withdrew them prematurely, as they were needed for work. So the children grow up as they began, and the Sierra Indians are quiet, withdrawn, submissive and passive, chewing coca leaves to forget their poverty and hunger. Illiterate and unable to speak Spanish, they are excluded from national life, even from voting.

The Peruvian government of General Velasco, which took power after an army coup in 1968, realized that pre-school education was not a luxury, but a crucial chance to compensate for the home deprivations of poor children. As part of an educational reform that transformed the whole educational system, nurseries were to be provided for infants up to three years old and kindergartens for the three- to five-year-olds. These kindergartens, known as child-houses (*wawa-hutas* in Aymara) are a unique attempt, supported by UNICEF, to break out of

265

the vicious circle of poverty and educational failure. They aim to provide the stimulation and good nutrition that the children lack at home, and to introduce them painlessly into the unfamiliar atmosphere of school.

At Makerkota, a scattered community of smallholders near Puno on Lake Titicaca, the *wawa-huta* is a humble, one-roomed building which the villagers themselves built and equipped. The day begins with an untidy line-up, boys in colourful stocking caps, girls in bell-shaped felt hats, chanting their daily song: 'My *wawa-huta* is my second home, where I shall come all my childhood.' The nursery leader, Julia Cervantes, is a local woman of twenty-four, herself a mother and wife of a peasant. Four foot six tall, she dresses in the traditional pleated woollen skirt and bowler hat. Thanks to a prudent father, she completed eight years of formal schooling (the minimum requirement is seven). Julia is perfectly suited to her task – maternal and homely, firm but encouraging.

After the morning line-up, she lets the children choose one of five corners, each one designed to develop a different aspect of their minds. In Britain or the USA the equipment provided would be standard in every middle-class home. The silence corner, marked by a gawkish drawing of a face with finger over its lips, is full of toys and games to develop cognitive skills, the senses of space, size and order – pyramids of coloured discs, holes to post different shapes through, and the like. In the home corner there are little dolls' chairs, tables, cups and pans, and children can play at housekeeping. The workshop corner is a miniature quarry of stones and bricks for building. The earth corner is outdoors, for making mud bricks and growing vegetables. The art corner is for creative expression, painting, modelling and music. None of the children, when they arrive, have ever had any of these things to do or play with. At noon comes a special meal of fortified gruel to supply the protein, vitamins, minerals and calories deficient in the children's normal diets, largely made up of potatoes. The *wawas* conclude their day with boisterous dances, swinging their arms from side to side and pretending to play the pan pipes. Julia commented on how confident they had become: 'Before, if they saw a stranger, they would cry and run away. Now they run up and say hello.' The first batch of *wawa-huta* graduates had just moved up to primary school, and the teachers said they were the brightest and best of their year.

The *wawa-hutas* do not only aim at changing the child. Julia teaches the parents, too, to stimulate their children, caress them more, reason and talk with them rather than terrorizing them. The programme has deliberately involved the community around each nursery, for both motivational and economic reasons. Julia, like the other nursery leaders, was elected at a village meeting. The villagers supply the vegetables for meals, and mothers come in on a rota to cook them. There is a *wawa-huta* committee which meets once a fortnight to discuss administration. All this means that the *wawa-hutas* cost no more than a quarter of what formal pre-school education would require. On the adobe wall at Makerkota, a poster rhetorically proclaims the *wawa-huta*'s purpose, and, indirectly, that of all education in developing countries: 'Peruvian peasant, your child must be strong and intelligent, valiant and a good worker, so that never again in Puno will there be exploitation, ignorance and poverty.'

Education for what?

Extending education to all became problematic as costs rose. For many poor countries, to achieve universal primary education would involve spending so much that other essential sectors would suffer. Governments started looking for ways to cut costs and corners. Western ideas of how to improve education – creating smaller classes, providing better facilities and more highly trained staff – were unattainable and in any case often questionable. Class size, for example, does not seem to affect performance very much, so there is little need to try and improve teacher–pupil ratios. And perhaps people were being overtrained at all levels. With a hard look at content and objectives, many countries have been able to cut the length of teacher-training courses without affecting quality. A reduction from three to two years would mean that 50 per cent more teachers could be trained with the same resources. School cycles could also be pruned by a year or two. Four years of relevant practical education can replace six years of academic twaddle with no loss, and probably great gains, to pupils. Many Third World schools have raised their productivity by working double shifts – in many parts of India, for example, one group of children comes early in the mornings till noon or one o'clock, and has the afternoon off. Then another shift clocks in and works until five or six. Scarce school resources are spread around more widely – and children are available for half the day to help their parents or to do part-time work, an important bonus for the poor.

The cost dilemma has led to an even deeper questioning of the aims, methods and target groups of education than this. The blinkers of formal, Western-style schooling are beginning to fall away. As the International Commission on the Development of Education reported in its 1972 report *Learning to Be*, education does not have to be limited to the young, with rigid entry and exit ages that condemn people who miss them to lifelong ignorance. It does not have to follow the set pattern of primary, secondary and higher education, with highly competitive, selective barriers at each stage and exams acting like Saint Peter at the Gates of Heaven. It does not even have to take place in schools. Formal schooling is expensive. It cannot, in the poorest countries, with low enrolment ratios and small budgets, promise education for all within any acceptable time-scale. It cannot reach those who are not in school, or adults who have never attended school, yet these groups need education too, if they and their communities are to develop.

The new approach to education had to start with some fundamental questions about who needed education, what kind of education they required, and what were the best ways of getting that education to them. Everyone needs education in the Third World: not only the unschooled, but the many who had spent one or two years at school and never quite succeeded in picking up reading, writing, arithmetic or anything else of value. These people needed a second chance. Farmers, artisans and housewives needed education to improve their working and domestic lives, and they needed to perfect and update that education on a continuing basis. Education could no longer be seen as something to be passively absorbed between the ages of five and twenty or not at all. It had to be a lifelong active learning process, helping towards the improvement of the individual and the community.

The new educational thinking takes a hard look at the content of education, relating it to its practical function in the real lives of recipients. Educationists like Philip Coombs have sketched a list of minimum learning needs dictated by the demands of survival, self-improvement and national development. These would include: functional literacy and numeracy – the ability to read newspapers, read and write letters to authorities, keep simple accounts and do craft and farm measurements; skills and knowledge needed for work, on and off the farm – including new techniques to improve productivity; knowledge about improving family life – nutrition and childcare, family planning methods, health and sanitation; the development of a scientific, pragmatic, problem-solving outlook based on an elementary knowledge of the natural processes of one's home area; knowledge enabling people to take part in civic and political life, such as legal rights, what authorities to apply to for what and so on; and the development of a cooperative attitude and willingness to join with one's neighbours in the effort of community development. This minimum package could be regarded as a kind of human right, comparable to other basic needs like adequate food and health care, which governments ought to make it their priority to deliver to all their citizens. This minimum package would make up a 'basic education'.

What are the best ways of delivering this basic education? Even in developed countries formal school right up to university delivers only a minute fraction of this need-to-know list. British children may memorize all there is to know about 1066, Americans about 1776, French or Germans about 1789 or 1871, and yet most leave school not knowing how to apply for a job, how to eat well, how to rear children, or what their rights are. In most of the Third World, formal school does not even make its pupils securely literate. More relevant, practical, work-oriented knowledge is generally provided through non-formal education: apprenticeships, evening classes and training courses. But in the Third World non-formal education also reaches only a small minority, perhaps as little as 10 per cent. In almost all countries most people pick up the knowledge and skills they use in everyday life and work as they go along, informally, from parents, friends and workmates.

Governments cannot structure informal education. But non-formal education has immense promise. As Philip Coombs has pointed out, it is not tied down to buildings or hierarchies, and can reach any chosen target group. It is better placed to use untapped resources in the community – such as buildings empty in the evenings, local experts, the educated unemployed who can be used to teach their uneducated brethren. And it can more easily use newer styles of teaching method such as learning by doing, the combination of part-time education with work, and a freer, more egalitarian relationship between teachers and pupils. The choice is similar to that in health or in housing. If poor governments insist on providing a high-cost service depending on equipment, buildings and highly trained personnel, they may only be able to afford to give it to a minority. If they opt for something cheaper which involves the community in self-help, they can reach a much greater number, and provide a service which is more cost-effective in achieving its aims.

For the people, by the people

Popular participation in education has been less widely encouraged than in other spheres – but its potential impact is enormous. As with other programmes, the community can help to cut the cost of education, for example, by providing free land and labour to build a school. But if participation is to be meaningful, a much closer linkage of school and community is essential, and the interchanges will be mutual. The school may become a learning resource for the whole community, offering education to all age groups and both sexes, allowing everyone to make use of its facilities and equipment round the clock, giving the services of its pupils for community tasks. Conversely, the resources and experience of the community can be harnessed to help education. In an experimental project in the Philippines and Indonesia, children are taken to the fields to learn the techniques of cultivation from farmers, and get practical lessons in woodwork from the village carpenter. The untapped expertise of the people is utilized. The teacher loses his monopoly of teaching, and becomes a manager of learning resources of all kinds scattered throughout the area.

Even these more developed forms of participation still leave the experts in charge of the basic form and content of education. The highest level of participation involves giving the community power to influence the curriculum and teaching methods, and even to select the teachers and head teachers. This amounts to a real transfer of power in education, taking it out of the hands of the élite, the bureaucracy and the experts who may use it as an instrument to further their own cultural and social domination, and placing it among the people themselves, who know best what knowledge and skills they want to be taught in order to develop their community.

Nowhere has community control of education been taken further, nowhere has the struggle between participation and bureaucratic direction been more clear-cut or more acute, than in China. Official policy has oscillated between two poles, which one could call the élitist and the populist conceptions of education. As these poles appear to exist in almost all modern educational systems, the Chinese experience has lessons for them all.

One extreme is exemplified by the mandarin approach. This is academic, administered by bureaucrats and taught by professionals. Emphasis is laid on the authority of teacher and text. Pupils and students learn by rote, and strive for individual excellence in competition with their colleagues, tested by difficult examinations. This model is selective at all stages. The lower levels are often nothing more than preparations for the higher, but many fall by the wayside. It is the education of a hierarchical society with pronounced inequalities of power and income, and aims at producing an élite to run that society, who should be highly intelligent, expert and competent. In practice, even where equality of opportunity is encouraged, it tends to favour the children of the existing élite.

At the opposite end of the spectrum is the populist model, which is the education preferred by an egalitarian society with widespread diffusion of responsibility. It is designed so that all its pupils may emerge, at any level, commanding a wide range of skills and capable of adapting to new tasks. This model emphasizes a close linkage of theoretical and practical work, or learning by doing. It does not consider teachers a caste apart, but holds that every capable person can teach those things he has experience of. It is run by the community, for the community. The relation between teacher and pupil is more democratic. Students' creativity is encouraged, and learning is mainly by discovery and self-motivated study in which the teacher is a guide, not an authority. Cooperation and collective effort are stressed instead of competitiveness. Ranking, marks and examinations are toned down or abolished, and promotion to higher grades is automatic.

These two alternative souls of education have fought out their battle in China, first one leading, then the other. The cultural revolution of 1966 resolved the struggle decisively in favour of the populist approach, leading to what was probably the most radical education reform in the world. At its heart was the question of power: if élites controlled education, they would mould it in their own interests. If education was to be for the benefit of the masses, the masses had to control it. After the schools began to reopen, from 1967 on, many changes were introduced, but spontaneously, from the lowest levels, not organized from on high. Selective middle schools for the academic élite were phased out. Management of many middle schools was taken over by communes and factories.

The most comprehensive guidelines for the new system were drawn up for Lishu country in Kirin province. The Kirin programme was published by the *People's Daily* on 12 May 1969 as a model for others to follow. Control of rural primary and middle schools was to be placed in the hands of the brigades and communes. They would be run by revolutionary committees made up of commune and brigade cadres, poor and middle peasants, and teachers and students. The local community would thus be in charge of fixing the programmes, appointing the teachers, and even financing the schools, with some government help.

As the localities wanted above all young people who would be able, adaptable and willing workers, great emphasis was placed on productive labour. Two weeks a term were often set aside for work experience in factories or farms. Schools had their own fields and workshops, not just for play or practice, but actually producing food and manufactures which they would sell to help cover their costs. One rural middle school in Kwangchow, for example, grew rice, sugar, fruit and vegetables, raised poultry, ran a weather forecasting unit and a workshop producing herbal medicines. Many urban schools had workshops which did subcontract work for factories, making components such as oil filters, radio parts, printed circuits or brake treads. Teams of workers were often permanently seconded to larger middle schools to teach mechanics or industrial work, and to ensure the proletarian spirit was respected.

After Mao's death the élitist tendency once again reasserted itself. 'Experts' were needed rather than 'reds'. Practical work was de-emphasized, academic, intellectual knowledge prized. Examinations, abolished in 1974, were reintroduced in middle schools and universities. Teachers' traditional authority was reasserted. Selective schools for the brightest children opened their doors again. There was a clear danger that the new approach might mean that once again the children who succeeded in the competitive academic rat-race would be the children of the already privileged.

The Chinese reforms, while they lasted, took place, significantly, as part of a much wider transformation of social and economic life in which participation was encouraged in all fields. But even without vast social upheavals, much can be done to make education into a real tool for individual and community development, and to open it up to those who failed, or never even entered, in the formal school system. Provided education is practically oriented to the real needs of communities, it almost always involves self-help, in that it is essentially teaching people how to help themselves.

Radio for self-development

As the sun slopes down towards the cloud-wreathed *cordillera*, Mario el Rosario gets out the battered plastic radio and places it on the bamboo table in the middle of his family compound.

His wife Angelita and his two eldest children pull up chairs, open their colourful textbooks and their dog-eared, plastic-covered notebooks and pick up their pencils. Mario tunes in to Radio Sutatenza, and the lesson has begun. The family are all pupils of one of the most innovatory and effective non-formal schools in the world: Acción Cultural Popular (ACPO) of Colombia. Every year around 140,000 people follow the broadcasts, beamed out from an antenna on the roof of the Bogotá office block that houses ACPO's studios. Two out of five listeners become literate within a year.

ACPO started from very humble beginnings. In 1947 a young priest fresh from the seminary, José Joaquín Salcedo, wanted to do something concrete to improve the lives of the 5,500 peasants of his new parish, Sutatenza. It seemed to him that education could help them in almost every aspect of their lives, but his parishioners were so scattered that he could not run regular classes. He hit on the idea of using radio. So he bought a cheap 100-watt transmitter, installed it in his little hut, and gave out receivers to peasants who wanted to follow his courses. After a year he had forty-five students, and had already discovered a principle that would inform his later efforts: radio was capable of bringing education to dispersed and isolated communities much more easily than formal schools could. It came straight into people's homes and could be timed so that it did not interfere with their agricultural work. In 1949 Salcedo, on a visit to the USA, picked up a cheap consignment of war surplus radio equipment that allowed him to go national. Within four years he had 15,000 pupils.

ACPO's stated aim is 'to form men who want to better themselves individually and socially and who are consciously committed to the tasks of development'. It wants to instil not just passive knowledge, but a creative and critical consciousness, and to foster solidarity, cooperation and community organization among peasants. Inevitably, this has attracted criticism from right-wing politicians and big landowners who prefer a fragmented, ignorant workforce. What Radio Sutatenza offers is what it calls 'basic integrated education'. Its curriculum is intensely practical, and continually revised every two or three years in the light of listeners' comments. Each course has a set of programmes and a colourful and lively textbook. The first, basic course teaches functional literacy and numeracy, based on words and calculations from the farmer's own experience. Most pupils repeat this course once, though in contrast with repeating a class in school this costs them and the government nothing. After this, pupils move on to five intermediate courses. 'Economy and Work' is a condensed course in farming, with hints on how to prevent erosion by contour ploughing and planting hedges, how to make compost or dig a drainage system, and precisely what seed, fertilizer and insecticide to use. There are detailed lessons on all the main crops and animals, do-it-yourself veterinary care and financial planning. The other four courses are on health; practical maths, for accounting a family budget or managing a farm; advanced literacy, focused on writing letters and speeches, to help peasant organizers; and Christian beliefs and morals.

Many literacy programmes fail because the newly literate can find nothing to read and lapse into illiteracy again. ACPO backs up its basic courses with follow-up material. There is a Peasants' Library of thirty or forty titles on anything from sex and marriage (the best seller) to beekeeping or guitar-playing, as well as more practical matters. These books sell 92,000 volumes a year, making ACPO one of Colombia's four biggest publishers. And it publishes a large-circulation weekly newspaper *El Campesino* (The Peasant) which I saw being read avidly, sometimes by three people at once, in sleepy villages and busy market towns. *El Campesino* is written in an easy-to-follow style, provides a valuable information service for the peasant and gives him reading practice to maintain and improve his literacy.

The strength of ACPO's approach, and the secret of its success, is that it does not rely only on the mass media. It backs them up with a network of face-to-face personal communication. Pupils are grouped into 'schools' made up of relatives or neighbours – altogether there are 18,000 schools in 1,200 villages. People study together as a group, help each other out with difficulties, make sure no one trails behind and motivate each other to persist. Each school elects a monitor, usually the most advanced learner, who guides and corrects his fellow pupils' work. And every district has a roving tutor. The tutors are volunteers who do a four-month training course and then work for three years on a very modest living allowance before leaving the scheme. ACPO sees this part of its work as training a large number of people who will become capable of village leadership.

The Rosario family make up one school, of which Angelita is the monitor. Their tutor is Victor Julio Mendes, aged twenty-four and himself a typical graduate of Radio Sutatenza. Mendes had to leave primary school aged only thirteen, because his father died and as the eldest son he had to work to keep the family. At fourteen he started following the radio courses to complete his education, and he found them much more useful than school had been. Mendes spends one night a month with each of the twenty-five schools in his area. His job is a dual one. He helps pupils with their work, correcting mistakes and explaining anything they have not understood properly. And he encourages them to try out the practical suggestions contained in the courses so that they learn by doing and, at the same time, improve their lives. He is at one and the same time a teacher and a community development worker.

The Rosarios are still working their way through the basic course, so they have not had much time to change their lives. Other families have started on a positive whirlwind of self-improvement. The Mesa Valencias, for example, built a compost heap, dug irrigation ditches, planted cacti to stop erosion, started raising poultry, bees and trout, cemented over their mud floor, bought a tin roof, pierced windows in the blank walls for ventilation, and turfed out the assorted dogs, pigs and chickens that used to enjoy the free run of their house. All this was in response to course recommendations. ACPO acts as a kind of disseminator of innovation. Surveys have shown that its pupils are three times more likely to adopt innovations than non-pupils. Non-pupils often copy successful improvements from pupils who are neighbours. ACPO spreads change by direct teaching, and change spreads out further by the demonstration effect. So the pebbles of knowledge for self-help drop in wherever there are radio schools, and the waves ripple out to cover the whole country.

The world war on illiteracy

ACPO's form of education works, as much as anything, because it is so directly linked to the real lives of its students and its teaching is aimed at real possibilities of changing them. The war on the scourge of illiteracy has been waged with similar weapons.

One of the pioneers in this field was the Brazilian educationist Paolo Freire, who ran his country's radical National Plan for Adult Literacy until the right-wing military coup of 1964. Freire held that the peasant's ignorance was part of a 'culture of silence' imposed on him or her by the oppressive political and economic system. As he was landless and powerless, he had no means of effecting change, improving himself or making his voice heard – and hence he had no motivation to know or understand, no reason to read or write, because he was responsible for nothing. The task of education, Freire held, was therefore to teach the peasant to analyse his own economic and social situation and make him realize it was possible to change it by organized action. Freire believed that literacy should be taught by way of awakening this critical consciousness, a process that he called conscientization. Conventional literacy campaigns had worked with alien, meaningless material based on sentences like 'Eva saw the grape,' 'Mary likes animals,' or 'Charles is a good, well-behaved and studious boy.' (These are actual examples.)

Freire's literacy method was based on studying the everyday vocabulary of the target group and selecting what he called 'generative words'. These would be simple, familiar terms which, between them, introduced all the basic sounds and letters of the language and could also be used to lead into discussions about the pupil's social situation. The list for Rio de Janeiro, for example, included *favela* (slum), *terreno* (land), *comida* (food), *trabalho* (work), *governo* (government) and *riqueza* (wealth). The class would break down each word into its phonetic components – *fa-ve-la* – and students would then build up new words using each bit – e.g., *fala* (speak), *vela* (sail). A discovery sheet was then drawn up with all the syllables that could be derived from the generative word – *fa-fe-fi-fo-fu; va-ve-vi-vo-vu; la-le-li-lo-lu* – and the students would invent as many new words as they could using these. Thus the learner felt that he had mastered the basic mechanism of human language – at the same time as he was being guided towards an analysis of his social situation and what he could do to change it.

Freire's method has a lot to recommend it, especially in Latin America where social relations of exploitation and oppression are perhaps the principle barrier to development. But, not surprisingly, few governments have been willing to back literacy programmes aimed at politicizing and radicalizing their citizens and perhaps making a rod for their own backs. However, some of the guiding principles of Freire's approach, especially its concern with practical relevance, have been applied in many other literacy programmes, including those in the sixteen-nation Experimental World Literacy Programme launched in 1966 and masterminded by UNESCO. The basic philosophy of the programme was expressed in the conclusions of a world conference of education ministers in 1965: 'The very process of learning to read and write should be made an opportunity for acquiring information that can immediately be used to improve living standards.' Each project was linked with some specific development task – in India, for example, farmers were to be taught literacy alongside methods of cultivation to be used with high-yielding seed varieties; in Guinea the programme was tied to learning improved working methods in factories and farms; in Iran there were programmes for women emphasizing family planning, home economics and childcare, and other programmes for handicraft workers. The world programme was a fertile testing ground for harnessing previously unused resources for education. Classes were held in desert mosques in Mali, factories and fields in Algeria and Coptic churches in Ethiopia. Farmers or farmers' sons, with only a few years' primary schooling, were used as course tutors in Syria and Madagascar. Their understanding of students' needs and problems more than made up for their lack of formal qualifications.

The overall results of the programme were something of a disappointment, nevertheless. Drop-outs and failure rates were high. Students (as ACPO had found) tended to be the more adaptable and resourceful members of whatever underprivileged group was being taught. Local economic and power structures sometimes frustrated the new literates in putting their fresh expertise into effect – in Mali, for example, students were taught literacy in tribal languages, yet the national language policy remained unchanged, and all official documents were in French.

Education for innovation

Several countries have tried to use education, especially of the non-formal variety, as a lever for the development of whole communities. This approach may not necessarily involve local people in participation in education. When you are dealing with populations at a very low level of skills, knowledge and technology – as, for example, in rural black Africa – no one in the community may have the perspective required to suggest solutions for their problems. They may simply not know the most basic things about the causation of disease, the best weaning foods, how to use fertilizers or how to prevent erosion. Hence the measure of expert guidance is essential. But that guidance must be based on a sympathetic understanding of poor people's priorities. So while participation in fixing the precise content of education is not always necessary, participation in defining the goals is: the community is always the best authority on what its own problems are.

The Ivory Coast's adult education TV was perhaps élitist in that it was formulated by experts. But it succeeded because it was based on a very sound diagnosis of rural people's needs and aspirations and was geared to stimulating practical action. As we have seen, the country was already using television for the dual purpose of teaching children and training teachers. It decided to make use of the 800 sets, one in almost every village, for adult education in the evenings. 'Télé pour Tous' (Television for Everybody) started broadcasting in 1973, and aims to stimulate villagers into a whole series of individual and communal development activities.

I sat through one evening session in a little classroom on the rural fringe of Abidjan, on the shores of Banco Bay. There's not a lot to do in the evenings, and this was like a free film show, so the place was packed out with at least seventy sweating bodies in togas, vests and T-shirts. Programmes are broadcast two evenings a week and are grouped to cover certain themes. The theme for the current series was village improvement. That day's broadcast was an introductory documentary on the family compound, the dangers of letting animals live there, the need for clean water supplies, a shower and a latrine. There were snaps of film from the poorer northern areas. Suppressed laughter rippled across the room at the bare-breasted women (down south they've been covering up for a long time). 'Aha, they've got better women up there than we have,' shouts one voice in the darkness. When the film is over the *animateur* gets up – a volunteer for each village whose job it is to get people to come to the sessions, and then stimulate discussion and organize community action along lines suggested by the programmes. In this case the *animateur* is also the headmaster of the local primary school where the TV set is located. He has only just taken the job on, and can't quite hit the right tone, treating his audience like a bunch of infants. 'Were all the compounds we saw alike? No. What was different about them? Who's going to speak up?' One man has a go: 'In the old-fashioned compounds the people eat together with the dogs. The chicken is equal to the man.' Hoots of laughter wake babies out of sleep in their mothers' arms into noisy crying.

Later programmes in this series would get down to specifics: how to build a ventilated roof so that it would not blow away in a gale; how to build a brick house with cement foundations; how and where to build a latrine so it doesn't contaminate the water supply; how to build a village market and a communal laundry; where to apply to get money from the government to help improve the village. Each animator is supplied with detailed notes and diagrams so he can advise and guide people with the work. Our inexperienced headmaster would learn his job with time. All over the Ivory Coast the programmes of 'Télé pour Tous' have stimulated a flood tide of innovation. Films on farmers' cooperatives resulted in the formation of dozens of new co-ops. Health programmes led to the setting up of village health committees. A programme on filtering water, which was backed up by a marketing drive, was followed by an eightfold increase in the sale of filters.

Education can be used as the stimulus to economic development for depressed rural areas – in place of its dominant role, to date, of contributing to their decline. There is a growing trend towards the vocationalization and ruralization of education, aiming to prepare children to take up innovative roles in their own village rather than getting on the first lorry to the capital as soon as they get their school leavers' certificates. Students' ambitions are channelled away from purely selfish self-advancement in career terms into the desire to improve their community, so they can help create work opportunities where they live instead of seeking them in the cities.

Such intentions underlie the Young Farmers' Education Centres in Upper Volta. The country had been one of the first to try and break the academic monopoly on mass education. Way back in 1961 it began to open rural education centres for teenagers who had missed out on formal schooling, and by 1973 there were 750 of these centres. But the scheme was acknowledged to be a failure, because it was contaminated with the faults of the formal school system. Everything was taught in French, so two of the three years of the course were virtually wasted teaching pupils enough French to understand the third year's lessons. Teaching was theoretical rather than practical. The centres became so unpopular that compulsory recruitment was introduced to fill all the empty places. In 1973 the government decided to phase out the old system and replace it with a new style of centre, with the help of aid from the World Bank and the European Development Fund. The new centres also recruit unschooled teenagers, but they use the local vernacular languages and place the emphasis on agricultural practice.

I visited one of the first of these restyled centres, at Bassanko, a Mossi village not far from the capital, Ouagadougou. The register of the old-style centre here had dropped to just two pupils. The new instructors, Bassirou Sawadogo and his wife Sidonie, managed to recruit forty-eight. The villagers had been impressed with the hardware that arrived to prove the place meant business: two oxen, a plough, a donkey and cart, wheelbarrows, watering-cans, forks, rakes and hoes.

The centre's base is a bare, one-storey hut, surrounded by six acres of land where the pupils spend every morning working. They built a great mud enclosure to make compost – virtually unknown in the region – out of regularly watered millet straw and animal droppings. They were taught to handle the cattle for the plough – again, an unknown instrument in traditional Upper Volta where all cultivation is by hoe. Students are being taught to rotate crops to conserve soil fertility. When they leave they will understand the theory and practice of mixed farming and horticulture. Not everything they have done is a raging success, of course. They built a model vegetable garden, and planted lettuce, onions, carrots and cabbages, and watered them assiduously from the well. The garden should have been protected by a stout straw fence, but the school did not have enough millet stalks as they had been used for compost. So foraging cattle and goats, desperate for a bit of juicy greenery in the desiccated yellow groundcover of the dry season, trampled their way through the flimsy stockade and ate every single vegetable down to the stump.

The idea is that villagers will see with their own eyes the good results the school gets (aside from its vegetable fiasco) on its land, and copy its methods. This is already happening in Bassanko. And as they become farmers in their turn, ex-pupils will spread the practices further. One problem with the old centres was that they overlooked the village power hierarchy. Their graduates were still young men subject to their fathers' authority and with no control over the use of land. They were unable to put their knowledge into action. With the consent of the village land chiefs, the new centres will provide substantial areas of land for ex-pupils to work as cooperatives. As they will probably consistently outperform their elders, more and more villagers will be pushed into using their methods.

Education is a part of any society, and while it often has faults peculiar to itself, many of these are strengthened by faults in the social system. Overemphasis on academic education, for example, is linked both with the status value of Western-type culture and with the excessive growth of government bureaucracies in the Third World. Government services and other providers of high-paying jobs in the modern sector usually insist, to an even greater degree than in the West, on paper qualifications and exam results when choosing new recruits. As long as they do so, this reinforces and strengthens the academic bias in school, as well as the obsession with rote learning and the tendency for lower-level schools to become institutions preparing for entrance to the next higher stage. Making the entire school system more practical and utilitarian depends partly on changing job requirements so that people are chosen more on the basis of continuous assessment at school, aptitude tests closely geared to the work they will be doing or, better still, on the basis of performance on the job with everyone being recruited at the lower levels first.

The curse of educated unemployment is linked to this job market. Pay differentials are often grotesque in the Third World, and educational qualifications are usually the path to the higher reaches. Naturally everyone aspires to these rewards, so more hopefuls throng the higher levels of education than there are openings requiring that degree of schooling. Heads full of exaggerated expectations, the surplus of students prefers to stay unemployed rather than take a job below their aspirations. Educated unemployment can only be reduced if pay differentials are considerably narrowed, and this is desirable in any case.

The knowledge and skills that can be imparted in the new style of education are like seeds of the future, capable of transforming the communities in which they are planted. But, like seeds, they cannot grow well without good soil, water and fertilizer. If they are to have their desired effect, the social system must be capable of absorbing them and making full use of them. As we have seen, the existing structure of inequalities can often frustrate them. Without access to land, Acción Cultural

Popular's splendid advice on farming is useless to the landless labourer. The Indian smallholder may find literacy useful in reading instructions on fertilizer sacks, but he must have access to credit to buy them and a good market to sell his produce. The young adolescents of Bassanko will no doubt become expert mixed farmers – but can the authoritarian, patriarchal family of the Mossi accommodate them, or will they be so frustrated that they head straight for the capital city or the Ivory Coast? The *wawa-hutas* of the Andes may save the children of the poor from automatic failure at school, but what will they do with success at school? Unless smallholders' land can be made more productive and more industries built up in rural areas, there will be no work for them and they will go and set up their little straw houses on the outskirts of Lima.

Education alone cannot transform underdeveloped communities. Unless it is integrated with social and economic change that puts more resources and power into the hands of the rural and urban poor, it will simply lead to frustration, bitterness and revolt.

12 Reform will not be a Sunday school tea-party

In 1976, the International Labour Office estimated, two thirds of the population of the non-Communist developing countries, some 1,200 million people, were living in serious poverty. Seven hundred million of these were destitute, with incomes more than 50 per cent below the poverty line. These are the absolutely poor, and their low income is simply the numerical expression of a series of multiple deprivations that, taken together, add up to lives that are hardly worth living. These are people with poor land, little land or no land, people with not enough work, people on inadequate diets, people with perpetual illnesses, people without the most basic knowledge and skills to improve their lives. They are people who have been denied the right to develop their full potential.

Two thirds of the world's poor live in Asia, and the signs are that in this overloaded continent absolute poverty is worsening. Landlessness is on the increase everywhere and real wages have declined in many areas because of the surplus of labourers. In all three continents the soil is being overworked by smallholders and their yields are falling.

Poverty is intimately linked with inequality, and is always more acutely felt when the poor person compares himself or herself with a richer neighbour. The typical Third World country is much more unequal than most Western countries, and the prevailing model of economic growth that has been pursued – based on expanding modern industry, government and cities and neglecting the urban and rural poor – has brought with it an increase in inequality. The share of the poorest two fifths in national income appears to decline as national income rises. Proponents of this model of growth claim that it guarantees rapid growth and an early end to poverty. But if inequality increases faster than total growth, the poor get poorer in the meantime and it may be a long meantime. The strategy of unequal growth attempts to eliminate absolute poverty by increasing relative poverty, to reduce material want by increasing psychological want.

The new development strategy holds that the reduction of relative poverty and of inequality is essential if absolute poverty is to be quickly eliminated. Social justice does not have to be adjourned to a distant future. Growth and justice are both necessary if subhuman conditions are to be eliminated within any foreseeable timespan.

Growth and equality

Some analysts believe that there is an inherent conflict between growth and equality, that inequality is necessary both to provide material incentives for enterprise and surplus funds for investment. The evidence points, if anything, to the opposite conclusion. One of the most equal capitalist societies, Japan, has grown fastest. The most equal Communist society, Czechoslovakia, has the second highest per capita income in the Communist world. And there are Third World countries that have managed successfully to combine growth with an increase in equality. Nor are they, as one might expect, all socialist states: the equitable growth strategy can be pursued by capitalist nations, too.

Taiwan and South Korea have both followed the capitalist road and achieved rapid growth with a considerable measure of social justice. In Taiwan the income of the poorest 40 per cent grew twice as fast as that of the richest 20 per cent. This was due in large part to a radical land reform and to the widespread distribution of capital among a large number of small and medium entrepreneurs. Agriculture has been based on labour-intensive cultivation and industry has focused on exports of labour-intensive goods, so employment and wages have been kept relatively high.

Tanzania and Sri Lanka have both pursued a greater degree of equality out of socialist convictions. Tanzania has nationalized all land and many industries, and investment has been consciously redirected into the rural areas. Differentials between high and low paid have been narrowed. Party leaders, top civil servants and public sector employees or their families are forbidden to own any business or to have incomes from second jobs, land or share ownership. This prevents politicians and government servants from becoming a new privileged class sharing economic interests with the wealthy. In Sri Lanka, too, the ruling élite has proved unusually altruistic. The Sri Lanka Freedom Party enacted a land reform which divested many of its own leading members of much of their land. It gave a monopoly on distribution to the cooperative sector, thus limiting opportunities for profit. The emphasis was placed on boosting production of rice – grown mostly on smallholdings – and on developing small-scale enterprise in the villages. An extensive welfare state – with free primary education, free health care and food rations – bolstered up the real incomes of the poor and gave Sri Lanka one of the lowest rates of illiteracy, mortality and infant mortality in the Third World. The share of the poorest two fifths in national income rose from 21 per cent to 27 per cent in the ten years from 1963, while that of the richest 10 per cent fell from 31 per cent to 22 per cent.

How much redistribution?

Both growth and redistribution will be essential if the basic needs of the poorest sections are to be achieved by the end of this century. If economic growth alone were pursued without redistribution, the International Labour Office has calculated that developing countries would have to grow at between 9 and

11 per cent each year to achieve basic needs for the poorest 20 per cent by AD 2000, almost double the rate that most of them have been actually making. If income were redistributed radically – say, to Chinese levels – then much lower growth rates would be needed, between 5 and 7 per cent, and these are realistic growth targets. Redistribution to this degree is unlikely – after all, the Chinese required three revolutions, in 1911, 1949 and 1966, to reach it. A more moderate degree of redistribution would mean developing countries would have to grow at 7 to 9 per cent a year to meet basic needs by the end of the century. To help them to grow at this rate, redistribution would also be necessary between rich and poor nations, and six times as much aid would be needed as is presently given.

Income can be redistributed directly, through taxation, welfare payments and subsidies. Alternatively, the productive assets that create income – such as land, capital and government infrastructure – can be redistributed. These alternative methods have been carefully examined by World Bank economist Hollis Chenery and colleagues in the seminal work *Redistribution with Growth*. They give low marks to the idea of transferring current income from rich to poor by way of tax and subsidies. This would, they argue, tend to reduce the overall level of investment in productive assets, and in the long run could lead to lower incomes for everybody, including the poor. Nevertheless, some forms of income redistribution are necessary. For example, most Third World governments raise the bulk of their revenues from indirect taxes on goods which the poor buy as well as the rich, and from taxes on cash crops which small farmers produce as well as large. This is actually a form of redistribution from the rural areas and the poor to the cities and the rich, since the money raised is spent largely to the latter's benefit. Indirect taxes on basic essentials need to be cut, while those on luxuries could be raised, and income taxes on higher incomes raised too. Another needed measure of income redistribution is a reduction of income differentials in pay structures.

The most promising form of redistribution, Chenery and co-authors argue, is to redistribute the assets that create wealth, such as land (rural and urban), but also public assets and services. Credit and expert help need to be channelled more to the small farmer and small businessman. Health, education, electricity, clean water and roads must be located more evenly, giving the rural areas the share to which their population entitles them. All these are investments that help to raise the productivity of people, land and machines and therefore raise incomes too.

Most observers, and many governments, agree that some redistribution is necessary. The real disagreement is about how much, and this area is a political minefield. A radical redistribution will involve real sacrifices on the part of the privileged. They are sacrifices they can easily afford, but they are likely to be bitterly fought, and governments may have great difficulty mustering political support for such moves.

Aware of these distasteful realities of the situation, Chenery and colleagues suggest a less painful course of action. Redistribution can come out of the proceeds of growth. Governments should divert much of the *growth* in national income towards investment to benefit the poor. They propose a redistribution amounting to 2 or 3 per cent of national income each year. This need not even entail a cut in the income of the rich. For most countries, it would mean only that the incomes of the rich rise 15 to 30 per cent more slowly than otherwise. This degree of sacrifice seems politically feasible, provided the élite is not totally ruthless in its egoism (and some are). Such a redistribution could, if carried on over thirty years, increase the share of the bottom two fifths in national income by as much as a half in a typical developing country.

This kind of redistribution from the proceeds of growth,

however, is unlikely to prove sufficient to correct the gross imbalances and inequalities that have arisen in many countries. What may be needed here is a slowdown in the growth of the privileged urban modern sector and a channelling of all new investment into the rural, poor and small-scale sector.

The politics of economic reform

It is one thing to call for reforms to help the poor, but quite another to achieve them. The central obstacle to redistribution in non-socialist countries is political. The privileged, who are likely to be hurt most by reform, often have the political pull to frustrate reform. In those few Third World states that are still democracies the rich can easily translate their economic power into political influence. The national press is usually controlled by a few rich families. Local potentates control (or can buy) many votes, while businessmen can exert control over national political parties because of their need for massive funds to fight elections. A government that has gained power through such a system cannot easily set about reforming it, as it risks undermining its own support. Moreover, many politicians and top bureaucrats are themselves rich, some of them through corruption, and this makes them less likely to legislate away their privileges.

The influence of wealth is no less powerful in dictatorships. In theory, an authoritarian régime should have the power to enact radical reforms, and some left-wing ones have done so. But in practice most dictatorships survive by placating the key sources of power in their country, such as the military (inclined to the right in most countries), big business, big landowners, multinationals and the international financial establishment. These power groups are likely to be alienated by radical reform programmes. Even if such programmes do become law, the privileged can use their influence at local level to prevent administrators and police from enforcing them.

Against all this, the voice of the poor is weak. The poor are unarmed. They are usually unorganized or weakly organized, so there are few strong pressure groups putting their case and defending it. In most non-socialist countries they are fragmented, making organization even more difficult: the landless may see no common interest with smallholders, the urban poor have no contact with the rural poor or the self-employed with factory workers. The poor tend to seek false solutions in ethnic, religious, linguistic or caste conflicts. Indeed they may, in the most exploitative of societies, be submerged in what educationist Paolo Freire has called the 'culture of silence' – a state of passivity, ignorance and self-depreciation born of their powerlessness to control the most basic circumstances of their lives.

The political weakness and lack of organization among the poor have to be corrected. Genuine, meaningful reforms may be impossible unless the poor are organized into groups able to demand their rights and defend them. The sort of community groups and cooperatives that are being organized as a back-up for the new style of development programme are an important first step. Through them the poor begin to learn that they are not utterly helpless, that they can create part of their own destiny. These organizations can be established around some particular issue such as health or the re-planning of the village or shantytown, and later generalized as democratic forums with a voice in all development matters affecting their members. The people can move on, with experience, from simply being consulted about plans and helping to implement them to formulating the plans and petitioning governments for more resources. This pressure, in itself, will help redistribution.

Organization of economic groupings is equally important. Urban factory workers in the Third World are often unionized, the urban poor live close together and are easily gathered into a riot: this greater degree of organization among urban groups is one of the main reasons why the cities have been so favoured in development programmes of the past. Organization of the rural poor is now an urgent priority. Farmers can be organized into pressure groups to fight for better prices for agricultural produce. Labourers and smallholders can be organized into peasants' unions to press for better wages, better tenancy conditions and land reform. They are also needed to monitor whether reform is actually being carried out and the law respected or not, and to raise a hue and cry when – as so often happens – land reform is evaded or regulations on tenancies and minimum wages ignored.

Political parties can be important channels of popular participation through which the poor can make their needs known, and this can work even in one-party states. The local party can act as a watchdog over the bureaucracy, while the party's local cadres can become all-purpose community developers and educators. A single party is, in theory, quite compatible with democracy. Alternative policies can be put forward within a single party, and where a genuine choice is offered candidates for office usually require greater local popularity than in multiparty systems, where candidates are often imposed by national party hierarchies.

The cows stand together when it rains

I was privileged to be present at the formation of a typical local organization of the poor, a new branch of Colombia's National Association of Peasants (ANUC). ANUC was created in 1968 by the Colombian government as a back-up to their plans for land reform. ANUC organizes peasants into local branches to conduct wage bargaining and to petition the government for land. Though its headquarters are in the Ministry of Agriculture's building in Bogotá, it is no puppet organization. It opposes violent tactics such as illegal occupations of estates – but it has denounced Colombia's land reform programme as an insignificant token measure, and has demanded radical redistribution of land.

Reform will not be a Sunday school tea-party

Guamo is a quiet little town in Tolima province. The two bright yellow towers of its church flank a flowered central square with the inevitable statue of some bourgeois hero of the past. On the big estates near by, bright red spraying planes whine over dense crops of maize and sugarcane, while labourers' shacks are squeezed into the unusable spaces, by roadsides and streams. The hamlet of Bringamosal is reached down a dirt track leading off Guamo's square. It passes through *terra quebrada* (broken land) with poor soil, few trees and deep gulleys eating into the earth. This is marginal land and therefore smallholders' and tenants' land, because if it had been commercially exploitable the big landowners would have got their hands on it centuries ago.

The peasants of Bringamosal live in one-roomed mud and bamboo shacks planted on widely scattered promontories like little fortresses. They believed themselves to be tenants of state land. Most of them had been there for ten or twenty years, but for the past five years they had bad harvests and had not paid any rent. A local businessman claimed to have acquired the title to the land by paying off their debts. What the true position was it was impossible to discover, but the peasants themselves understood only two things. First, they worked the land for years and depended on it for their survival and their independence; they had, as they said, bought it with their sweat. Second, the new landlord wanted to evict them and re-hire them, or others, as labourers.

A week earlier one of the peasants had been working his cassava plot close by the house when three strangers came up the path and started beating him. Immediately afterwards a truckload of police pulled up. José understood what the game was. His attackers were thugs hired by the prospective landlord. If he retaliated with violence, the police would arrest him for assault and drag him off to jail, where he would be unable to resist any further moves to take over his land. (This is a frequent landlord's tactic in Colombia.) So he defended himself

295

passively. The police left saying they would get him next time.

The district office of ANUC heard of the incident and called a meeting to try to organize the tenants. It was a Sunday evening, and the sun was low behind the jagged mountains and grey clouds of the *cordillera*. About forty people turned up, men and women, in Sunday shirts and dresses. Under a huge mango tree hung with green fruit they began with a service around a little table with two big wax candles. A woman who could read led them in a prayer contrasting with the realities of their situation: 'Our lives are in God's hands. No evil can happen to us without His permission. We are pilgrims on our way to heaven; faith guides our way. Our destiny is not here on earth. The goal is eternity, our fatherland is heaven, hope is our guide.'

The Guamo peasant leader had come to help them create a destiny for themselves on this earth and to combat the fatalism inherent in the prayer. When the service was over he addressed the meeting, pacing up and down with anger in his voice. 'The government serves the interests of a small number and two or three citizens take all the land in the area. How can this happen? Because, friends, we don't talk together, we go drinking beer or gin, lose all respect for ourselves and our families, lose our consciences and our morality. Now there is a land reform law, but the peasant can die at the feet of this law because the capitalists can take other peasants, put them in police uniforms, give them rifles and let them kill us. This can only happen because we are disorganized. The only way to resist is to organize ourselves. The cows stand together when it rains. We must fight together, not betray a single one of our company. If you are not organized, the police will take every one of you to jail, but if there are fifteen of you, they will hesitate. Unity makes strength. You have the right to live honourably here.' The peasants agreed to form a committee, and ANUC would help them with their legal battle against the take-over of their land. With organization, that battle would now be

Reform will not be a Sunday school tea-party

much more evenly matched. Without it, the poor would not stand a chance.

The rich will not give in without a fight

It is not easy to organize the poor to take their share in decision-making and to defend themselves against exploitation. The culture of silence is deep-seated. Even if grassroots organizations are formed they are easily dominated by the professionals, managers and bureaucrats whom they are set up to supervise. Participation, moreover, is not always a pleasure. It involves a cost to the participants in time, effort and sacrifice of private leisure. People may become active around one particular urgent issue, yet lapse into apathy when that is solved.

Unless they are backed up by radical economic reforms, organization and participation may not solve anything because they, like every other political institution, can be captured by the rich. The privileged have a way of twisting every project, diverting every programme to their own advantage. Using their local pull over government officials they manage so often somehow to distort every initiative for reform, hold off every assault on their privilege and corner the lion's share of any new resources being given out, even if these are intended primarily for the poor. Canals, wells and new roads get located, mysteriously, close to their land. Extension workers, by pure coincidence, choose them as model farmers. They have the good fortune to get credit to set up new enterprises. When service cooperatives, residents' associations and village development committees are created, they just happen to get elected on to the executive committees. In one-party states they end up as the local party chairman. They are the survivors, the self-righting dolls that you cannot knock over. The reason is that they have a lead weight in their base; their weight is their economic power. Only when the weight is equalized with the other dolls do they take their place as mere mortals.

Real community participation may, in fact, prove difficult to awaken in many rural settlements of Latin America, North Africa, the Middle East and Asia. A collection of people who happen to live in the same place is not necessarily, in any real sense, a community, capable of arriving at decisions that will be in the common interest. Families may be scattered physically, like the *baris* of Bangladesh on their isolated mounds above the floodwater. They may divide by race, language or caste. They may be split into economic groupings whose interests are diametrically opposed: landed and landless, employers and labourers, landlords and tenants, moneylenders and debtors. On the central economic issues of life there is not much more chance of such groups reaching agreement than of lions and zebras drawing up a 'community plan'. Instead, there will be bitter conflict over scarce resources, in which each side will use every weapon at its disposal. One group or another will come to dominate the organ of community participation and use it for its own ends – and that group will usually be the rich.

Bangladesh, in the mid-seventies, softened its military rule with a mild degree of local participatory democracy. Elected village and district councils were given a voice in development planning and in choosing several types of grassroots worker. What happened was that the larger landowners used their patronage and pull to win places on these councils, and proceeded to use their new powers to allot extra privileges to themselves. Any paid positions, for example, would naturally go to relatives or clients.

Real community participation can only exist where people have common interests – where everyone can expect an equitable share of the benefits of development and everyone has access to sufficient land or other means of earning a livelihood. So redistribution of land, assets and income may be a precondition of meaningful community participation.

Even without such reforms, however, it should be possible to devise participatory institutions that will secure the interests of

Reform will not be a Sunday school tea-party

the majority. To follow the Western model of representative democracy in grossly unequal societies is to invite domination by economic élites. In a polarized society a representative will usually only fairly represent people whose interests he or she shares. Council members who are landlords can only be fully relied upon to represent the interests of landlords. The zebras of the poor countries all too often elect lions to represent them, and when they do they can only expect to be eaten.

Other models of participation are needed. Few non-Communist countries may go as far as Red China, where former landlords and rich peasants were deprived of political rights; but different socio-economic groups could, for example, be guaranteed a fixed number of seats on participatory councils, in proportion to their numbers in the community. The model constitution of Bangladesh's *swarnivar* (self-help) villages provides a certain number of seats for the landless and the landed, for youth and for women.

Even here, though, there is always the danger of the representatives of the poor being bought off by the rich and becoming their stooges. The interests of the poor are more likely to be furthered where the basic participatory institution is actually the assembly of all adults, or at the least all family heads, in the settlement. The typical Third World settlement is small and manageable enough for this to be feasible for all major topics. Bali's *banjars*, as we saw in Chapter 1, meet once every five weeks. If a small committee is required to do detailed work, its members could be delegates rather than representatives. They could be mandated by the village assembly on the main issues, subject to instant recall if they went against the mandate. Their decisions would have to be approved by the village assembly.

But it is naïve to imagine that political reforms as radical as these would always, or even usually come about in an orderly and peaceable manner. In the most polarized societies, those most desperately in need of reform, the organization of the poor can unleash a process of acute social conflict that ends in open class warfare leading to revolution or right-wing dictatorship. The beginnings of this process are visible in India, where attempts to form unions of landless labourers are often met by landlord violence. Its later stages are exemplified by the events in north-east Brazil from 1955 to 1964. Efforts to organize the peasants of this, the poorest of Brazil's regions, began after the Second World War in an attempt to end the naked and brutal exploitation that prevailed. In 1955 the peasant leader José dos Prazeres started up the Agricultural Society of Planters and Cattle Ranchers of Pernambuco. Its first object was to collect money to hire a schoolmaster, to teach members' children to read and write, and to form a vegetable growers' co-op. Later its aims expanded, and it began to fight the illegal imposition of compulsory free labour on tenants (known as 'the yoke'). The landlords' response was violent. When peasants went to law to challenge the yoke, landlords would intimidate witnesses and bribe judges and assessors. Peasants who refused to give free labour had their crops trampled, their animals killed, their lives threatened by landlords' hired thugs. When peasants defended themselves, landlords would get local and state officials to send in police or troops. This pattern of events was repeated at national level. The peasant leagues began to spread and recruit the support of students, left-wing intellectuals and even some industrialists who saw the semi-feudal social structure on the land as an obstacle to progress in the north-east. Proponents of agrarian reform began to win local and state elections, as the landlords' traditional political hold over their workers weakened. The landlords stepped up their resistance, while the peasant leagues organized demonstrations, strikes and illegal occupations. The north-east was in a state of undeclared but open class war. But the forces of reform were not well enough organized or equipped to win the fight. The disorder provided the excuse for the military coup of 1964 which established a right-wing régime. The peasant leagues were disbanded, their leaders jailed or exiled. All talk of agrarian reform was shelved and remained shelved. Strikes were made illegal. Wages stuck at a low level, so that most of the benefits of Brazil's rapid economic growth went into the pockets of the rich.

So the outcome of the battle for reform is always uncertain. For every reform there is potential counter-reform. And the greater the gap between rich and poor, the more bitterly the former will fight to hang on to their privileges and the more resources they will have at their disposal to do so. Recent history is littered with sad examples of radical reforms brought to a premature end by a combination of internal and external pressures: Bolivia's reforms, cut short by the right-wing coup of 1971; Sukarno's move leftwards in Indonesia, halted by the coup of 1966; Allende's experiment in democratic socialism in Chile, brutally truncated by Pinochet's coup of 1973; the 1968 revolution in Peru, put on ice after 1975 as the demands of debt management (so often the cause of failure) weakened the hand of reformers.

These failures point to some lessons for reform régimes. They should foster organizations of the rural and urban poor; but organization alone is not enough. The poor are hard to organize in large part because of their poverty: many are ready to break ranks, to work for lower wages or to be hired as thugs to intimidate their brethren. Therefore the strategy of organization can only work if it is pursued in tandem with reforms to strengthen the economic position of the poor. A reform government needs to create jobs in large quantities to increase the demand for labour, and push a vigorous family planning programme to reduce the supply. Parallel with this it should carry out the redistribution of assets, especially land, with all possible speed so as to create an irreversible shift in the balance of economic power. The delay of promised reform has proved fatal for many régimes.

A reform government must be careful to guard its rear. It should keep out of international debt, or it will fall into the arms of the International Monetary Fund which will, if it continues according to previous form, enforce an austerity programme that will cause riots, jeopardize public support and possibly lead to a coup. Keeping out of debt means on the one hand avoiding grandiose spending schemes involving heavy imports of Western machinery, and on the other moving out of volatile commodity production and towards self-sufficiency in food. As military coups happen usually when military status or salaries are interfered with, reform governments should be careful to avoid creating such a stimulus.

In the unstable polities of poorer countries, sudden and violent change by revolution or left-wing coup is just as likely as gradual reform. Here the outcome is even more uncertain. Success is possible where societies are acutely polarized into rich and poor and the oppressed classes are conscious and organized – or strongly represented in the officer class. The likelihood of success is strengthened where nationalistic feeling also demands change, because of the previous régime's involvement in military defeat, colonial rule, the excessive power of foreign companies or other national humiliations.

A successful revolution or radical coup does not, however, as some simplistic observers believe, solve all problems. The central questions of the degree of inequality and of people's participation remain open. Socialist society may be arranged hierarchically or cooperatively. Excessive differentials in income may remain between bureaucrats and managers on the one hand, and workers, on the other, or between city and country. Education may remain élitist. So the new development models have important lessons for socialists as well as capitalists.

The dangers of tokenism

The new development strategy is not a collection of piecemeal reforms for unconnected sectors. It is a total approach to the development of entire nations, and to be effective it has to be applied to the whole structure, root and branch.

If reform is confined to a single sector it cannot work. Urban improvement may accelerate migration to the cities unless it is pursued simultaneously with development of rural areas. Industry on any scale cannot be developed without gross inequalities, unless agriculture is also developed. Better nutrition cannot be achieved without better health services, and neither may do a great deal of good if they are not accompanied by vigorous family planning programmes. Broader and more relevant education will merely generate frustration unless programmes in other spheres provide opportunities for putting learning to productive work. None of these programmes can work properly without social and economic justice – nor can justice alone produce growth without programmes to boost productivity.

It is not enough, either, to apply the new strategy to the grassroots. It has to change things from the top down as well as from the bottom up. Yet in so many countries the élite seems to expect to carry on as before while the masses are uplifting themselves through self-help. In some countries the new development strategy is being used piecemeal to buy off the poor with minimal reforms that do not significantly affect the privileges of the rich. Worse, the worthy principle of 'community participation' is not infrequently perverted into a way of making villages provide and pay for their own new services – a way of hiving off the poor into an economy of their own that, though improved, is still grossly underpriviledged *vis-à-vis* the modern sector. A new dualism may emerge to replace the old dichotomy of modern sector versus traditional and informal sectors. It will be the modern sector versus the 'new improved' backward sector, but still backward and discriminated against for all that.

Despite the change in development thinking, actual practice has not changed in very many, perhaps most countries. Agriculture and the land may get a little more attention, but the cities and industry continue to be favoured. Intermediate technology may be fostered on a small scale in the rural and fringe urban areas, but Western, capital-intensive technology continues to dominate the modern sector and to destroy jobs in traditional and informal sectors. Squatters may get their standpipes and community latrines, but civil servants still get their subsidized model housing and the desirable suburbs get the surfaced roads, the street lights and the refuse collection. Community health care is introduced, but the big hospitals go on being built and the doctors stay in the cities. Basic and non-formal education may provide some learning for those who previously had none, but the obsession with formal schooling continues, preoccupied with academic diplomas leading to inflated salaries. The new education then becomes a way of providing second-class instruction for the poor, to turn them into a class of more efficient menials and mechanics. Participation, meanwhile, may be fostered in minor, trifling matters, but dictatorship may still continue at the centre, and bureaucrats may still boss people around. When 'participation' crosses the line drawn close around it, it becomes 'rebellion' and the troops will be sent in. Participation may, sometimes, be no more than a slogan to describe what is really the drafting of the populace as forced coolie labour to carry out projects decided on by the government, while the funds saved thereby may be spent on more prestigious modern-sector projects benefiting the privileged élite.

If change is really to benefit the poor and powerless, it has to hurt the rich and powerful. Real resources have to be massively diverted. That means that big industry, large-scale farming, expensive buildings, prestige medicine and academic education cannot expect to go on growing as before. They have to slow down or stop so investment can be transferred to the neglected sectors and groups. Real powers have to be devolved to democratic organizations at the base. That involves consequences which ruling groups may find uncomfortable. Governments will have to lose part of their power to act without consulting the people. Local administrators and managers will lose some of their autocratic power and the status they derive from it. Economic élites will lose their exclusive or privileged access to the ears of rulers – and will find their economic interests further threatened as a result.

None of these things will happen without political upheavals. But if they do not happen, or are delayed intolerably, the political troubles will be much more protracted, and more bloody.

13 Fair shares: a new international economic order

When you consider the degree of inequality that exists between nations, it does not seem surprising that the leaders of the Third World are so concerned to close the gap or catch up with the advanced countries. In 1976 the average per capita income of the industrialized countries was more than eleven times the average for the developing countries. The average annual *increase* in the industrial citizen's income was greater than the *total* average income of the Third World. Far from catching up, in absolute terms the poor nations were falling further behind.

Part of the reason for the vast income differences undoubtedly lies in the physical conditions of the tropics: the poor soils, the uncertain rainfall, the droughts and floods and disasters natural and unnatural, the ideal breeding grounds which heat and moisture offer for humanity's enemies, diseases and agricultural pests.

The old international economic order

Part of the blame, however, also lies with colonialism and its aftermath. The colonial powers transformed their colonies into hewers of wood and drawers of water. Much of the industry that did exist was largely dismantled, and the colonies became producers of raw materials as well as captive markets for Western manufactures. Political independence did not alter the situation greatly – indeed in Latin America, the new oligarchies of commercial bourgeoisie and feudal landowners conspired to prevent the development of national manufacturing industry.

By the mid-seventies three quarters of the exports of developing countries were still made up of primary products and the Third World as a whole produced only 9 per cent of world manufactures. Many countries depended on the uncertain earnings of just one or two commodities to provide the bulk of the foreign exchange earnings they needed.

Primary commodities are a risky business for a nation to rely on for a livelihood. In the unpredictable political and agricultural conditions of the tropics, supplies tend to fluctuate even more than demand in the Western consumer countries. Prices rise and fall, further destabilized by the commodity dealers and speculators, who buy and sell hysterically at the merest whiff, for example, of ground frosts in Brazil's coffee-growing areas. The net result is that most commodity prices ride a dizzying switchback of excessive peaks and deep troughs, while the producer countries reap windfall gains one year and face bankruptcy the next. Over the past twenty-five years the trend underlying these fluctuations for many commodities has been heading slowly downwards. The oil producers secured a massive increase in the price of their product in 1972–4; but among non-oil developing countries, a given quantity of exports in 1975 bought 21 per cent fewer imports than two decades earlier. Not many developing countries were willing to delay their development plans to suit the vagaries of the commodity market, however, and continued to import machinery and manufactures at high levels.

Partly as a result of this, their balances of payments tended to clock up massive deficits during the 1970s, and to cover these they sank into increasing debt. The combined debts of the developing countries rose from $74·7 billion in 1970 to a staggering $366 billion in 1979, and repayment of this debt ate up a large chunk of their earnings from exports. Country after country came knocking on the door of the International Monetary Fund for loans to tide them over. The fund's policies are controlled by the Western countries, whose votes vastly outnumber those of the Third World. It grants credit on stringent conditions such as devaluation, heavy cuts in government spending, wage controls and increases in the prices of essential goods. These IMF packages hit the poor hard and are very often followed by serious political disturbances.

Debt, plus the hunger for manufacturing jobs, has led more and more countries to open their arms to Western-based multinational companies. These came to dominate leading sectors of industry in many Latin American and south-east Asian nations. In the early seventies they were taking out in profits nearly $8 billion a year more than they were putting in in new investments. The brain drain, caused by the international income gap, was also a heavy cost on poor countries, amounting to more than $5 billion a year. Against these heavy debits of the international economic order, the only substantial credit was aid. But as Western countries grew more prosperous they also grew more niggardly, and the aid given fell from 0·52 per cent of their gross national products in 1962 to only 0·32 per cent in 1978, when total aid (including Arab and Communist funds) was $22·7 billion.

The New International Economic Order

These inequities in the world economy led the nations of the Third World to demand, with increasing urgency, a new, reshaped international economic order which would be more just and give them more resources for investment in rapid development. The essence of their demands was expressed in the Declaration and Programme of Action for a New International Economic Order, adopted at the Sixth Special Session of the United Nations General Assembly in May 1974, and elaborated in greater detail in the Manila declaration, adopted by the so-called Group of Seventy-seven (which actually includes around 115 developing countries) in 1976. As the 1974 declaration stated, the aim was to set up a system 'whereby the prevailing disparities in the world may be banished and prosperity secured for all'.

The first target was to secure a square deal for commodities, to achieve 'a just and equitable' relationship between the export and import prices of developing countries. This would be achieved by an integrated programme for commodities, at the core of which would be a giant commodity fund financed by producing and consuming countries. This fund would back up individual commodity buffer stocks, which would buy and sell produce with the aim of keeping prices stable. The integrated programme would cover eighteen commodities of major interest to the Third World: bananas, bauxite, cocoa, coffee, copper, cotton and yarn, hard fibres, iron ore, jute, manganese, meat, phosphates, rubber, sugar, tea, timber, tin and vegetable oils. The programme would also finance studies and development projects to strengthen natural products against their synthetic substitutes, and to allow Third World countries to diversify so as to reduce their dependence on a single commodity. To prevent commodity prices from declining in relative value, some countries proposed that they should be index-linked to the price of manufactures. Most commodity producers also demanded that the take of Third World countries from their own products – much of it siphoned off by Western shippers, processors, packers and distributors – be increased, with producer countries taking over a greater share in these activities.

The second aim was a massive increase in manufacturing in the Third World. The target, fixed at the second general conference of the United Nations Industrial Development Organization in Lima, 1975, was that their share of world manufacturing should be raised from 7 per cent to 25 per cent by the year 2000. This would be achieved by way of a new international division of labour, whereby more labour-intensive manufacturing needing less capital or skills would be redeployed to the Third World, where wages were cheap, leaving

the advanced nations to specialize in high-technology industries. This move would come about more or less automatically
if Western countries removed the protectionist barriers against
Third World manufactures and granted them preferential
access. As infant industries in the poorer countries would need
tariff protections in order to develop, these concessions would
have to be one-way and non-reciprocal. The poor nations
should no longer have to pay through the nose in fees, royalties
and licences for such Western technology as they would need
for specific industries. Instead, they should be granted 'unre-
stricted access to existing technology irrespective of the ownership of such technology'. Much of the desired transfer of
industries and technology would take place through the multinationals, yet the Third World countries also demanded the
right to control multinationals tightly and to nationalize them
if they considered it necessary.

The third set of demands related to increasing the financial
resources for this new surge in development. In 1971 the
United Nations' Second Development Decade had set a target
for aid of at least 0·7 per cent of the gross national product of
the developed countries. The Manila declaration reiterated this
target, and demanded that aid should in future be measured
much more rigorously, excluding funds paid out to colonies and
dependencies, which both the British and the French class as
aid. Eventually aid, which has unwarranted connotations of
charity, might be replaced by an international development tax,
which would levy fixed proportions of national income from
the rich and give the money to the poor. The burden of debt
would be alleviated by waivers or deferment of interest, and in
needy cases by the cancellation of the principal owed. Finally,
the much-hated International Monetary Fund would be reformed, giving much greater representation in its governing
councils to developing countries. The promotion of development would become one of its major aims. It would make much

greater funds available to cover shortfalls in export earnings, and make its loans with far fewer nasty conditions attached.

The potential benefits

The different elements of the New International Economic Order would not benefit all developing countries equally. Removing protectionist barriers against manufacturers would help primarily the newly industrializing countries such as South Korea or Brazil, though it would also assist commodity producers who want to set up factories to process their commodities before they are exported. Improved commodity prices would help the less industrially developed countries who rely on primary products for their foreign exchange earnings, but it would not help the resource-poor countries. Increased aid and concessional loans, finally, would help mainly the poorer and poorest countries.

The benefits of individual aspects of the new order could be considerable. British economist H. F. Lydall has calculated that if imports from developing countries were increased enough to displace just one American worker, this would result, directly and indirectly, in the creation of anything up to thirty-three jobs in the poorest countries, while displacing one Common Market worker would generate up to twenty-three jobs.

Increased aid flows could have a revolutionary impact on growth in the poorest countries. If all Western nations were to meet the target set for the second United Nations Development Decade in 1971, and gave 0·7 per cent of their gross national products in aid, the sum actually given in 1977 would have more than doubled, from $14·7 billion to $33·2 billion. If the extra $18·5 billion were channelled exclusively to the 1,200 million people in the poorest countries (with per capita incomes below $250 in 1976), then the aid these countries received would be approximately trebled – and at no cost to the other developing countries. And if this additional aid were all invested, not used for immediate consumption, then the poorest countries could boost their investment rates from 19 per cent of GNP to the very high level of nearly 29 per cent. This would enable them to more than double the growth rates of their economies.

Abolition of all tariffs would, of course, affect employment in the Western countries. Extra imports from the Third World would mean so much less production at home in the affected sectors. The International Labour Organization has calculated that removal of all tariff barriers against the developing countries could involve an initial loss of some 800,000 jobs in the West, or $1\frac{1}{2}$ per cent of employment in industry. If tariff abolition were phased over ten years, this would amount to a relatively painless loss of 80,000 jobs a year. Studies of the effects of increased imports from the Third World in such sensitive areas as textiles show that they have resulted in only relatively small losses in employment, especially when compared to the effect of improved productivity, which has destroyed many more jobs.

But job losses due to Third World imports occur in particular sectors, and do not necessarily mean an equivalent increase in overall unemployment. The poor countries can earn more foreign exchange from increased exports and spend this, for the most part, in the West, thus creating new jobs in other sectors. One International Labour Office estimate suggests that increased imports of manufactures from the Third World could generate indirectly perhaps 50 per cent *more* jobs than they destroyed directly. The Western consumer stands to benefit, too, as the developing countries can produce labour-intensive manufactures much more cheaply than the West. This would help to curb inflation. One study has shown that if the USA were to abolish all tariffs of foreign products that competed with American-produced goods, the gain to the consumer would be in the order of $11·5 billion. Some 475,000 people would have to change their jobs, at a total cost of roughly $800 million. Net profit on the deal: $10·7 billion. This sum would be spent on other products, thus stimulating further growth in the economy.

There would, of course, be some temporary sacrifices demanded of workers and firms in developed countries in the directly affected sectors. These could be helped by what is known as adjustment assistance, under which governments, not individuals, would carry the cost of changes in trade patterns. Only a few countries have introduced legislation for adjustment assistance. The United States Trade Expansion Act of 1962, updated by the Trade Reform Act of 1974, provides for employees who lose their jobs as a result of new trade agreements to get two thirds of their lost wages for a year, while affected companies get technical advice, tax relief and loan guarantees to help them move on to new and more competitive activities. In 1974 the Netherlands introduced a programme offering finance for scrapping old machinery in industries in a weak competitive position. Unfortunately, none of the programmes has had a strong impact in reducing protectionist pressures – perhaps because none has found a satisfactory solution for what is the greatest problem of adjustment: the impact on towns and entire regions which specialize in affected industries. A comprehensive system of adjustment assistance would include help to workers – maintaining incomes in periods of unemployment, paying the cost of moving to a new area, and retraining. It would help affected companies to move into new and more dynamic lines or pay them compensation if they closed down completely. Most important of all, it would ensure that new and more varied industrial enterprises moved into affected areas to prevent regional decay and make regions less vulnerable to future shifts in trade patterns.

Freer trade and greater resource flows to the Third World could boost the prosperity of developing and developed countries, increasing growth rates and income levels everywhere.

Just how much difference they could make has been estimated by International Labour Office economist Keith Marsden. Using a sophisticated computer model of the world economy, Marsden contrasted the results of this kind of strategy with the outcome of defensive, protectionist strategies like those currently being followed.

The first strategy Marsden names is the cooperative, one-world scenario. This would involve rich and poor nations setting specific goals and timetables for the eradication of poverty. Western countries would increase their aid to 1 per cent of GNP, socialist countries to $\frac{1}{2}$ per cent, and all of this would be channelled to the poorest countries. Private investment in the developing countries would be more than doubled, and one third of the total would go to the poorest. Meanwhile Third World governments would pursue poverty-oriented economic policies. Contrasted with this harmonious outlook is Marsden's 'beggar thy neighbour' scenario, in which countries are chiefly concerned with their short-term self-interest and enact defensive measures which lead to tit-for-tat retaliation from others. In this version, sadly reminiscent of present-day reality, protectionist barriers go up, aid stagnates, and private investment in the Third World declines.

The world of AD 2000 looks startlingly different depending which line is pursued. Under the cooperative scenario, Marsden estimates that world GNP would reach $27,407 billion by the end of the century, and would be growing at 5·2 per cent a year. Absolute poverty would have disappeared entirely – no one would find themselves below an ambitious poverty line of $600 per head. With 'beggar thy neighbour' policies world GNP would be $8,000 billion lower, growing at only 3·7 per cent a year. The numbers of absolutely poor would rise from 900 million in 1975 to 1,500 million in 2000, even with a much lower poverty line of only $300 per head. In absolute terms Westerners might benefit even more than the poor. The increased rich–poor flows would cost them some $523 per head, but the more rapid growth rates of the one-world strategy would produce average per capita incomes of $12,990, against only $9,900 in the selfishness scenario. Net, every Westerner would be more than $2,500 better off. In the jargon of games theory, international economic relations under the beggar's scenario are a minus-sum conflict, in which all the participants lose out. Cooperation, by contrast, is a positive sum game in which everyone can go home with a prize, and the welfare of all can be promoted without any group having to make long-term sacrifices.

Unfortunately, on current performance the world looks headed for Marsden's 'beggar thy neighbour' scenario. While limited progress has been made in some respects, the major Western governments have pursued 'looking after number one' policies. Protectionism is rampant, aid has been stagnating, concessions to the new international order have been insignificant tokens. The developing countries, despairing of winning advances by gentlemanly means, have been forced into strident, aggressive postures.

Progress towards a new order: industry

The new international division of labour has been slowly developing, with little help from Western governments, for some time now. The share of non-oil manufactured goods in Third World exports has seen a steady rise from 19 per cent in 1960 to 45 per cent in 1976. The greatest progress has been made in labour-intensive industries, not only the expected ones such as textiles, cloth and clothing, leather products, glassware and pottery, toys and games, but also in more advanced activities – hand and machine tools, cutlery, electric power machinery, domestic electrical goods, telecommunication apparatus, optical and measuring instruments.

The multinational companies have been among the most active promoters of this new division of labour. Originally the transnational corporations, 'TNCs' as they are known in United Nations parlance, set up branches abroad to duck tariff barriers, aiming at the home markets of larger countries in which they set up business. When the Japanese became a major threat with their lower wage rates and greater efficiency, TNCs were forced to look for ways to cut production costs to meet the competition. They began, in the second half of the 1960s, to set up 'export platforms' in Third World countries with low wage rates but adequate infrastructure and enough skilled workers to be serviceable. These were mainly in Latin America and south-east Asia. As the US watch company Bulova's president Harry Henshel remarked: 'We are able to beat the foreign competition because we *are* the foreign competition.' As Japanese wage rates rose, Japanese companies too began setting up shop abroad, mainly in south-east Asia.

This process is likely to continue and indeed accelerate unless protectionist forces in the West halt it. The nations chosen to be export platforms are rapidly upgrading their workforces and are becoming capable of more and more sophisticated operations. Because of this, and because of rising Western protectionism, they can be expected to diversify their production into a wide range of goods. Brazil and South Korea are already challengers in steel and ships and are becoming so in cars. But at the same time their own wage levels have been rising rapidly, and the most labour-intensive, least skill-intensive operations are moving out to countries with even lower wage costs. The new centres for labour intensive manufacturing will be countries like Sri Lanka, India, and – most significant of all – Communist China.

So the international redivision of labour appears to be in a permanent state of flux, responding to changes in wage and skill levels and in technology. It is possible that the new microprocessors may shift the cost balance back somewhat in favour of the developed countries. As the chips allow many more processes to be automated, labour requirements can be so reduced that wage levels become a minor consideration compared with transport costs or the need for skilled labour. But this development is more likely to affect consumer electronics than clothing or footwear.

The new protectionism

Western reactions to progress towards a new international division of labour have so far been largely negative. Instead of helping it to come about, many Western countries seem to be doing all they can to stop it. Instead of assisting their own industries to adjust to new roles, they are helping them to stagnate in old ones. And while they give preferential entry to some kinds of goods and some exporting countries, they discriminate against the most important items from the fastest industrializers.

From the end of the Second World War until the early 1970s, free trade was the ideal and largely the practice of Western nations. The dangers of protectionism had been learned from the experience of the twenties and thirties, when rising tariffs failed utterly to protect jobs, bringing only stagnation, chaos and war. Trade liberalization was a strategy that paid dividends. International trade expanded almost twice as fast as national economies were growing, and helped to speed up growth. The free trade ethic was badly shaken, however, in the prolonged recession that followed the massive rise in oil prices in 1973–4, which faced governments with a double load of worries: large balance-of-payments deficits coupled with worsened inflation. For the first time since the war they could not use the normal Keynesian weapons against recession such as cutting taxes or increasing government spending (which might have worsened the inflation and balance-of-payments problems). On occasion some of them even had to deflate their economies, thus making the recession worse and leading to levels of unemployment higher than any known since the war. This conjunction of high unemployment plus fears of worsening balance-of-payments deficits provided the background to the new protectionism. The strongest Western economies, Germany and Japan, managed to export their way out of the quandary – but their very strength made the problems worse for everyone else, adding to their payments deficits. Thus most Western governments found themselves in a situation of needing to preserve jobs and to cut balance of payments deficits.

The 1948 General Agreement on Tariffs and Trade, under its nineteenth article, permits countries to impose temporary import restraints when external competition is damaging domestic industries. But these restraints must be non-discriminatory – that is, they have to apply to all trading partners, right across the board. As this would run the serious risk of retaliation, article nineteen has remained something of a dead letter.

Therefore the new protectionists have avoided general tariff increases – the usual weapons of the old protectionists – and chosen a range of precision rifles aimed at particularly troublesome intruders. The most prevalent of these measures are known as 'orderly marketing agreements' or 'voluntary export restrictions'. Exporting countries agree to slow down, halt or cut back exports of specified items to individual countries. As the threat of more stringent unilateral action is always present, these 'agreements' are not really voluntary at all. The EEC, for example, obliged the major Asian exporters of textiles and clothing to cut their 1978 exports to the Common Market below the level for 1976. These and similar restrictions in North America are expected to cut the growth of developing-country exports of textiles and clothing to 5 per cent a year in the late seventies, less than one third of the rate for 1967–76. Developing country exports of footwear have been hit by restrictions in Australia, Canada, the USA, the UK, France and Sweden. Then there is a range of domestic measures which amount to disguised protection. Employment subsidies enable uncompetitive industries to sell below cost price. Britain's

Temporary Employment Subsidy paid companies to keep on their payrolls workers whom they would otherwise have been forced to make redundant. Around half the benefits of this subsidy in 1977 went to the industries most threatened by new Third World producers – textiles, clothing and footwear.

All in all, the new protectionism amounts to a kind of negative or retrograde adjustment assistance. It protects industries that are losing their competitiveness in the international market. Yet it actually discourages companies in these industries from making changes to make themselves more competitive. And it hampers the movement of labour and capital out of these lines into activities where they could be used more productively. The result is to preserve low-skilled, low-paid jobs, and to forgo higher-paid, higher-skilled jobs, and to pay more than necessary for the goods involved. What is worse, protectionism tends to be self-perpetuating and self propagating. Thus countries who put up protectionist barriers against Third World imports are taking a cut in their potential national wealth, as well as risking an international escalation of protectionism.

In reality, the new Third World manufactures exporters are not at all the threat they are perceived to be. The share of developing countries in Western consumption of manufactures is still minute. It rose from 1·2 per cent in 1959–60 to 2 per cent in 1973–4, and the World Bank predicts that it will amount to only 2·7 per cent in 1985. By contrast, Western exports of manufactures to the Third World are booming. The Common Market's balance-of-payments surplus in manufactures with developing countries rose from $13·5 billion in 1972 to $46 billion in 1977, while the USA's surplus rose from $3·5 billion to $11·5 billion. The Third World is now perhaps the most important market for Western manufactures. The non-oil developing countries took a greater proportion of North American exports of manufactures in 1977 than did Western Europe, a bigger share of Europe's than did North America, and a larger slice of Japan's than did either Europe or North America. And developing countries also offer the fastest-growing market for the more slowly growing West. While the growth rate of trade in manufactures among industrial countries declined dramatically from 12 per cent a year between 1963 and 1973, to 3 per cent a year after 1973, growth in exports to developing countries accelerated from 7 per cent to 12 per cent. Anti-Third-World protectionism damages this booming market. Developing countries usually spend all the foreign exchange they earn, and they spend the great bulk of it in Western countries. Limiting their exports to the West simply limits the amount they can spend on imports from the West. So nothing can be gained from this kind of protectionism, but much can be lost.

Why, then, if the benefits of free trade with the Third World are so clear, is protectionism on the increase? Why do Western governments act against the long-term interests of their own citizens? The answer lies in those democratic institutions of which the West is proudest: plural societies and representative democracy. Those who stand to gain from protectionism have very much more political impact than those who would benefit from free trade. The benefits of freer access for Third World goods would accrue to three groups who have no organized voice to put pressure on governments. First, the entire population, as consumers with an interest in cheaper goods. Second, the potential workers in expanding export industries, who don't even know what they're missing. Third, future generations who are unaware of the extra prosperity they are losing through protectionism.

By contrast, the costs of freer access are borne by a much smaller number of people with well-developed political and trade union channels for voicing their demands. These costs, there is no denying it, are considerable. Workers are attached to their jobs, their homes, their neighbourhoods, relatives and social links. The choice between unemployment or pulling up roots is a hard one that most people would prefer never to have to make. Trade unions channel and express the resistance of workers to threats to their jobs – even when government measures for redundancy, removal and retraining are generous. In Western societies that are no longer willing or politically able to crush trade union opposition, the demands of workers through their organizations have to be taken very seriously indeed.

The costs are concentrated not only occupationally, but also geographically. Industries have a historical tendency to be concentrated in a few areas where they can share specialist services, subcontractors and a pool of skilled workers. An area that has specialized for decades or even centuries in a trade threatened by Third World imports faces an uncertain future. Residents may take direct action – as in the redundancy-threatened French steel towns of Denain and Longwy in 1979. Or they may use their votes. All Western democracies elect their representatives on an area or at least a regional basis. All have strong opposition parties waiting in the wings to take over. All governments depend for survival on area and regional votes – none can afford to risk losing a region's votes by damaging its key industries. None have a long enough period of office to be able to carry through a successful adjustment programme before facing another election.

What can governments do to counter pressures towards protectionism? Any progress towards more normal levels of economic growth in the West can help. It is prolonged recession that has brought protectionism. In boom times a more progressive form of adjustment is much easier because there are plenty of alternative jobs for affected workers to move into. In the meantime very much more positive schemes of adjustment assistance could be introduced. These would aim not just to help older industries adjust, but also to stimulate the development of new industries, with higher levels of technologies and skills, that have a real future.

Ensuring a proper match of supply and demand of skills will demand far-reaching educational reforms. The shift from labour-intensive to skill-intensive industries has been happening for many years, and few Western economies have been able to adapt their labour forces to it fully. There have often been shortages of skilled workers during the recessions and surpluses of unskilled workers during boom times. The present mismatch between skills and changing opportunities results from the failure of most Western educational systems to turn out adaptable, practical, work-oriented people, or to attract and retrain workers with no skills, or outdated skills. So, ironically, the changing international economic order will require Western countries to reform education along the lines suggested in Chapter 11 for the Third World: improving access to education for all age groups, and making education at all levels very much more practical and less academic.

At the same time a major effort of propaganda will be needed. Ordinary people have little understanding of national or international economics. When their jobs are threatened they look for simple explanations, often blaming outsiders. Racialism increases in times of recession. Protectionism is a sort of international racialism, blaming developing countries for domestic unemployment. In resisting protectionist pressures, governments will need to explain at every opportunity how freer trade with the developing countries can create more jobs at home.

Progress towards a new order: commodities and finance

On the commodity front the Western countries are able to be a little more generous than with industry. Like the exporting countries, they too dislike wildly fluctuating commodity prices, which make a mockery of financial planning. They have an interest in getting stable and secure supplies of commodities at fairly predictable prices. And so, after long negotiations, they agreed in 1979 to set up a common fund for commodities, though on a much more modest scale than that desired by developing countries. The Third World originally wanted a giant $6 billion fund, financed by government contributions raised according to ability to pay, and acting as a financial reserve for a series of individual commodity stocks. A significant sum would be set aside for a 'second window' which would help countries producing the weakest commodities (or none at all) to diversify into other lines. It would also finance research to improve production and quality, and develop new uses for commodities, and help with initiatives in marketing. Some Western governments – notably the USA and West Germany – were distinctly unenthusiastic about the whole idea, so the Western line was to dig in and wait for the Third World's demands to be scaled down, as indeed they were. The eventual fund involved government contributions of only $400 million, with an additional voluntary $350 million for the second window. This meant that the fund's impact would be limited, especially as, at the time of the agreement in March 1979, only four commodities would be covered: tin, coffee, sugar and cocoa. There was, however, one notable new feature of the fund: the Third World would be able to outvote the West, even though the West were the main paymasters.

The experience of existing commodity agreements points to the problems the fund and future commodity agreements may face. These agreements have aimed at stabilizing prices within a band agreed in advance. There are often problems in agreeing on floor and ceiling prices. The agreements have used different methods to stabilize prices. The sugar and coffee agreements did this by way of export quotas, restricting exports if prices fell below the agreed floor and increasing them if they rose above the agreed ceiling. But quotas are always vulnerable to being busted by countries who need the money too badly. Buffer stocks are more reliable. If the price falls below the agreed minimum, the stock buys in the commodity and this raises the price. If the price goes above the maximum, the stock starts selling, which brings the price down again. The effectiveness of a buffer stock of fund depends on its size and the flexibility of its floor and ceiling prices. The smaller it is, the more often it will have to revise its floor and ceiling prices up or down following the market trend. The tin agreement, working with a small buffer stock in a rising market, sold out in January 1977, and was powerless to affect prices. No buffer stock can be big enough to keep prices permanently stable. All it can do in practice is to iron out the short-term fluctuations. Apart from this, it cannot alter the long-term market trend, so the line becomes a smoother up and down wave (or up and up, or down and down) instead of an erratically wiggly one.

This kind of buffer stock or agreement does little, moreover, to help with the main concern of Third World commodity producers – how to maintain or raise the real value of their export earnings in terms of what they can buy in imports. Although they have been cooperative about stabilizing prices, Western governments are unwilling to help improve them and have steadfastly refused any idea of index-linking them to manufactures, which, they say, would interfere with the natural play of market forces. If producers were paid an artificially high price, this would simply encourage them to produce more of a given commodity than the world had use for, and would result in banana or bauxite mountains just like the butter and milk powder mountains created by the Common Market's high prices for farmers.

On the financial aspects of the new economic order, the West has been none too generous either. While most Western nations have accepted in principle the aid target of 0·7 per cent of gross national product, only four countries – Norway, Sweden, Denmark and the Netherlands – had reached it by 1978. The rest, by refusing to set target dates for attaining the 0·7 per cent, have left aid at the mercy of political vagaries. The World Bank projects that aid – 0·32 per cent of Western GNP in 1978 – will be only marginally up in 1985, at 0·35 per cent.

There has been some small progress towards channelling aid to the poorest countries. In 1975–7 countries with average incomes below $400 made up 61 per cent of the world's population and received exactly the same proportion of aid. This was an improvement on the 54 per cent they were receiving six years earlier. But the whole of the increased share went to the thirty-one nations designated by the United Nations as least developed. The share of the rest, including such needy giants as Egypt, Pakistan, India, Indonesia, as well as Sri Lanka, fell from 45 per cent to 41 per cent.

On the debt question, welcome progress was made in 1977 and 1978, when ten Western nations wrote off the official debts owed to them by the poorest countries (or, in the case of Finland and Norway, by all developing countries). The total capital involved was around $6 billion, but all the donors were forgoing were service payments amounting to perhaps $300 million a year. As practically all new aid to the poorest countries was in the form of grants, these debt cancellations amounted to a retrospective change of past loans into grants. It did not affect commercial loans, which account for most of the debt of the middle-income countries.

Even the hated IMF was changing slowly in the right direction, though not enough. In 1969 the Fund introduced a buffer stock facility, allowing countries to borrow so they could finance purchases to build up buffer stocks of key commodities. In 1974 it brought in an extended credit facility allowing more borrowing and longer repayment periods for countries with severe balance-of-payments problems. And since 1963 it has had a compensatory finance facility, which allows countries with declining export earnings to borrow more. Perhaps its biggest gesture to date has been the setting up in 1976 of a trust fund, financed from the sale of IMF gold, which is loaned at nominal rates of interest to the poorest countries. In its first two years the Trust Fund realized $1·3 billion, with which it made loans to forty-three poor countries. Such measures are welcome in that they tend to increase the amount of credit countries can call on automatically, without conditions. But for larger loans, conditionality remains, though it is beginning to take a little more notice of political and social impact.

All these aspects of the New International Economic Order add up to one fundamental issue: the need to transfer more resources from the rich countries to the poor, so as to speed up equitable development and end absolute poverty as soon as possible. The poor countries have a historical right to this, in view of the damage they suffered through colonialism. They have a moral right, because existing inequalities are obscene. The strongest argument of all is that it is in the long-term self-interest of the advanced countries if the poor develop faster.

Prospects for a world welfare state

The world economic situation at the beginning of the 1980s seemed to be descending into chaos. Three problem situations coexisted uncomfortably: chronically underused industrial capacity and high unemployment in the West because of lack of demand; 800 million absolutely poor in the Third World needing, yet unable to buy, the barest essentials – a huge demand with no money to back it up; and massive balance of payments surpluses in the countries of the Arab peninsula – huge wealth that was not being spent. These surpluses were taking demand out of the world economy, reducing the global level of trade, growth and employment. The full impact of recession in the West was softened by developing countries, who borrowed heavily to pay for their higher oil bills without cutting back other imports, thereby saving an estimated three million jobs in the EEC alone. But Third World debt could not go on deepening for ever: it looked as if borrowing through normal commercial channels would have to slow down in the early eighties. Imports would have to be cut – and more jobs would be lost in the West, adding to the effects of micro-chips, continually rising oil prices and savage monetarist deflation. There was no escaping the feeling that catastrophe was just around the corner.

What seemed to be required – along with greater energy economies and crash development of alternative energy sources – was a sort of global Keynesianism, a massive coordinated effort to create more demand in the world economy. And the three central problems could perhaps be used to solve each other. The West, and hopefully the Communist states, could make some small immediate sacrifices, doubling aid to the South and channelling it overwhelmingly to the poor countries with per capita incomes below $500 or $600. More of the gigantic surpluses of the Arab oil-exporting nations could go into longer-term development loans which would go mainly to the middle income countries. These loans would not be, as with most aid, for 'projects', which take too much time to prepare, slowing down the flow of funds, but more flexible 'programme' loans. The fund administering these loans could attach conditions – as the IMF does – but conditions that equivalent sums would be spent to benefit the poor, buying land for the landless, redistributing investment into rural areas, encouraging small enterprise. This could help to overcome political resistance to reform. This massive transfer of resources, aimed at abolishing absolute poverty, would simultaneously stimulate demand in the world economy in a non-inflationary way, and Western sacrifices would be more than paid back in increased exports and faster growth. Several recent studies have shown the great mutual benefits of such an approach. The Interfutures project of the Organization for Economic Cooperation and Development, published in 1979, calculated that interdependence policies (freer trade, more resource transfers) would produce per capita incomes in AD 2000 60 per cent higher in the West and 30 per cent higher in the South than would policies of confrontation (see also page 314).

Considerations like these lay behind the recommendations of the Independent Commission on International Development Issues chaired by Willy Brandt. These included a doubling of aid, a doubling of World Bank lending, creation of additional IMF Special Drawing Rights and so on. Eventually there might be an international development tax, levied from richer countries according to ability to pay and given to the poor according to need, partly funnelled through a new World Development Fund in which West, South and Communists would participate. Brandt made more strongly than ever before the crucial point that it is in the long term self-interest of the North to make significant transfers to the South now.

The question that will determine the future of the world and of the world's poorest is whether political leaders will have the vision and commitment to plan and execute a programme of enlightened self-interest. Much hinges on the attitudes of the West. But Western political systems tend to encourage short-sighted moves. Elections are never far away, and programmes that cost money now and pay off a few years later may lose you the next election, handing the credit to your opponents. Public opinion in many countries, especially the USA and the UK, is often insular and self-seeking. Threatening war may win more support than rationing petrol or increasing aid. But public opinion is not immutable: it frequently changes in response to a lead from government. Politicians must now have the courage to lead, to educate the public about the potential benefits of a new order instead of pandering to fears and prejudices. Third World leaders can help by adopting redistributive, egalitarian policies. If resource transfers continue to be used to bolster up privileged élites, then the case for them is seriously weakened. The New International Economic Order must progress hand in hand with new and juster national economic orders.

14 Self-help economics: collective self-reliance

The blockage to change which the developing countries came up against in the 1970s inevitably encouraged them to seek alternative strategies. If neither the West, nor the oil-surplus countries, nor the Communists would help significantly, then the developing countries would have to help themselves and each other. If the north would not agree to improved commodity prices, developing countries could band together and force prices up. If the West would not open its markets, then the developing countries would have to create their own markets among themselves.

The new strategy became known as collective self-reliance. It tied in neatly with the new philosophy of development. Self-help, mutual help, organizing the poor to strengthen their hand against the rich: these were the domestic solutions being urged for individual countries. What could be more natural than to extend them to the international plane?

Commodity cartels

Ever since the Organization of Petroleum Exporting Countries dropped their bombshell on the world economy with their price increases of 1973–4, the model of militancy among commodity-producers has fascinated the Third World. The underlying theory is simple enough: as price is the outcome of supply and demand, producers of a given commodity can raise its price by coordinating their production and sales so as to reduce supply. OPEC's success was like a sensational rags-to-riches story holding out hope for the rest of the Third World. Between

329

1972 and 1976 the average exporting government's take from a barrel of oil rose from $1·47 to $11·15. The price of manufactures rose too, but by 1976 oil could buy 385 per cent more of them than it could four years earlier. That change was pregnant with symbolism: for the first time a group of developing countries had turned the tables on the West, thanks not to gracious concessions but to vigorous unilateral action. The vicarious pleasure non-oil developing countries took diminished somewhat, of course, as the increases rocked their own economies.

Whether it was good or bad for the Third World as a whole, OPEC seemed to offer a possible model for action for other commodities. Indeed, after 1973, twelve new producers' associations were set up covering pepper, rubber, mercury, timber, iron ore, jute, sugar, tea, coffee, bauxite and bananas. The latter three – Café Mondial (1973), the International Bauxite Association (1974) and the Union of Banana Exporting Countries (1974) – have been among the most active. At the time there was great optimism among producer countries, and a certain amount of anxiety among consumers, about the possibilities of commodity militancy. But as the seventies rolled by with no repeat of OPEC, it became clear that the particular combination of factors accounting for its success was exceptional. First there was the importance of oil as the lifeblood of industrial countries, without which their economies would have come to an immediate standstill. Because of this, demand for oil was relatively inelastic – that is, people would not buy a great deal less of it even if the price went up steeply. There was no ready substitute – you couldn't suddenly switch cars, lorries, power stations or chemical plants on to coal or gas, and the changeover would take years and involve heavy investments. At the time, all major Western nations were dependent on oil imports, Western Europe and Japan totally so, and the USA to a significant extent – and OPEC countries controlled the great bulk of those imports. The governments of the OPEC countries had, since the beginning of the seventies, increased their control over the oil companies, raising the level of taxation and royalties, as well as the national share of ownership. This put them in a position to control supply. Another essential factor was the political unity among OPEC members. Two thirds of the oil came from Arab nations where, despite ideological differences, the spirit of pan-Arabism was strong and reinforced by shared hostility to Israel. Moreover, the biggest producers, from the Arabian peninsula, were not poor nations desperate to sell. Their currency reserves and small populations gave them considerable staying power, and oil was easily and cheaply storeable, simply by leaving it in the ground.

So a provisional checklist of requirements for total success in a commodity cartel might read as follows: Demand should be fairly inelastic, or people will simply buy a lot less if the price goes up steeply, and producers may gain nothing or even lose out. The commodity should have no ready substitutes, or consumers will shift to the alternative when prices go up. The product should be easy to store or cut back in production, and must be one in which the cartel members produce an indispensable share. Governments must have enough control over production to be able to regulate it – and must be sufficiently strong and united to agree and stick to whatever reductions in production are necessary.

During the 1970s even OPEC began to lose some of its strength on several of these counts. Members began to split economically and politically. On the one hand were the radicals like Libya, plus the poorer or more heavily populated countries who badly needed price rises. On the other, the Saudis and the Gulf sheikhdoms had immense surplus funds invested in Western currencies, and were ruled by conservative régimes wanting to purchase Western armaments. The Saudis especially exerted a strong braking effect on further price rises. Then the supply situation began to ease, as more non-OPEC sources came on tap in Alaska, Mexico and the North Sea. Demand eased too, in response to the earlier price rises, as Western countries began to economize on fuel. Oil was not such a totally magical commodity after all: higher prices could bring higher-cost supplies on tap, and induce people to cut back consumption, though both adjustments took longer than they might with most other commodities. 1979 saw a return of the early seventies' crisis. A reduction in supply followed the overthrow of the Shah of Iran. Prices shot up, and once again OPEC appeared to be a mighty force. The truth was that its strength depended on the market situation for oil, waxing and waning with changes in supply and demand.

Few commodities other than oil comply with the demanding checklist for cartel success. Tea and bananas deteriorate with storage. Cotton, tobacco, sugar, meat, maize and soyabeans are all produced by Western farmers who are usually induced to overproduce by government subsidies and external tariffs. Synthetic substitutes are a perpetual headache for cotton, jute, sisal and rubber. The oil price rises have helped to make them more competitive, but the existence of alternatives will always place a corresponding ceiling on the prices these commodities can command.

Another OPEC does not seem really on the cards, therefore. Nevertheless, there are some promising contenders where concerted action could produce worthwhile, if not spectacular, gains. The Third World produces more than 90 per cent of world coffee exports, with the top four producers (Brazil, Colombia, the Ivory Coast and Uganda) accounting for a half. Almost all cocoa is produced in developing countries, three-quarters of it in four countries (Ghana, Nigeria, the Ivory Coast and Brazil). Even tea faces little competition from Western producers, and two countries alone, India and Sri Lanka, produce more than half the world's exports. These beverages are not of vital importance – but the price rises they all enjoyed in the mid-seventies showed that demand was inelastic enough (because of Western caffeine addiction?) to result in higher total income when prices rose. Some of the minerals share (though to a lesser degree) oil's key characteristics: economic importance, high share of Western consumption produced in the Third World, concentration of production in a manageable number of countries. Four fifths of tin exports come from the Third World, and the top four producers account for three-quarters of world exports. The same proportion of world exports of phosphate rock (for fertilizer) comes from the developing countries, and the four leading exporters account for two thirds. The Third World controls three quarters of the world's exports of bauxite (from which aluminium is made) and two-thirds come from the top four exporters.

The biggest obstacles to successful cartel action arise from the sheer poverty of many commodity exporters. Cutting back production or supply involves costs that poor producers and poor countries may be unable to carry. The beverage plants have a long life. Producers, especially smallholders, are not going to uproot them if the price drops; indeed they will go on selling their cocoa pods or coffee beans at almost any price. Mines involve fixed overheads for maintenance and key staff, which go on mounting up even when there is no production. Most developing countries desperately need the foreign exchange their commodity exports provide, and will often sell as prices are dropping, when any prudent trader would wait until they bottomed out. In some cases they may even increase production to try to maintain earnings when the price falls. In this situation, quotas may not be adhered to: the poor countries face the constant temptation of breaking ranks to make a fast buck.

These problems emerge clearly in the case of copper. CIPEC, the copper equivalent of OPEC (the initials stand for the French Conseil Intergouvernmental des Pays Exportateurs du Cuivre) was set up in 1967 by Chile, Peru, Zambia and Zaïre. All four countries had acquired considerable control over production, and copper is easily storeable under the ground. But CIPEC's members could not agree to cut back supplies. Peru nursed ambitions to treble her production of the metal. At the same time production was increasing in non-CIPEC countries such as the Philippines, Papua New Guinea, Mexico and Iran. Copper prices started to fall after 1974 because of industrial recession in the West. In 1976 CIPEC decided to cut back production by 15 per cent in an attempt to raise prices, but Chile refused to enforce a cutback. Eventually copper prices began to improve not as a result of cooperation among producers, but in consequence of the invasion of Zaïre's Shaba province which disrupted production of mines in the area, and of strikes in Peru.

The price a commodity fetches on world markets is only one aspect of a more general issue: how to boost a country's earnings from its commodities. There are other ways of increasing revenue by unilateral or cooperative action, perhaps more straightforward than cartel action on prices. Such methods include introducing or increasing taxes and royalties on foreign-owned companies, nationalizing them wholly or partly, or increasing the country's share of the value added to the commodity between its raw and finished states by processing, packaging, transporting and marketing. The case of bauxite shows that there is a lot individual countries can do to increase their own revenue, as long as the commodity involved is a fairly strong one and they are sitting on an important source of supply. Jamaica accounts for about one fifth of world bauxite production, and bauxite makes up two thirds of her exports. Raw bauxite is only a small proportion of the value of the eventual aluminium ingot made from it – but until recently all the processing took place outside Jamaica. Between 1950 and 1973 Jamaica's take from the $17 billion final value of the ingots was only 2 per cent. After a disastrous decline in revenue in 1973, Jamaica passed legislation increasing levies and royalties per ton to more than four times what she was getting previously. To increase the value added locally, Jamaica has for some time conceded new mining licences only on condition that the bauxite will be locally processed into alumina (the halfway stage to aluminium). One ton of alumina can generate twice as much revenue, four times as much foreign exchange and four times as many jobs as one ton of bauxite.

In some cases the best thing a country can do with a weak agricultural commodity is to cut down its production and turn the land over to high-value crops (such as market vegetables or flowers) or, if it is having to import food, to food production. This might be the case with much of the sugar in Latin America and the Caribbean, with Bangladesh's jute or Sri Lanka's tea. The latter two countries are trying to cut down the cash crop acreage (thus freeing land for food), but to keep up production by increasing productivity.

Regional markets

Another, and increasingly popular, form of collective self-reliance involves the creation of regional common markets among developing countries. Third World industry is slowed in its expansion by lack of demand. Rising protectionism is blocking off the biggest existing market, in the West. And in most countries internal markets are small, almost always because of the poverty of the masses. Faced with these two obstacles, developing countries are increasingly associating for trade among themselves, to create larger markets that will make manufacturing operations more viable.

One of the most important preconditions of trade is the existence of communications links. But most road and rail systems in Third World countries lead straight to the main port, a visual expression of past colonialism and continued dependence on the West. Regional cooperation has already made some progress in developing road and rail links between developing countries. The earliest of these was the Pan American Highway, first approved in 1923, which now stretches from

Chile to Mexico with only a single break at the swampy Darien gap that severs Colombia from Panama. A parallel route is planned east of the Andes – the forest margin highway. For Africa a network of regional roads is projected. One of the major routes will be the Transafrican, from Mombasa in Kenya to Lagos, Nigeria's capital, via Uganda, Zaire, the Central African Republic and Cameroon. The Trans East African, from Cairo to Gaborone in Botswana, passing through Sudan, Ethiopia, Kenya, Tanzania and Zambia, will realize Cecil Rhodes's dream of a Cape to Cairo railroad, though in an entirely different spirit.

By 1978 there were fifteen associations of developing countries for trade, and no less than nine of them were created after 1973. Latin America has the Latin American Free Trade Association (LAFTA) and the Central American Common Market (both initiated in 1960); the Andean Pact (1969); the Caribbean Community (1974); and the Latin American Economic System (1975). In Africa there are the West African Economic Community (CEAO) and the Central African Customs and Economic Union (UDEAC), both set up after independence by former French colonies; the Mano River Union between Liberia and Sierra Leone (1973); the Economic Community of West African States (ECOWAS: 1975); and the Economic Community of the Great Lakes (1976). In the Middle East there are the Arab Common Market (Egypt, Iraq, Jordan, Syria and later Sudan: 1964) and the Regional Cooperation for Development (Turkey, Iran and Pakistan: 1976). In the east there are the Bangkok Agreement, comprising seven south and south-east Asian states (1975), and ASEAN, the Association of South East Asian Nations (1975). In addition several developing countries from all continents have signed a protocol to the General Agreement on Tariffs and Trade, providing for mutual tariff concessions. The protocol came into force in 1973.

These groupings vary considerably in their scope. Most include provision for mutual tariff cuts and common external tariffs. The more ambitious (LAFTA, the Andean Pact, ASEAN, ECOWAS) involve joint planning of industrial projects so that members' economies can become more complementary and different countries can specialize in different products. ASEAN planned a series of major industrial ventures, under which Singapore would produce diesel engines for the whole area, Indonesia and Malaysia ammonia and urea, Thailand rock salt and soda ash, and the Philippines synthetic fertilizer. Without the assurance of a larger market, these projects might not be viable on a purely national scale. Joint planning of agriculture, to achieve self-sufficiency in food, has been tried out by the Caribbean Community. Some of the regional associations are developing joint research and marketing facilities, and have development banks able to put bigger sums of money into ventures than individual countries could afford. They can also develop common codes on foreign investment, to prevent multinationals switching to another country in the area so as to avoid controls. The Andean Pact, for example, stipulates 51 per cent local control of foreign investment.

As with commodities, however, the path of cooperation rarely runs smooth, and there have been more than just teething problems. Free trade within an area can accelerate the unevenness of development, pushing industries towards areas that are already more favoured with resources, skills or communications. The poorer countries may gain little, yet pay more for their products than they would on the world market. Therefore regional markets of developing countries have to be more directed and controlled than Western versions. Industries sometimes have to be sited in countries that may not be ideally suited for them, and naturally there are tugs of war between countries as to who will take home the most goodies. Balance-of-payments problems, which most developing countries run into from time to time, have also interfered with regional markets. In 1977 CARICOM sailed into stormy waters when Guyana and Jamaica, facing trade deficits, had to cut down on imports from other countries in the region. Ideological differences were involved when Chile withdrew from the Andean Pact in 1976, because it wanted to open its doors to foreign investment. One of the oldest and most comprehensive of the regional markets, the East African Community, broke up completely in 1977 after political and economic squabbles between the partners, Kenya, Uganda and Tanzania. Formed in 1967, the EAC had internal free trade, a common external tariff and shared development bank, posts, railways, harbours, shipping and airline.

Technical cooperation among developing countries

Economic cooperation among developing countries requires the technical back-up of organization, management and expertise. In the later 1970s the idea of technical cooperation among developing countries (TCDC) spread, with the help of a United Nations conference on the subject in Buenos Aires in September 1978. 'The key to development,' declared the conference's plan of action, 'lies in the achievement of greater national and collective self-reliance.' The conventional idea of north–south relations, whereby northern expertise can solve southern problems, was outmoded. Many developing countries had themselves evolved appropriate solutions, which might be applicable in other countries. This experience should be exchanged, on a permanent south–south basis, allowing the perspectives of developing countries to be applied to development problems. To this end a global focal point was needed for TCDC, to encourage and organize exchange of experience and cooperative research. Technical cooperation might also involve, as Commonwealth Secretary Shridath Ramphal has proposed, setting up a sort of Organization for Economic Cooperation and Development equivalent for developing countries. The 'OECDC' would research issues in the north–south dialogue and formulate common negotiating positions and tactics.

TCDC so far has reached only an embryonic stage, and once again poverty is the main stumbling block. Most developing countries have a serious shortage of top-level administrative, managerial and scientific personnel. Much of this is siphoned off by the brain drain, or by the need to staff embassies and United Nations bodies. What remains usually needs to be mustered carefully to solve a country's own problems. Few countries have emerged as significant contributors to TCDC. Among them, India is pre-eminent, but then she has the world's third largest body of trained scientists.

The southern nations lack not only technical back-up for cooperation, but even their solidarity is weakening. There is the split between the newly industrializing countries, the commodity-producers, and the poorest countries who have practically nothing to sell. Each group has an interest in maximizing Western concessions in the sphere that will help it most – trade, commodities or aid respectively. Most of the industrializing countries might actually prefer cheaper commodities. Moreover, Western intransigence has induced behind-the-scenes splits within each group. Many governments put greater effort into negotiating special deals for themselves than into pursuing a better deal for everyone.

Close off your borders?

Overall, the record of collective self-reliance has not so far been very encouraging. In commodities, trading groups and technical cooperation, progress has been slow against a contrary wind of difficulties due to poverty and diversity. That does not mean the strategy should be abandoned – quite the opposite. Every effort should be made to overcome these problems.

Some writers have gone so far as to suggest that national and collective self-reliance should replace entirely the idea of interdependence with the West and increased transfers of resources. As colonialism and neo-colonialism have distorted Third World economies and made them subservient to the West, they may only be able to achieve economic viability, these authors suggest, if they sever all links: no trade, no aid, no nothing. 'Close off your borders,' is British writer Richard Gott's advice. Things may take longer, and there may be mistakes and inefficiencies in the early stages. But these drawbacks have to be accepted as the inevitable costs of learning how to stand on your own feet – like the knocks and bumps a child gets when it is learning to walk.

Not surprisingly, this doctrine has found few takers in the Third World. The real choices facing developing countries are more complex. Some aspects of their relations with developed countries are damaging and should be regulated or eliminated. Others are beneficial and should be welcomed. Indeed, these beneficial aspects can help to speed up achievement of national and collective self-reliance. The multinationals are the real Trojan horses of Westernization and cultural imperialism, and need especially tight control – if, indeed, they are admitted at all. But there are aspects of relations with Western countries that help towards self-reliance, and could help a good deal more if they were stepped up. In the field of commodities, development finance from the north is essential for increasing productivity, improving quality and marketing, and diversifying. Cuts in Western tariffs against processed commodities would do more to help local processing than any other measure. Regional markets have been hamstrung by the fact that the structure of production in developing countries is complementary to that in the West. As a result, three quarters of their exports go West and less than a quarter goes to other developing countries. Until these relative shares are reversed, the best hope for rapid growth of manufactured exports obviously lies in freer access to Western or Communist markets for labour-intensive goods.

Multilateral aid, channelled through the United Nations family of agencies and the development banks, has perhaps the most important role of all to play. The investment it provides is no longer (as it may have been in the sixties) designed to push Western models or encourage dependence. Increasingly the agencies are helping to transfer non-proprietary and appropriate technology to developing countries, as well as helping to build up local capacities in all fields. In this way they can help to reduce the need for Faustian bargains with the multinationals, and perhaps replace them altogether. For example, the World Bank is now lending to finance exploration and development of minerals and fuels, the World Health Organization is helping to start up manufacturing units for non-proprietary drugs, and the UN Industrial Development Organization is disseminating industrial technology free from patent restrictions. The development agencies are gradually becoming the principal channel for technical cooperation among developing countries: their know-how is derived from experiments inside the Third World, and transmitted by experts increasingly recruited from the Third World.

The ideal of collective self-reliance, then, is not in conflict with a beneficial interdependence of developed and developing countries. The two approaches complement each other. All in all, interdependence is not an option that either side in the north–south dialogue can reject. It already exists, a curious blend of parasitism and symbiosis. Now it needs to be purged of its destructive elements, so that it can genuinely benefit both sides. Collective self-reliance in the south will be more successful with help from the north. Northern growth will be faster with concessions to the south.

15 Development for what? Lessons for the world

The word 'development' is often bandied around among observers and participants in the process as if there were a general consensus on what it means. In reality, there is bitter disagreement over the central questions: Development for what purpose? Development towards what end? Everyone is agreed on one point: that development must mean the eradication of absolute poverty and hunger and want. But after that, what? The field is wide open.

In most Western minds, and in those of the majority of Third World élites, development equals modernization, and modernization equals the triumph of Western materialism. It means the build-up of mass production and factories and cities, the mechanization and chemicalization of agriculture, the extension of drug and surgery-based modern medicine to all. It means the development of a consumer society of one kind or another, either on American lines with the apotheosis of the privatized individual, or on Soviet lines with more (but only a little more) emphasis on social responsibilities. It means modern armies equipped with the most devastating technological weapons available. It means the endless pursuit of growth, without question as to the goals or even the shape of that growth or whether the sum of human welfare is being advanced.

It may be that the benefits of this type of rapid growth led by the modern sector will eventually trickle down. But eventually can mean many generations. The choice of this model also implies the choice of a certain pattern of society. On the way there, social values of a higher order are being sacrificed. Traditional society, with its values of cooperation and mutual help, is dying fast under the slings and arrows of commercialization and material greed. The extended family is breaking into nuclear fragments through migration and urbanization. The community support of the village is wearing away under the drip of cash. Egalitarian modes of sharing round work and food are disappearing as social polarization continues. It is now every family, every individual for himself or herself. The means chosen to eradicate poverty, in other words, are undermining the central goals of any civilized society.

There has to be another way: a way to remove the curse of want while conserving the original values of Third World societies. There must be a set of means that do not just expand material wealth, but also point towards, and are in harmony with, a worthwhile set of ends and values.

The new development strategies were developed primarily as means of eradicating absolute poverty more rapidly, so that men and women could look forward to a life free from poverty, hunger, disease and ignorance, if not for themselves, then at least for their children or grandchildren. But the new strategies also contain implicit values and goals, which are in keeping with the idea of development not only or primarily of things, but the development of humanity and all men and women to their full social, aesthetic and intellectual potential.

The industrialized nations too are developing, and few of them seem to know or even ask where to. They are equally in need of a set of goals and a set of means in keeping with these goals. The model proposed for the developing countries is equally adaptable to the developed.

The central value implicit in the new strategies is equality, of wealth and of power. They point to a society without pronounced contrasts between rich and poor, where the rewards of intellect and of manual labour are not grossly divergent, where people are not consumed by envy and motivated by the desire to catch up with or get ahead of one another. They do not answer the question to which no country in the world has offered a definitive answer: How much equality? The most equal distribution of income yet measured was that of Czechoslovakia in 1964, when the average income of the top 20 per cent was only two and a half times that of the bottom 40 per cent. That seems a realistic goal for other countries to work towards.

Much greater equality of power is the second major goal, implicit in the ideal of participation favoured by the new development approaches. Participation reduces costs and mobilizes the most valuable of all underused resources: human energy and creativity. But participation also implies grassroots democracy in the workplace and the community. As a minimum it must mean that plans should no longer be imposed from above, but must involve those who have to live with them. This ideal, like that of economic equality, cannot be halted at any particular cut-off point: people will always compare present reality with the ideal, and demand greater equality. Ultimately, equality of power must mean participation by workers in controlling the means of production, and control by residents over their own housing and neighbourhoods. Control by way of elected representatives is not enough: participation means that everyone has to become involved in making the decisions that affect them directly through neighbourhood and factory assemblies, permanent ongoing democracy, not the occasional right to choose a new set of rulers.

Equality of power also means the dethronement of the professional, implicit in all the barefoot technician programmes of the new development. Professionals of all kinds – doctors, lawyers, architects, planners – attempt to control important aspects of people's lives. They mystify the practice of their skills so as to exclude others from them. The spread of the barefoot technicians is a major blow to professional mystiques. The success of this movement shows that, with a very modest amount of specialized knowledge, almost anyone can deal with the major problems that crop up. Through the local committees that support and guide them, the professionalized experts should remain under the control of their clients. Their major function is to guide and educate people so they can improve their own farms and businesses, build their own houses, control their own fertility, plan their own diets, look after their own health and learn how to learn for themselves. The ideal of self-help – which is the converse of the idea of professionalism – means the development of a new, autonomous, creative human being possessing most of the skills needed for his or her own self-realization.

The third major common strand in the new strategies is cooperation. In community development, in farming and in manufacturing, cooperatives are being set up throughout the Third World. Self-help has to be strengthened by mutual help. Learning of development skills is speeded up when it is pursued collectively. The ideal becomes a network of egalitarian communities whose members pursue cooperative self-improvement, not individual self-advancement.

The final principle is respect for nature. Growth that does not respect the natural world, its complexity and its sensitivity, limits itself. Resources are exhausted, ecosystems collapse, species disappear and our own physical and mental health and even our survival are threatened.

In many respects the West is no further advanced than the Third World towards these goals. Considerable inequality between classes and regions persists in most countries, stimulating everyone to pursue an unnecessary multiplication of material wealth to catch up with the next person. Except in a few advanced countries, like Sweden, democracy is little more than the opportunity to select, every four or five years, a group of people to take decisions without consulting you. Participation is limited, in practice, to self-selected pressure groups. The mass of the people are not involved in the planning of their settlements or the running of their factories or farms, but are dominated, on both sides of the Iron Curtain, by bureaucrats and managers. Major aspects of people's lives have been expropriated and are monopolized by the professionals in anything from health to entertainment. Self-help may be widespread, but mutual help and cooperation is a rare phenomenon. The supportive extended family died many generations ago, and even the nuclear family is disintegrating, leaving a collection of isolated individuals pursuing egotistical goals.

The West is in no position to provide an example of the development of humanity to the Third World. Though they are materially overdeveloped, in the important human respects the industrialized societies are as underdeveloped as, or more underdeveloped than, the agricultural nations, and they can learn a lot from the new development models.

Western agriculture will eventually have to find new ways. The wisdom of the eighteenth-century British agricultural revolution, based on mixed farming, crop rotation and the return of all organic wastes to the soil, has been largely thrown to the winds. Farming is now based on pumping oil-based chemicals into the ground and cultivating it by oil-driven machinery. It has been farming oil, not soil. The soil itself has become progressively mined of its trace elements. Sooner or later the West will be forced to return to its senses and adopt less energy-intensive, more organic methods of farming.

Industry is the second major field where the West is headed for trouble and can learn from the new development models. Technology is now moving so fast that new investment threatens to destroy more jobs than it creates. The new technology of microprocessors may saddle Western countries with a labour surplus that could grow to Third World proportions. This surplus will be heavily weighted with the unskilled and under-educated, aggravating the problems of crime, drugs, vandalism and terrorism. Machinery will produce more wealth than ever before, but a smaller number may be employed in producing it and there will be considerable problems in distributing the benefits to those excluded: a situation exactly comparable to the contrast between rich modern-sector industry and the mass of poor in the Third World. Socialist countries will find this problem of distributing the work and the benefits of advanced technology much easier than non-socialist ones.

The West may be forced to seek its own versions of appropriate technology and appropriate management. It too needs, as social philosopher Ernst Schumacher has pointed out, a new, gentler technology, one that is less wasteful of resources, that does less violence to nature and to human nature. As it has been in the Third World, the employment effect of new technology should be increasingly scrutinized. We may see a new wave of Luddism or protest against new technology. There will be temptations to freeze technological advance at a given level to prevent further loss of employment. Cooperative, worker-controlled or state-owned enterprises will be best placed to adopt new labour-saving technology and to spread its benefits evenly among their workers, without cutting back the workforce. Small-scale enterprise is coming back into favour in the West, as it is in the Third World: more human in scale, more adaptable, more labour-intensive than large-scale enterprise and large-scale technology, with its impersonality, alienation and anomie.

In the cities, the older planners' habit of demolishing viable houses, communities and scattered small workplaces, to replace them with sanitized estates or tower blocks without local work opportunities, is thankfully going out of fashion as Western countries practise their own version of 'slum upgrading'. Absurd planning regulations cry out for repeal. British home-owners, for example, have considerably less freedom than Lima squatters to house themselves as they see fit. People ought to be allowed the right to alter, extend and improve their homes as their income improves, rather than being forced to move and lose their community links. The practice of zoning, separating residential and work areas, may make sense where big factories are concerned, but to ban small businesses from residential areas is as destructive of work opportunities in the West as it is in the Third World. Many people might start up businesses if they could use their homes as premises. The workplaces thus created would be near to where the people are – hence saving on transport costs and reducing city traffic congestion.

In health and nutrition the West can learn a lot from the new approaches in the Third World. Western countries now face the same problem as developing countries: their medicine is still hooked on cure rather than prevention, and as medical technology grows more sophisticated health care gets so expensive that it can no longer be afforded, either by individuals in private systems like the American, or by national insurance schemes like those in most of Europe. De-professionalization is urgently needed here. Health volunteers in each neighbourhood or street could take some of the load off doctors. Self-medication, with the advice of pharmacists, should be encouraged for a much wider range of drugs. Health education should be stressed in schools. Health problems in the West are just as often environmental in origin as in the Third World, and effective preventive measures could cut the workload of the health services so as to make them affordable again. The banning of smoking and closer control of industrial chemicals could combat cancer more effectively than chemotherapy or radiation therapy. Improved nutrition, such as the banning of refined flour and sugar, nutrition education and encouragement of exercise could further reduce health problems.

Education in the West is way behind some of the more adventurous experiments in the Third World: no Western state educational system prepares its pupils for life anywhere near as effectively as Colombia's Radio Sutatenza (see page 275). In most cases young people are flung into the world with their heads full of academic irrelevancies without any knowledge of law, the welfare system or the working environment, let alone family planning, health or nutrition. Education in most Western countries needs totally remodelling along functional lines. The same questions have to be asked as in the Third World: What do young people need to know in order to survive and prosper in the real world? What skills and knowledge do their communities and countries need them to have? A functional approach to education would minimize the alienation at school felt by many of today's youth, who rightly cannot see the purpose of so much that they have to learn. Methods of delivery need re-examination too: non-formal education, in which work would be combined with school from an earlier age, has much to recommend it.

Finally, the West can learn from those valuable aspects of traditional society in the Third World which are now under threat of extinction. There is in the West a great hunger both for a supportive community and for forms of religion that would express and celebrate our relation with nature and with other human beings. This need is clear from the spread of communal living arrangements and the flourishing of esoteric religions, many of them directly imported from the Third World. It will be the task of architecture (under the guidance of the people, of course) to devise settlement patterns that fuse the need for privacy with the need for community support.

Adoption of more egalitarian and participatory, less polluting and wasteful lifestyles will, not only contribute to the North's well-being, it will actively help the Third World and help avoid social disintegration and possible nuclear holocaust. If the North wasted less energy and raw materials, the price of resources for the essential needs of the South – industrialization and food production – would be lower. But incessantly and senselessly rising consumption is encouraged by social inequality, as everyone pushes to catch up with the rich. Greater equality is essential in cutting down waste, and also seems to make people more willing to give aid. It is no coincidence that the best aid givers are those countries which have egalitarian philosophies and a greater degree of grassroots democracy at home and at work – Scandinavia and the Netherlands.

In the more divided societies, the social bonds seem to be weakening. Individual and sectional egoisms increasingly disregard the common good, as resource shortages, inflation, unemployment and deflation bite. As social peace at home grows more fragile, the threat of war looms larger. Resource shortages and internal social conflicts have been the causes of most of the wars in history. Once again we should note that the world's pacifist nations – Sweden, Switzerland, Costa Rica – all enjoy social peace at home, based on participatory democracies inherited from egalitarian, smallholding peasants.

Reforms will not come easily in the North, any more than in the South. Managers, professionals, bureaucrats and representatives will not readily concede reductions in their powers or privileges, and they have much more political pull than ordinary people. Reforms are beginning on a voluntary basis. More movements are needed like the Norwegian 'The Future is in Our Hands', which links changes in northern societies with help for the South. Carnations can sometimes halt tanks, but only if there are enough of them.

If the world pulls through the gloom of the immediate future, the new development patterns will have much to teach us all. Mankind has reached a point where it is not enough to develop material wealth. It must now learn how to distribute that wealth fairly, and how to develop all humans to their full physical and psychological potential, in harmony with nature. West, East and South should be engaged in a process of learning from each other the concrete ways of achieving this.

16 Equal burdens, equal benefits: development for women

East Africa's Rift Valley is an alien landscape: a broad expanse of grassland and sparse thorn bushes, extending endlessly like a lane between walls of mountain. It is dry as tinder most of the year, but in the rains it becomes a swamp. Giraffes startle as you pass and lope off in slow motion, while goats on hind legs strip the leaves from between the thorns. There are no roads or even paths to the Masai homesteads; they merge almost imperceptibly into the background: stockades of branches surrounding a circle of low huts, whalebacked humps of bent poles plastered with dried cow-dung.

The women age prematurely. Nehai Sowakla, for all her beaded necklaces and long earrings trailing from split lobes, looks two decades older than her forty-odd years. One of her eyes is half closed with trachoma. She is feeding a tiny baby from a long leather bottle with fermented milk. A three-year-old boy, with only a thin linen cloth draped over one shoulder, trembles with fever. His face is patched with white, healed scars from a fall into the fire. The compound, which houses the cattle and goats at night, is a mire of mud and droppings, alive with flies that cluster around the children's eyes, mouths and noses.

The Masai males are out all day with the herds. To the women fall all other chores. They build the huts. They cook, in the dark, windowless interiors, in a thick cloud of choking smoke. But the worst of their tasks is the collection of fuel and water. Nehai sets out soon after dawn each morning, an old oil drum on her back, for the nearest spring, eight kilometres away at the base of a low hill. The round trip takes her five

351

hours. Meanwhile her daughter-in-law and her two co-wives are out, scouring the plain for miles around for dead branches and twigs, breaking off live ones where all else fails. They return towards evening, fifty pounds of wood on their backs, supported by a leather thong across their brows.

Women's burdens – heavy throughout the Third World – are enough to break a camel's back in much of Africa. The task of alleviating them, and of raising their incomes and status, is a crucial one, and not only out of fairness, for women play a central role in the production and processing of food, in the getting and using of fuel, and in the gestation and rearing of children. The ground to be covered is vast: traditional roles, except in a few regions such as South East Asia, are oppressive, and the process of development has often reduced women's incomes relative to men's. Even where women are the principal farmers, they usually have no rights in landownership. Their education is neglected in favour of males: two thirds of the Third World's 800 million illiterates are women. Their health falls far below its potential: though by nature they should live longer than men, in some areas their life expectancy is shorter.

Kenya is perhaps the best location to study what can be done for women. The problems are especially acute here: the distance of water sources, the dwindling of fuelwood supplies, above all the fact that, in some areas, half or more of rural households are headed by women with farms to run as well as families, while their husbands are away working in cities or on the 3,200 large farms that occupy half the country's farmland. Wages are low and family smallholdings tiny; the income from both is required for subsistence, and wage employment is rarely to be had within reach of the villages. Poverty and inequality tear the family apart.

Kenya's hardy, well-built women have learned to cope by themselves, ever since the Mau-Mau emergency when their menfolk were away fighting. The country now has a network of around 6,000 grassroots women's organizations, about one for every 600 adult women. They run savings clubs to help each other, in rotation, to buy tin roofs or high-grade cattle, or to pay secondary-school fees. Helping these groups is the government Women's Bureau, set up in 1975, International Women's Year. With technical and material help from UNICEF and UNDP, the Bureau finances some 400 projects a year aimed at raising women's incomes, but requests for funds run at ten times that number. So most women's projects in Kenya are, of necessity, entirely self-reliant. It is women, above all, who make the national slogan of *harambee* (Swahili for 'pull together') a reality.

Reducing the burden of housework

The excessive workload of women does not only affect their health, and that of any babies in their wombs or breastfeeding, it also acts as a powerful incentive to have more children who will be able, from the age of six or so, to lend a hand; Kenya's women rate as the world's most fertile, averaging eight live children in their reproductive life.

Making clean water supplies more accessible can save anything from half an hour to five hours a day. Much of the effort to improve water supplies in Kenya is directed at women's groups. The National Council of Women is helping scores of groups to instal water pipes and dig wells. One of those projects is just a few kilometres from Nehai Sowakla's homestead. Looking south down the Rift Valley from the shoulder of the Ngong hills, you can see a bright patch of clay-brown water glinting on the dull green plain. It is the dam of Olosh Oibor, where a unique partnership between a tough American missionary and a wily old tribesman is working a total transformation of Masai life. Simeon Olesaguda is somewhere between 75 and 80 years old – he has lost track of the exact figure. He looks about fifty, and has five wives and thirty-five children, the youngest still at the breast. In 1970, he heard that a missionary was looking for Masai land on which to build a church. The other family heads were not interested, but Olesaguda had a simmering interest in Christianity. His mother, a Kikuyu woman, had taught him to read with a copy of the Bible. So he invited the missionary, Danny Grindall, to build on his grazing land. Grindall was willing to work as well as to preach. 'Danny asked us what we needed most,' Olesaguda explained. 'I said, we need water so my people can rest from wandering, and my children can get away from the flies and the dung.'

Grindall mobilized external finance, while Olesaguda, his wives and his children chipped in with hard labour. The dam was completed in 1972, and it provides water all the year round for the cattle. Settled life also brings other possibilities. There is a school, filled with Olesaguda children. There are permanent houses, made of half-cylinders of concrete moulded over chicken wire, and sited on a dry promontory. Four tall windmills raise the water close to the houses and irrigate a vegetable garden bristling with rows of healthy spinach, onions, carrots, beans and tomatoes. The dam is stocked with fish – tilapia and black bass. But the most dramatic benefit has been to the women. They used to trek to a spring four kilometres up the steep sides of the Ngong hills; now they can draw water from a tank less than a hundred yards from their houses. They have an extra four hours a day, and use it to trade in Ngong town, or even to rest or chat.

In the beginning, Olesaguda was a laughing stock among the Masai for allowing the missionary a place on his land. Since then they have learned to take him seriously, as they watched his herds expand to 200 cattle and 500 goats, and saw him become the proud owner of a bar-cum-hotel in the market town of Ngong. It's hard to say whether Danny Grindall has used Olesaguda to spread the gospel among the Masai, or if Olesaguda has used Grindall to attract funds for development.

Either way, the lot of the women of Olosh Oibor has been totally transformed, though they are still a very long way from equality.

Spreading village technology

In the suburb of Karen, just outside Nairobi, is a compound filled with exotic machinery. It is, as one UNICEF official put it, an appropriate-technology 'zoo', and most of the items there have to do, in one way or another, with lightening women's burdens. It is AT applied to everyday housework, much more labour-saving than traditional ways, and much, much less expensive than electrical goods.

There is a maize sheller, a large wooden wheel embedded with fence staples that tear the corn off the cob; a handmill that saves an hour or more a day of pounding maize into flour. There are hydraulic ram pumps that use the kinetic energy of rivers and streams to lift their water uphill; water filters made out of charcoal, sand and stones; raised washing-up stands to keep pots away from dirt floors; fly and rat-proof food safes. Many inventions here are concerned with saving fuel, and the labour and deforestation that goes with gathering it. The 'stove' that village women use is a pot balanced on three stones; it takes 5 kilos of wood to heat a single pot, and 90 per cent of the wood's heat value is wasted. The Karen raised platform stove is an oblong of clay bricks with a chimney at one end; with the same 5 kilos of wood, it can cook two pots of food and heat up the water for tea. The hot box cooker cuts fuel consumption even further: the pot is brought to boiling point, then placed on a hot stone in an insulated haybox. The use of solar energy can eliminate the need for fuel altogether. The solar water heater passes water through a long, meandering pipe, painted matt black, under glass. This feeds warm water into a large insulated storage jar, where it rises, exits at the top, and circulates through the pipe again. On the solar cooker, four concentric rings of aluminium reflectors concentrate the sun's rays on a pot suspended at the focal point.

Inventing such items is a pleasant pastime for a socially conscious boffin, but it is very much harder – and very much more important – to ensure they are put into use on as wide a scale as possible. There has been a tendency with all appropriate technology to concentrate on the glamorous business of discovery and development of pilot models, and to neglect the crux of the matter, which is diffusion.

The village of Karai, not far from Nairobi, became the human testing ground for Karen's inventions. A village development committee was set up to decide what were the priority needs. In a place where 18,000 people had to share four wells, often out of order, the answer, once again, was water. The *ghala* water-tank was developed to answer this need. It is an enormous fat jar made of cement plastered over a basket framework. It holds anything upwards of 1,000–2,500 litres of rainwater, collected from a tin or tiled roof. It costs about £30 ($60) or the equivalent of one or two months' family income, but it is two or three times cheaper than its rival, the corrugated tin tank, which soon begins to rust and leak.

Karai women who have adopted village technology can testify to its value. Margaret Wariara is a bulky matriarch in a pink cardigan and headscarf. She has two large water jars, which cut out all need to go to the well during the rainy season and last her a month or two into the dry. She also has a raised platform stove. Three times a week she used to spend up to eight hours collecting firewood – an indication of just how far the firewood crisis has progressed in the Kenyan highlands. Now she goes out only once a week.

The water jar and the raised stove look like winners: they make economic sense, are socially acceptable and technically sound. Yet after three years work in Karai they had hardly spread at all. Despite a subsidy of half of the cost, less than one Karai home in ten had a water jar in May 1980, and only one home in two hundred had a raised stove. Meanwhile, inferior commercial rivals had saturated the market. The tin water tank is visible wherever you travel in Kenya. The jiko, a tiny, inefficient charcoal burning stove made of scrap metal, is found in every urban home, though it burns up two sacks of charcoal a week at a cost of 40 to 50 per cent of the average wage.

The slow progress of village technology points to some deep-rooted problems. The stove repays its cost in only three months, and produces massive savings thereafter. But raising the capital cost of 330 shillings presents an insuperable problem for most families. The spread of fuel-efficient stoves is absolutely crucial to reducing women's burdens and eliminating the terrible environmental damage of deforestation; government programmes of cheap credit should be set up to allow people to buy them. The second problem relates to the method of diffusion that has been chosen. The basic idea is that village technology should be introduced with the full consent and participation of the community, and should be capable of local manufacture. This model works well for large-scale community facilities such as water pipes or school buildings but it is far too cumbersome for household items. The commercial rivals have made massive headway simply by using market networks. What is needed for village technology is a high-powered national campaign of social marketing (see pp. 190–91) using advertising and media as well as village level workers and leaders, to create a prestigious brand image for the stove or the water jar. Trained craftsmen could be supplied with notices saying 'come to your local buffalo jar dealer'. The tale of the water jar – often retold as a great success story – is rather the opposite. The lesson is that the whole thrust of AT programmes should in future place far less emphasis on invention, and far more on diffusion. For that, after all, is the only point of the exercise.

The Third World Tomorrow

Raising women's incomes

It may seem curious to talk of raising women's incomes separately from men's – and if most men were as good fathers as most women are mothers, there would be no need to. But men have an unfortunate propensity to squander family resources on drink, gambling, whoring or prestige – all the more, in much of Africa, as they are often living apart from their families.

The main road from Nairobi to Mombasa runs, straight as a ruler, through the dry scrubland of Machakos and Taita-Taveta, where marabou storks, bald, bejowelled and gangly, perch on fat baobab trees. Two thirds of the Taita region is national park where settlement is not allowed. The parks bring in foreign tourists and dollars, lining the pockets of hotel owners and tour operators; but for the many, they add to the pressure on the remaining land. Out of this desiccated plateau rise the Taita Hills, incongrously green and fertile. Rainclouds that pass by invariably shed their load here, where the mountain heights cool the air below dew point. So the hills are densely populated, their steep slopes terraced with tiny *shambas* of an acre or half an acre, growing maize, cassava, potatoes, beans, leeks.

The area is fertile, too, in women's projects of an impressive diversity. One group in Voi had just taken on a disused five-acre field to grow cowpeas. They had to keep guard to chase off baboons eating their seedlings. Other groups were raising poultry and small livestock, building rooms to let, running butcher's shops and bakeries. The groups are often desperate for funds and stage touching formal receptions for foreign visitors in the hope of attracting grants. One group in Wundanyi were building their own nursery school – children would not be admitted to primary school unless they had attended nursery first, but the nearest one was eight kilometres away. We sat on benches, putting umbrellas up and down as showers alternated with sunny intervals, while a spokesman – significantly, a man – read out the group's annual report and accounts. In the two years since they started, they had collected 4,000 shillings (£250 or $500), barely enough to dig the foundations. To complete the building they would need another £7,000 ($14,000). They were clearly far too enamoured of expensive concrete, when strengthened mud bricks would have done just as well.

As my tour progressed, other problems became all too apparent. The 'Weruga woman pig project' (*sic*) consisted of a long, tin roofed shed with concrete floor and timber walls. Here thirty-five large pink pigs were being fed and tended by a male swineherd in a shabby khaki raincoat. Six women's groups clubbed together in 1976 to get it going, buying ten pigs and having four studs donated by the Women's Bureau. But it was obvious to any mathematically minded observer that something was going seriously wrong. The women could sell a 60-kilo pig for about 1,000 shillings. But they were feeding the pigs, not on wastes and scraps as they should have been, but (on the advice of the local extension worker) on the best processed meal, bought locally at a cost of 100 shillings per pig per month. Hence pigs would have to be fattened and sold within nine months to make any money. In fact, they were taking an average of about two years, making a loss of about 1,500 shillings (£100 or $200) per pig. The sad truth was that the pigs were eating their money, and only the herder and the feed merchant were better off.

One of the most heroic women's ventures in Kenya is the Mraru Women's Bus Company, based in a tiny village on the drier eastern slopes of the Taita Hills. Three quarters of the women's husbands are working away from home, and because of the low rainfall women depend for survival on the profits of small trading in Voi, 12 kilometres away. But the Wundanyi–Voi bus used to speed through Mraru already full – even when a woman had a sick child to take to the clinic. On the return journey, they would often find themselves chucked off the bus before it started, to make room for someone travelling further and paying more. So, in 1971, the local women's group conceived the notion of buying their own bus to run a service between Mraru and Voi. Four hard years followed, scrimping and saving – women without cash donated pawpaw, eggs, charcoal or baskets for auction; chasing funds and loans; trying to coordinate negotiations with bank managers, bus salesmen and local bureaucrats. On 3 May 1975, the shiny white 21-seater arrived in Mraru from the Mombasa factory. The bus did a brisk trade, three or four round trips a day. Within only eighteen months the women had paid off their loans and had a handsome surplus of $2,000. They should have banked this to cover the cost of repairing and replacing the bus. Instead they distributed half to the members, and with the other half began to over-extend themselves, diversifying too far, too soon. They put the other half of their profits into building and stocking a village co-op shop. As further earnings came in, they started up a 'goat project' with 100 UNICEF goats and 56 donated by members.

It was in 1978 that things started to go badly wrong. By then the pitted dirt roads had taken their toll on the bus. Repair bills mounted and earnings fell while the bus was off the road. One major patch-up cost £1,250 ($2,500) and a police safety check incurred a fine of £125. Early in 1979 the old crate, no longer able to earn its keep, was finally cashiered. Naturally the women wanted to keep the bus service going, but inflation had raced ahead of them, and their savings of £2,500 were less than one tenth of the sum needed to buy a new bus. The same year, two thirds of the 'goat project' died in a drought. The shop was badly hit by the bus's absence, for the manageress could no longer travel free to Voi and buy in bulk. At the time of my visit, the shelves were only thinly stocked with Omo, Fanta, salt, matches, umbrellas, malaria pills and the like. The women said the place was earning enough to pay the manageress her salary of 400 shillings (£50 or $100), but they were not keeping any systematic records of income, expenditure and balances, so they may have been making a loss and not have known about it.

Miraculously, the women managed to raise the 120,000 shillings deposit on a new bus – half from the sale of the old one, the rest from savings and loans. But their prospects looked bleak. Competitors had stepped into the market opening they identified; a local subchief opened a rival shop, and bush taxis – much more economical than a massive bus – started running the route. On the figures the women quoted to me, it looked as if their expected monthly profits would be £250 ($500) less than the loan repayments, and if they defaulted even once, the bus would be repossessed. The Mraru Women's Bus Company would have to fight for survival. Chairwoman Eva Mwaluma, a petite lady in her fifties, active in local church and politics, told me: 'When we started, we did things without knowing if they would make money. But we have overcome problems in the past, and we have faith we shall overcome them in the future. We are unstoppable.' I sincerely hope they are, but to me it looked as if another income-boosting project had turned into a scheme for increasing workloads and reducing incomes.

Many of the projects I saw had common failings: their technical and financial viability had not been properly thought out, management and accountancy were bad, and there was a tendency to go for glamorous, over-ambitious ideas. The fault lay not with the women but with their local government advisers, most of whom were male: they were not providing sound technical advice, or sufficient training in management and accounting, to back up the women's proven energy and determination.

Building women into development

Women's income-raising projects are becoming increasingly common throughout the Third World, from fruit-bottling co-ops in Honduras to sewing centres in India, embroidery in Upper Egypt and jute products in Bangladesh. Yet there is perhaps a risk, in creating special 'women's projects', that male local government officials will treat them less seriously than other projects. Perhaps it would be better simply to build a strong women's element into regular national programmes. What is essential is that the women's angle on every project, every programme, every new law, should be carefully considered; always asking the questions: 'What's in it for women?' or 'What will happen to women as a result?' or 'How can we plan this so that women also benefit?' And, as men cannot be trusted to ask those questions, or to answer them accurately, it means setting up systems for consulting women on their needs, informing them, involving them in execution and in democratic control. It means building up the representation of women among government employees and politicians, not just in the traditional fields of health, nutrition and family planning, but in every field.

The answers will often be more complex than starting up 'women's projects'. In Kenya, for example, the deeper problems that lead to the separation of families need to be tackled: land reform, to create new, viable holdings for the poor out of large farms and part of the national parks; relaxing the restrictions on urban squatting, which keep the level of rents, even for single men, so high; creating more wage employment in rural areas.

Women need to be guaranteed equal services from all government departments, equal rights in ownership of property, especially land. Indeed in some areas, notably health and nutrition, they merit preferential treatment right up to the age of menopause – for the health and nutritional status of women from the months before conception to the end of breastfeeding has the strongest impact on the health and mental development of the newborn child. Using school and adult education to boost women's knowledge of hygiene, nutrition, food storage and processing, and child stimulation will improve the health and intelligence of the whole family.

The struggle for women's equality will be a long one, but it will make faster headway if it is combined with a wider struggle for equality between social classes. For a society that allows the blatant exploitation and oppression of one social class by another cannot be expected to mount an effective battle against the exploitation and oppression of one sex by another.

17 Success and failure of socialism: the Cuban experience

Calle Principe is a narrow, cobbled street that leads down from Avenida Menocal to the broad sweep of Havana's waterfront. The houses have a shabby, rundown look, with flaking paintwork and crumbling cement rendering – building materials, pre-empted for public projects, are hard to come by – but at least no one here pays any rent. In one of the front rooms, round a dining table decked in a flowered plastic tablecloth, the executive committee of the street's Committee for the Defence of the Revolution is holding its weekly evening meeting. Every Cuban street, block of flats or village has its CDR. There are 80,000 in all, with five million members – half the island's population.

from bureaucrats and politicians. The CDR is the principal of popular participation has been taken further – both in the sheer volume of work done by volunteers and, more recently, in the ability of ordinary people to demand accountability from bureaucrats and politicians. The CDR is the principle channel by which popular energies are mobilized to improve present services and build up future ones.

Calle Principe's committee carries out a long list of functions that now run to over 200, and all in members' spare time. They issue ration books, they check the scales in shops, they organize elections to local councils. They collect and salvage used bottles, paper and wood. They tour houses to see if lights or taps have been left on unnecessarily, to save on water and energy. Every night, in two three-hour shifts between 11 p.m. and 5 a.m., CDR volunteers patrol the streets or sit on a strategic corner to prevent burglaries. Every Sunday a brigade of twelve cleans the streets, while others lay out parks in open spaces and tend flowers. (One CDR leaflet for members is poetically entitled: *On the Cultivation of Roses*.)

Over and above the activities that directly benefit their own locality, CDR members donate free labour in vast quantities. The practice helps to overcome manpower shortages, and speeds up the process of development; the price, of course, is a heavy burden of work in evenings and weekends. Every Sunday around twenty people, out of Calle Principe's adult population of 270, put in three or four hours' hard labour on building projects. Calle Principe's organizer, Enrique Marcheco, a serious Afro-Cuban in his late forties, proudly relates how Calle Principe helped to build the stadium for the Latin American games, the massive Tallapiedra Thermoelectric plant, and (along with 1,200 other CDRs) the new 28-storey Central Havana Hospital. Individual members put in prodigiously long hours – Enrique Marcheco, by November, already had his certificate for 500 hours of voluntary labour that year.

Such a level of activity could hardly be raised by an organization imposed from above. The CDRs are genuine popular organizations, with their roots in the heady early years of the revolution. In the violent autumn of 1960 bombs were exploding all over Havana and factories were being sabotaged by supporters of the former dictator Batista in a build-up for the US-backed Bay of Pigs invasion in April 1961. The prospect of counter-revolution was a very real one: the regular army was too small to cope. There was no real alternative to mobilizing the people, who had only recently been liberated from the depredations of urban and rural landlords and were only too willing to help prevent a restoration of the old régime. The CDRs kept watch over streets and public buildings; they kept an eye on elements of the old bourgeoisie, or known supporters of Batista; they raised popular militias at the time of the Bay of Pigs invasion. But they soon began to expand their functions, organizing supplies of scarce foodstuffs, preventing black marketeering, supervising the occupation of property abandoned by émigrés or taken over from landlords.

What motivates today's volunteers? Many are genuinely inspired by communism's answer to material incentives: *emulacion*, socialist competition as to who can be most self sacrificing for the common good. The committed, devoted worker like Marcheco picks up a lot of kudos, visibly enshrined in a deluge of diplomas and certificates for hard work, over-fulfilment of norms, and the like. But for the more self-seeking or cynical, there are more concrete incentives to participate. Scarce consumer durables such as TVs, fridges or washing machines, and much-sought-after new housing (most of it built by volunteer labour organized by workplaces) cannot simply be bought or rented on a free market, but are allocated according to family needs, work performance, and the record of voluntary work.

Trade unions, factories, organizations of small farmers, and youth groups, all are involved in the massive level of volunteer work, but the second most important organization after the CDRs is probably the Federation of Cuban Women (FMC), founded in 1960 with the express aim of creating a revolution within the revolution. 'In the Sierra Madre we were nurses, messengers, literacy teachers, even soldiers,' explains Isobel del Rio, who led a women's platoon fighting side by side with Fidel and Che, and is now the stately Havana regional organizer of the FMC. 'Equality for women has been part of the revolutionary programme from the very earliest days.' After 1959, the FMC retrained domestic servants as day-care workers, rehabilitated Havana's huge army of prostitutes, and tried to get women out to work. It did not have a great success in the latter effort; by 1979, two out of three Cuban women were still housewives. To cater for these, the Federation created a pattern of activities outside the home to integrate women into the wider concerns of society: every week there is a two-hour meeting, sometimes on national political questions, sometimes on foreign affairs, sometimes on health education. And the Federation, too, raises a mass of unpaid voluntary labour.

Delegation 638 of the Havana region, for example, meets on the fifth floor of a modern block of flats close to the monolithic monument to José Martí, the 19th-century nationalist and socialist martyr. The attendance record of its thirty-seven members is over 90 per cent, though eighteen of them work. About half the women bear the grandiloquent title of 'mothers fighting for education'; they help out in their children's schools, visit absentees to find out what's wrong, and organize group homework sessions. Every month or two – more often at some seasons – around half the membership piles on the back of a lorry at 6 a.m. on a Sunday morning, off for five or six hours of digging up potatoes or cutting sugarcane.

Most privatized Westerners might shy at the sheer weight of hours demanded from Cuba's level of participation. For activists, it may amount to fifteen or twenty hours a week, or more if they are communist party members or delegates to local councils. During the mass education campaigns the burden doubles, with two-hour evening classes four nights a week. They began with the literacy campaign which, by the end of 1961, had enabled Cuba's one million illiterates to read and write. In the seventies there followed the 'campaign of the third grade' to give everyone the equivalent of three years' schooling. By 1980 the 'campaign of the sixth grade' had been completed, and the target ahead is that everyone should have completed the ninth grade by 1985 and the twelfth by 1990. In all the campaigns the teachers, too, are volunteers.

All this evidences the emergence of a new model of human being in Cuba: oriented towards activity rather than passivity in his or her spare time, towards production rather than consumption, towards cooperation and self-sacrifice rather than competition and egoism. By no means everyone, of course, is capable of living up to this ideal, but Cuba's education system does its best to turn out people who do. The Cuban secondary schools, by now all boarding schools in rural areas, educate children in their peer groups for a collective style of life. They aim to be as far as possible self-financing. Classes last only half the day; for the other half pupils work as labourers on the large, commercial school farms, whose output is sold to cover the schools' costs.

Education for cooperation begins even sooner for the 8 per cent of under-sixes who are lucky enough to attend the *circulos infantiles* or nursery schools, which take the children of working mothers from the age of six weeks. Teaching in the schools is highly structured: even the games and dances are carefully designed to be cooperative rather than competitive or individualistic. Fights are not allowed – teachers adjudicate and make the little combatants agree and embrace. There is an attempt to break down stereotyped sex roles by encouraging (but not forcing) boys to play at cooking and girls to drive lorries or build. Children are expected to help out, on a duty rota, with little jobs like picking up rubbish, cleaning plants' leaves, changing the water in the fish tank, or serving food at lunchtime. Perhaps the most impressive aspect of the *circulos* is the thorough programme of systematic stimulation for the under-ones, which helps to overcome any handicaps due to home background. Each child's progress in the most minutely detailed abilities is marked on a wall chart. If a particular capability, such as focusing on an object or smiling at a face, is late in appearing, the child gets extra attention, in a special raised playpen, to stimulate that facility, and parents are told how they can stimulate it at home.

Participation pays some of its richest benefits into the Cuban health service, widely recognized as one of the best in the world. Health care is based around polyclinics staffed not by general practitioners but by four specialists: a paediatrician, a gynaecologist/obstetrician, an internal medicine specialist and a dentist. Once a week specialists in other fields visit each clinic. Thus, far more cases can be dealt with at primary level, and hospital facilities can be reserved for those who genuinely need them. The service is heavily oriented towards prevention and screening as well as cure. The polyclinics deal with industrial safety and environmental health within their areas. People at risk of high blood pressure, cancer, asthma or TB have annual or biennial check-ups.

Health has been given a very high priority in Cuba. In 1959 half the country's 6,000 qualified doctors emigrated; today there are 15,000. But the level of service could not be so high without popular participation. For every doctor, there are approximately ten voluntary workers, each one putting in six or eight hours a week. Calle Principe CDR has its elected health officer, Maria Varona Miranda, a 64-year-old pensioner. She took an initial six-week training course and has a refresher course of six evening classes every year. She keeps a register of all young children and expectant mothers and makes sure – by repeated home visits if necessary – that they keep their appointments for vaccinations and routine check-ups. One day each year, she administers polio vaccine to all the children in the street who are due for it. She organizes blood donations – Calle Principe has agreed to provide fifteen a year. Each delegation of the Federation of Cuban Women also has a sanitary brigade: they persuade all women to go for cervical smears every two years, and once a month they spray potential mosquito-breeding sites in their area.

Accountability: the essential check on bureaucracy

Until 1976, participation in Cuba often meant the enlistment of mass labour for projects decided on by a distant leadership. The essential counterbalance to voluntary work – the right to participate in decision-making – was lacking.

Paradoxically, the USA was responsible for the absence of effective democracy in Cuba. Their economic boycott, their persistent efforts to reverse the impudent revolution on their doorstep, forced Cuba into the arms of Russia, stifled Cuba's joyful early outburst of liberty, and made necessary a level of internal vigilance against sabotage that – given the perennial popularity of Castro – would probably not otherwise have been necessary. In 1965 Castro's followers merged with the Cuban Communist Party. Overcentralization on the Russian model, already prevalent in the economy, came to dominate politics and the bureaucracy. But, like Tito and Mao, Castro has never lost his ability to analyse failures as well as successes and to develop new policies to deal with them. In 1970 he mobilized the whole island and staked his own prestige on the achievement of a ten million-ton sugar harvest. Cuba failed to deliver; indeed the following year the harvest dropped below five million tons. The disastrous failure led to a profound rethink, a realization of the need for a much greater degree of decentralization, democracy and popular involvement in decision-making. The idea of *Poder Popular* – a unique experiment in any communist country – was born. After a pilot run in Matanzas province, proposals for a new constitution based on People's Power were aired and discussed at all levels, from CDRs and women's delegations to the first congress of the Cuban Communist Party in 1975. The first nationwide elections were held in 1976.

Under People's Power, local administration – previously controlled by central government – was handed over to elected municipal assemblies. For every seat, the electorate must be offered a choice of at least two candidates, who are nominated by their neighbourhoods at open meetings. No one stands on a party ticket, and candidates need not be communists. Delegates to regional and national assemblies are elected not directly, but by their respective municipal assemblies. All the delegates are accountable to their electorates to a degree that is rare even in Western democracies. As in the Paris Commune so beloved by Marx, they are subject to recall at any time. They hold weekly surgeries for people with individual problems, and every three months they face their electors in a 'rendering of accounts' meeting, in which they must explain what they have been doing, listen to complaints of a more general kind and report back on action taken about previous complaints.

Carlos Notario is the full-time president of Plaza de la Revolucion municipal council, which covers thirteen square miles of Havana. The council's responsibilities are vast, covering not only expected areas like education, housing or health, but also the running of shops, snack bars, small hotels, buses, clinics, cinemas and small factories. In 1976 Notario faced seven rival candidates for his seat: but electors were so happy with his performance that in 1979 he was the sole nominee, and a special assembly had to be held to find another candidate to stand against him. His quarterly rendering of accounts meetings are so crowded that he has had to split them into five groups. I asked him what sort of things he had to deal with at his last meeting. He got out a thick pile of record cards – he keeps one on every point that is raised. There were complaints about the lack of choice on restaurant menus; the need for air conditioning in a stuffy new supermarket; the fact that Pio-Pio – Cuba's answer to Kentucky Fried Chicken – sometimes gives you tiny pieces of chicken, sometimes large ones, all for the same price; and the dogmatism of ice-cream vendors who insist that the only combination of flavours they will sell is chocolate and vanilla. Corruption, too, can now come to light in a way that was difficult before: one shop manager complained about a bread delivery van that regularly left five loaves fewer than the order, and whenever the manager complained, the driver threatened to take all the rest of the loaves away. 'The effect has been to shake up the administration,' says Notario, 'and to deal a body blow at bureaucratic attitudes.'

The accountability genuinely works at local level, for if a delegate does not deliver the goods he will be booted out straight away in blatant cases, or at the next election in less serious ones, and replaced with someone more effective or energetic. This sifting process is in fact much easier where no one stands on a party ticket than under a system of multiple parties each with only one candidate for a seat. Recall in mid-term is rather sparingly used – only one Plaza de la Revolucion delegate was kicked out in mid-term, because he didn't attend council meetings or render accounts. Re-election, however, is far from a walkover – only thirty-six of the original sixty-four Plaza members were re-elected in 1979.

The health service has gone further than most ministries towards its own system of accountability. To stamp out the arrogance and lack of consideration for patients' convenience, so common in health services, Cuba has a programme called 'Optimization of Service'. For each clinic the number of mislaid case notes, of cancelled appointments and patients' complaints, and the average time spent in the waiting room, are carefully recorded and the clinics that do badly get a rocket. Plaza de la Revolucion polyclinic has even created a People's Health Council, giving elected patients' representatives a say in the running of the clinic. The slogan posted on the notice-board at the entrance to the clinic, clearly visible to all patients as they enter, sums up the spirit of People's Power: 'To pass over a fault or deficiency, whether committed by a worker or a director, is incompatible with the condition of being a communist.'

There is still a good way to go towards full People's Power. At the regional and national assembly levels, Communist Party members are in the overwhelming majority, and the fundamental lines of policy in all spheres are still laid down by the Party rather than by the elected organs of People's Power. But since 1975 there has been a real attempt to involve wider popular organizations in policy formulation: the most important laws and policies have been discussed at meetings of every branch of all the grass-roots organizations, and modified to incorporate some of their suggestions. This represents a level of consultation that few Western democracies can boast of.

Moreover, the Cuban Communist Party itself is not an un-democratic, self-selected élite: party militants are elected by assemblies of all the workers at their factory, farm or office – though the party can turn them down if there are good reasons for doing so, such as a doubtful work record, any hint of crime or corruption, or an ambiguous political past vis-à-vis the Batista régime or the Bay of Pigs invasion. The stage has not yet been reached – and hopefully never will be – when the party is cynically viewed and used as the principal avenue for self advancement.

The achievements of the Cuban Revolution have been impressive. Before 1959, 8 per cent of landowners owned 70 per cent of the land, and the landless or near landless majority were lucky to find work for four months of the year at harvest time. Today the use of the army and of volunteers in harvesting has removed the need for this vast reserve of underemployed, and the ceiling on individual ownership of land is fifty-seven hectares. Life expectancy at birth is now 72 years – on a par with the United Kingdom. Malaria, polio, diphtheria and tetanus of the newborn have been wiped out. Malnutrition and illiteracy have been eradicated. Women's equality is unquestioned and aggressively promoted.

However, the performance of agriculture and industry have been disappointing. The degree of self-sufficiency that one might think desirable after twenty years of socialism has not been attained. There is an almost colonial reliance on cash crops, especially sugar, leading to an excessive dependence on massive aid or hidden trade subsidies from Russia (sugar is exchanged for oil at rates very favourable to Cuba). Despite recent liberalization measures, the economy is still too centralized and fails to produce enough goods of the type and quality that people want. Shortages were all too visible at the time of my visit (November/December 1979). Cement for house construction or repair was very hard to come by. Shops had a lean and hungry look, with only the bare essentials on sale.

Fresh vegetables and fruit were in short supply: watercress and limes were all that was available one day, and a long queue suddenly materialized out of nowhere when a delivery of taro roots arrived. Queueing was a familiar part of life: queueing for an hour or two for buses after work; queueing for most of your lunch hour for a seat in a restaurant. Taxi drivers – who get paid whether they get fares or not – were impossible to hail and were known as '*los incapturables*'. Basic things were very cheap – a family of four could eat for a month on four pesos (about £3 or $6) and rent was only 10 per cent of income. But most things were on ration, and the rations, in some cases, were parsimonious: one toilet roll and one and a half blocks of soap per person per month; one pack of cigarettes a fortnight; one pair of pants a year. Some rationed goods could also be obtained off-ration at a much higher price, but this provision benefited the better-off and was widely resented. Rationing may be spartan, but it is certainly fair.

To some extent one could reverse Galbraith's critique of the USA: in Cuba there is a good deal of public affluence, in particular superb nurseries and health centres, side by side with private squalor. Nor has the revolution abolished all inequalities: salary differentials range up to seven to one as between, say, a hotel cleaner and a norm-busting factory worker or a professor of medicine, and the latter would also enjoy the use of a free official car with free petrol.

It is not surprising, then, that there is a fair amount of discontent around (though I doubt if it is any more widespread than in the West). Some people are by now fatigued with the level of sacrifices and voluntary labour expected of them, and resent Cuba's assuming an international role which seems beyond her means. This discontent intensified greatly after Castro's decision to allow Cuban exiles in the USA to visit relatives on the island. They arrived with suitcases full of gifts of clothing, radios, watches, and bearing all the signs of the affluence of the Western hemisphere's richest country. Any foreign visitor to Havana is approached by malcontents: one man literally wanted to buy the shirt off my back, another asked me to go into the tourist shop of the National Hotel, open only to foreigners, and buy a sweater for him. A month after my visit, after a disastrous sugar and tobacco harvest, Castro opened the gates to emigration and 100,000 Cubans scrambled to leave the island. However, to get that figure into true perspective one should compare it with the *one million* would-be illegal immigrants apprehended *every year* trying to get into the USA from Mexico; by that yardstick, there would appear to be a great deal more discontent in booming capitalist Mexico than in spartan Cuba.

Capitalism or socialism?

Some reviewers of the first edition of this book criticized it for ducking what they saw as the central question facing developing countries: the choice between capitalism and communism. There was a very good reason for ducking it: the choice is not mine to make. The answer for each country will be decided, not on the merits of the case, but by the balance of historical forces; and whatever the outcome, reforms of the kind put forward in chapter 15 will still be needed. The problem, too, is clouded by gross oversimplification on both sides of the argument. For between the two extremes of centrally planned communism and free-market capitalism there exists a wide range of practical options even over the fundamental issues: the proportion of factories or farms that are socially owned varies along a continuum, as does the degree of market freedom and of income inequality allowed. Nor is the form of the state mechanically determined by the mode of ownership of the means of production.

It is possible to make certain generalizations. Most of the Third World socialist countries have a better record than the average for their income level in improving health, nutrition, education and the status of women. They have been able, in a way that few non-communist countries have, to enact the radical reforms in rural and urban property ownership that are usually needed to eliminate absolute poverty and gross inequalities. Through the vehicles of mass parties and state-owned media, they have been able to promote very large campaigns that radically alter undesirable traditional attitudes in areas such as health, nutrition or women's roles. In all these respects, most people in most socialist countries of the Third World are almost certainly far better off than they would have been had the previous régimes continued.

That does not mean, however, that socialist countries are in no need of reform. The one-party state is often liable to a rigidity that makes civil upheaval the only channel for significant reform. It is by now clear, too, that the command economy, with fixed production quotas for each enterprise, is incapable of delivering the goods that people want, and inevitably suffers from shortages and queueing; nor is it compatible with meaningful trade union rights. On the economic front, factories and farms must be allowed much greater freedom to respond to prices that are determined by market forces, and to keep some of the benefits of success, with the tax system stepping in to prevent excessive inequalities. Liberalization on these lines has made Hungary a showcase in Eastern Europe. On the political front, further experimentation with multiple candidacies and accountability, on the lines of Cuba's People's Power, could create a much more flexible and responsive political system.

To call indiscriminately for revolution in all non-communist Third World countries as the only way of removing poverty and inequality is, however, naïve and romantic. Nor is it valid to claim that capitalism is always and inevitably inhuman and irreformable. The reality is far more complex. There are, of course, a fair number of grotesquely repressive right-wing régimes in the Third World where revolutionary tactics are a reasonable choice. Just before Cuba, I visited Guatemala. Here the poor Indians and *ladinos* leave their minute smallholdings for two or three months every year to pick coffee or cotton on the great haciendas of the lowlands, where immense tracts of land are kept deliberately vacant. They are housed in straw tents and dormitories as cramped as slave galleys. Every call for even modest land reform, every attempt to organize the poor to demand better pay and conditions, is met with brutal repression, often assassination. No road is open to reform other than armed insurrection; whatever the prospects for success (and they are by no means clear) there is simply no other option available. Military dictatorships of this type are themselves the best recruiting sergeants for communism, and the more they are militarily aided by the United States, the more will guerrillas be forced to seek arms from Communist countries.

I had flown to Guatemala from Costa Rica – only a few hundred miles away – yet the contrast could not be greater. Costa Rica is still cursed with widespread poverty. Land is distributed almost exactly as it was in Cuba in 1959, and there is a growing invasion of multinationals. Yet Costa Rica has a democracy as free and as real as any Western industrial nation, a commitment to national and international peace so powerful that it has had no armed forces since 1948, and a welfare state in some respects more advanced than Britain's. There is universal primary education and social insurance, and the average life expectancy and infant mortality are equal to Cuba's. There has been a gradual progress towards greater equality of incomes. The basic needs of the poor are actively guaranteed: every pre-school child from a needy family attends an education and nutrition centre where it gets a balanced diet and early stimulation. The primary health-care system is the best I have seen anywhere: every rural family is visited once every two months by a health auxiliary who provides vaccinations and checks for early warning symptoms of cancer and heart disease, gives advice on health nutrition and family planning, and keeps a special eye on children and pregnant and nursing mothers. Participation is no less pronounced than in Cuba: village committees build and maintain health centres and schools and install water supply systems. Both the leading parties in the country share a consensus commitment to increasing welfare provision and participation and reducing inequality. Call it paternalism, call it reformism, the reality is undeniable: here is a capitalist country in which the basic needs of the poor are met, regardless of their income levels, by means of redistribution through the tax system. Where there is a real prospect of such significant reform, working for reform is the only rational strategy with any prospect for success in the short- or medium-term. Reform, in any case, will not prejudice the prospects for more radical changes in property ownership, should the prospect or pressure for these alter in the future.

Costa Rica and Cuba demonstrate clearly that neither capitalism nor communism is always and inevitably as grotesquely oppressive as its opponents paint it, nor so perfect as its proponents claim. Both systems must move towards greater equality and greater power for the masses, and towards enterprises controlled by their workers within a regulated market. And both systems are, in theory, capable of moving towards such reforms. Under rigidified régimes of either type, change along these lines will only come about by civil disturbance, riot or rebellion. Under flexible régimes, orderly reforms arising out of shared values or organized pressure from popular organizations will be the main mode of change.

The problem that faces the world is that the superpowers are not content to let each nation choose for itself, but intervene to reinforce rigid régimes, giving them a staying power they would otherwise not possess. Thus the conflicts within each country, over ownership of the means of production and access to political and trade-union power, are transformed into confrontations between the USA and the USSR. The problem seems likely to grow more critical in the years ahead, particularly as regards the USA. The seventies saw a consistent trickle of countries turning to socialism through successful guerrilla wars or army coups (South Vietnam, Ethiopia, Angola, Mozambique, Afghanistan, Nicaragua, Zimbabwe); such transitions tend to be irreversible.

Given the social tensions within many Third World countries, this trickle towards socialism will inevitably continue. In the process, however, the USA is likely to see its economic and security interests increasingly threatened: further incursions of socialism will shrink the sphere of action of US multinationals, and in some cases will jeopardize US military bases (or create new Soviet bases) and threaten US oil supplies. The grave danger is that the USA may one day stake world peace on the gamble of halting or reversing the advance of socialism in the Third World.

Postscript

Conservation: organic farming and community forestry

One of the central questions for the future of agriculture, forestry and fisheries will be: how to achieve the increases in production that will be essential, while preserving and, where possible, improving the natural resource base. Conservation is an absolute precondition of continued production.

In agriculture this will inevitably mean a move towards a more organic style of farming. In the past, the organic and inorganic approaches have been upheld by two mutually exclusive and mutually hostile schools, or, one might almost say, churches. In the future it seems likely that a new synthesis and symbiosis of the two approaches will emerge.

Recent studies from the FAO (*Soils Bulletin* nos. 33, 35, 36, 40, 41, 43, 45) have underlined the enormous potential of organic methods for the tropics. Applying a *mulch* of organic material to the soil surface has been found to reduce the loss of water in run-off by 79-98 per cent, to cut soil erosion by 93-96 per cent and to boost yields by 40-73 per cent. *Minimum tillage,* where seeds are planted through the dead residue of a previous crop, or weeds, has an even greater impact, boosting yields of cowpeas, for example, by 50-100 per cent. More revolutionary still is the idea of a *living mulch* – a cover crop of leguminous nitrogen-fixing creeper such as *centrosema* or *desmodium* – through which the food crop can grow. Living mulch has the greatest impact of all in increasing yields, reducing erosion and run-off, as well as reducing the labour needed for weeding.

Biological fixation of nitrogen offers a very promising av-

enue towards a free, ecologically sound fertilizer. Food legumes
have been found to fix anything up to 550 kilos of nitrogen
per hectare (broad beans) and forage legumes up to 862 kilos
(*pueraria phaseoloides*). When the legume seeds are mixed
with peat containing specially selected strains of bacteria,
yields can increase spectacularly. In one Zambian test, inoculated soya bean yielded 93 to 103 per cent more than non-
inoculated, at a cost of only $5 per hectare – a greater increase
than was achieved by adding 200 kilos of chemical fertilizer
at a cost of $100 per hectare. And a good deal of the nitrogen
remains in the field for the following crop – when maize follows a legume, for example, the yield rises by 20–30 per cent.

It is doubtful whether organic farming unaided by any sort
of chemicals will be able to produce the kind of yield increases
necessary to cope with population growth and growing incomes. The sheer quantities of mulch and compost required
in the tropics, where organic material breaks down much
faster, would be prohibitive in their demands on land and
labour. It seems likely that organic and inorganic methods
will be combined in scientifically designed packages. The
Chinese, for example, typically apply three parts of mineral
fertilizer to seven organic: the minerals help to improve the
balance of nutrients in the organic matter, often deficient in
nitrogen, potash or phosphorus. Conversely, farmers relying
mainly on chemical fertilizers would be unwise to add less
than three parts organic material to seven chemical: use of
organic material has been shown to improve the uptake of
chemical nutrients, as well as conserving and improving the
soil.

The same fusion of organic and inorganic approaches will
apply to pest control. The use of massive doses of chemical
poisons is not only dangerous to human health and ecological
systems but, as insects develop resistance, it is becoming increasingly counterproductive. The trend is now towards *integrated pest control* which complements small, carefully targeted

doses of safe insecticides with organic methods such as clean cultivation, crop rotation, companion planting, the breeding of pest-resistant seeds, and the common-sense idea of ignoring pest damage if it is only minor. Pests of stored food can be combated by cleanliness, use of improved containers, better methods of drying (moulds love moisture) and the use of organic pest deterrents.

Perhaps the greatest contribution to conserving the environment in the tropics can be made by trees. They protect the soil against burning sun and battering rains, they prevent erosion and floods, attract rainfall, and raise up minerals from deeper soil layers. But the Third World's fuel crisis is a grave threat to the stock of trees. By AD 2000, the potential demand for firewood will reach 2,600 million cubic metres per year, but production may be only 1,500 million cubic metres. Some of the shortfall will be made up by the progressive eradication of the tree stock scattered around farmland and on the forest margins.

To meet this crisis, the whole idea of forestry is being revolutionized (see *Forestry for Rural Communities*, FAO, 1979). The old concept of trees as simple timber is being replaced by *multi-use forestry* in which forests and copses are developed and exploited not only to provide fuel and fodder, but foodstuffs such as fruits, nuts, mushrooms, honey and game, and commercial products like gums, resins, oils, herbs and fibres. On this resource base a wide range of locally based processing industries can be built. *Agro-forestry* involves the combination, in the same place, of farming and forestry, in a wide range of forms depending on local circumstances. Filipino farmers have developed a highly productive multi-level form of agriculture, combining fruit or fuel trees with medium-height crops such as coffee, maize or runner beans and low-level crops such as pineapple or soya beans. The different levels do not compete for light, nor do their roots compete for nutrients, and a protective canopy shields the soil as in the original rainforest. *Silvipasture* – where goats or cattle browse on vegetation growing under trees – is another possibility. One of the most promising techniques for Africa is *alley-cropping*. This involves growing food crops between rows of fast growing leguminous trees such as *leucaena*. In the growing season the trees are kept cut and pruned back to aviod competition with the crops. The nitrogen-rich leaves and twigs are used for mulch, the larger branches for poles or fuel. In the dry season the trees are allowed to grow freely. The benefits build up over time. On an infertile, sandy soil at Ibadan, alley-cropping gave maize yields of more than 3·5 tonnes per hectare in the second season, without any added fertilizer. This is four times the average yield for Africa. For more arid areas a *tree fallow* system can be adopted, in which the traditional fallow period of six to nine years can be used to grow an economic species such as the leguminous tree *acacia senegal* (which provides fuel, fodder, gum arabic, root fibres and edible seeds) instead of useless weeds and shrubs.

These new techniques have to be combined with new forms of social organization. *Community forestry* is spreading in South Korea, India, the Philippines. It means involving the local community in planning, executing, running and enjoying the benefits of forestry development. Subsidies are sometimes needed to tide villagers over the time before the trees become productive, or to compensate them for losses if the main benefit from tree-planting goes to farmers downstream who are freed from flooding and silting of irrigation canals. But, as in all types of project, great caution is needed, especially in highly polarized societies, to prevent landowners from monopolizing the benefits.

Conservation is often raised as an issue separate from the problem of distribution or of population size. In reality, it is often the maldistribution of land, and of government services to agriculture, that forces small farmers and the landless to farm steep slopes or arid areas where ecological damage is inevitable. Improved distribution and vigorous family-planning programmes must be an essential element of any conservation strategy.

Bibliographical note and recommended reading

A much fuller bibliography relating to the problems of the Third World, as well as a general survey of those problems, will be found in my book, *Inside The Third World* (Penguin, 1979). Most of the extended descriptions of projects are based on my own field trips.

Chapter 1: Back to the roots

My account of Balinese institutions is based on personal observation and the essay by Clifford Geertz in Koentjaraningrat, ed., *Villages in Indonesia* (Cornell University Press, 1967). An idealized view of Indian village society is given in Jawaharlal Nehru, *The Discovery of India* (Fourth Edition, Meridian Books, 1956), and partly demolished in Louis Dumont, *Homo Hierarchicus* (Weidenfeld & Nicolson, 1970). African village society is outlined in P.C. Lloyd, *Africa in Social Change* (Revised Edition, Penguin, 1972), while an idealized view is given, for example, in Jomo Kenyatta, *Facing Mount Kenya* (Secker & Warburg, 1953). The characteristics of the Andean *ayllu* are described in Chapter 2 of W. H. Prescott, *History of the Conquest of Peru* (Dent, 1908).

For Gandhi's ideas, see M. K. Gandhi, *Gandhi: An Autobiography* (Jonathan Cape, 1966); George Woodcock, *Gandhi* (Fontana, 1972); and any of several collections of Gandhi's shorter writings, e.g., M. K. Gandhi, *Socialism of My Conception*, ed. A. T. Hingorani (Bharatiya Vidya Bhavan, Bombay, 1966).

The best concise summary of Mao's agricultural and industrial policies I have come across is Bruce McFarlane and E. L. Wheelwright, *The Chinese Road to Socialism* (Penguin, 1973).

Bibliographical note and recommended reading

On medicine, education, etc., see David Milton, *et al.*, eds., *People's China* (Penguin, 1977).

Chapter 2: Basic concepts

On growth with justice, see Chenery, Hollis *et al.*, *Redistribution with Growth* (Oxford University Press, 1974), and the speeches of Robert McNamara to the World Bank's Board of Governors of 24 September 1974 (on rural poverty) and 30 September 1976 (on urban poverty). For basic needs, see International Labour Office, *Employment, Growth and Basic Needs* (ILO, Geneva, 1976); also D. P. Ghai *et al.*, *The Basic Needs Approach to Development* (ILO, Geneva, 1977), and International Labour Office, *Background Papers*, Vol. 1, for the Tripartite World Conference on Employment, Income Distribution and Social Progress (ILO, Geneva, 1976). On the concept of basic services, with some cases studies, see *Assignment Children*, No. 37, and the works quoted under Chapter 10. For eco-development see the United Nations Environment Programme working paper of the Intergovernmental Expert Group on Environment and Development (UNEP IG/4/3, Nairobi, December 1976) UNESCO's ideas on endogenous, human-centred development are outlined in Chapter 3 of United Nations Educational, Scientific and Cultural Organization, *Medium Term Plan* (UNESCO 19 C/4, Paris, 1977). The Cocoyoc Declaration is United Nations Document A/C2/292 of November 1974. On participation, see the excellent review, United Nations Department for Economic and Social Affairs, *Popular Participation in Decision-making for Development* (United Nations, New York, 1975), and the earlier survey, *Popular Participation in Development* (United Nations, New York, 1971).

Chapter 3: Land to the tiller

On the problems and prospects of land reform, see the Food and Agriculture Organization and International Labour Office, *Progress in Land Reform, Sixth Report* (United Nations, New York, 1976); Erich Jacoby, *Man and Land* (André Deutsch, 1971);

and World Bank, *Land Reform*, Sector Policy Paper (Washington, 1975). For individual country experiences, see Wolf Ladejinsky, *Agrarian Reform as Unfinished Business* (Oxford University Press, 1977), and Ingrid Palmer, *The New Rice in the Philippines* (United Nations Research Institute for Social Development, Geneva, 1975). For Egypt, see Samir Radwan, *Agrarian Reform and Rural Poverty, Egypt 1952–1975* (International Labour Office, Geneva, 1977). On the case of Té Huyro, Centro Nacional de Capacitación e Investigación para la Reforma Agraria, *Té Huyro Ltda*, mimeoed, Study No. 33. (CENCIRA, Lima, 1972). For settlement and colonization, see Jacoby, *op. cit.*, and the excellent survey and summary of issues in World Bank, *Agricultural Land Settlement*, World Bank Issues Paper (Washington, 1978). On Upper Volta, Autorité des Aménagements des Vallées des Volta, *Bilan des Activités*, mimeoed (Ministère du Plan, Government of Upper Volta, 1975), For Indonesia's programme, see J.M. Hardjono, *Transmigration in Indonesia* (Oxford University Press, Kuala Lumpur, 1977).

Chapter 4: *The green, blue and other revolutions*

On rural development and integrated rural development, a useful summary is World Bank, *Rural Development*, Sector Policy Paper (Washington, 1975). For individual case studies, see Uma Lele, *The Design of Rural Development* (Johns Hopkins, Baltimore, 1975), and Philip Coombs and Manzoor Ahmed, *Attacking Rural Poverty* (Johns Hopkins, Baltimore, 1974). Estimates of potential for extra irrigation are from World Bank, *Agricultural Land Settlement* (Washington, 1978). For commercial and official rates of interest and non-coverage of small farmers see World Bank, *Agricultural Credit*, Sector Policy Paper (Washington, 1975). On agricultural extension, see Lele, *op. cit.*, Coombs, *op. cit.*, and Danial Benor and James Harrison, *Agricultural Extension* (World Bank, Washington, 1977). An overview of the current state of research can be found in *Consultative Group on International Agricultural Research* (United Nations Development Programme, New York, 1976). Progress at CIAT is recorded in CIAT's annual reports, Cali, Colombia, 1976 and earlier years, while *Fish Farming* (International Development Research Centre, Canada, 1978), describes some of the research on pisciculture.

Figures on the energy cost of Western and Third World agriculture are given in Food and Agriculture Organization, *The State of Food and Agriculture 1976* (FAO, Rome, 1977), and on the potential for organic manure in *The State of Food and Agriculture 1977* (FAO, Rome, 1978). Prospects for food production are more extensively surveyed in the *State of Food and Agriculture 1975* (FAO, Rome, 1976), and in the Food and Agriculture Organization, *Fourth World Food Survey* (FAO, Rome, 1978). Other good overviews are given by special issues of *World Development*, May–July 1977, and *Scientific American*, September 1976. On climatic hazards see John Gribbin, *The Climatic Threat* (Fontana, 1978), and the essay by Reid Bryson in *World Development, op. cit.*

Chapter 5: The house that Jack built

On the Peruvian squatter settlements, see William Mangin, 'Squatter Settlements', in *Scientific American*, October 1967, and on the growth of and conditions in squatter settlements generally, see United Nations Department of Economic and Social Affairs, *World Housing Survey 1974* (United Nations, New York, 1976). Appropriate construction methods are sketched in a special supplement in the *Guardian*, 3 May 1976. The savings that can be had from low-cost construction are outlined in World Bank, *Housing*, Sector Policy Paper (Washington, 1975), and in Orville Grimes, Jr, *Housing for Low Income Urban Families* (Johns Hopkins, Baltimore, 1976). The activities of Calcutta Metropolitan Development Authority are summarized in K. C. Sivaramakrishnan, 'Slum Improvement in Calcutta', in *Assignment Children*, No. 40. This same issue contains case studies of community participation in urban development from Tondo foreshore, Cebu City and Klong Toey. A discussion of the problem of participation is in the papers from the Habitat Conference on Human Settlements, Vancouver 1976, *Secretary's*

Bibliographical note and recommended reading

Report (A/CONF/70/RPC/9), and in Ben D'Souza, *Popular Participation and Community Action in New Towns,* (A/CONF/70/RPC/BP/16). The Cissin experiment is outlined in United Nations Development Programme, *Pilot Housing Project Ouagadougou-Cissin,* mimeo (Ouagadougou, 1974), and in M. Hundsalz, *L'Habitat spontané et so restructuration,* mimeo (Ouagadougou, 1976). See also World Bank, *Sites and Services Projects,* a World Bank Paper (Washington, 1974).

Chapter 6: Working models

Current rates of unemployment and underemployment are from International Labour Office, *Employment, Growth and Basic Needs* (ILO, Geneva, 1976), and *Labour Force Estimates and Projections 1950–2000* (ILO, Geneva, 1977).

On the concept of intermediate technology, see E. F. Schumacher, *Small is Beautiful* (Blond & Briggs, 1973); R. F. Congdon, ed., *Introduction to Appropriate Technology* (Rodale Press Emmaus, 1977); and the excellent overview, Nicolas Jéquier, ed., *Appropriate Technology, Problems and Promises* (Development Centre, Organization for Economic Cooperation and Development, Paris, 1976), which also contains a number of the case studies quoted here. See also Hans Singer, *Technologies for Basic Needs* (ILO, Geneva, 1977). Comparative costings of alternative technologies are given in A. S. Bhalla, ed., *Technology and Employment in Industry* (ILO, Geneva, 1975). On the prospects of biogas, see Khadi and Village Industries Commission, *Gobar Gas, Retrospect and Prospect* (Bombay, 1978), and Arjun Makhijani, *Energy Policy for the Rural Third World* (International Institute for Environment and Development, 1976). On fuelwood, see Brian Johnson, *Banking on the Biosphere* (Lexington Books, New York, 1978). Figures on the world distribution of patents are from UNCTAD paper TD/B/AC 11/19/ Rev 1. The impact of multinationals on national technological capacities is surveyed in Dimitri Germidis, *Transfer of Technology by Multinational Corporations,* Vols. I and II (OECD Development Centre, Paris, 1977). Estimates of the effect of transferring income to the poor on job creation are from the *Draft Five Year Plan 1978–1983* (Planning Commission, Government of India, New Delhi, 1978).

Chapter 7: From little acorns

On the characteristics and prospects of small-scale industry, see the excellent survey by Eugene Staley and Richard Morse, *Modern Small Industry for Developing Countries* (McGraw Hill, New York, 1965), and World Bank, *Employment and Development of Small Enterprises*, Sector Policy Paper (Washington, 1978). See also Ram K. Vepa, *Small Industry in the Seventies* (Vikas Publications, India, 1971), and Philip A. Neck, ed., *Small Enterprise Development: Policies and Programmes* (ILO, Geneva, 1977).

On credit measures for small companies, see World Bank, *Development Finance Companies*, Sector Policy Paper (Washington, 1976).

For India's small-industry programme, see *Draft Five Year Plan 1978–83* (Planning Commission, Government of India, New Delhi, 1978), on the overall employment situation and plans to cut unemployment. Ministry of Industry Report 1977–78, Government of India, gives current data on small-scale industry, the list of reserved products and a statement of industrial policy. For the functions of the new centres, see *District Industry Centres* (Ministry of Industry, Government of India, 1978).

On rural industry, see the useful summary of data and issues in World Bank, *Rural Enterprise and Nonfarm Employment*, World Bank Paper (Washington, 1978), and Staley and Morse, *op. cit*. On artisan training, see Philip Coombs and Manzoor Ahmed, *Attacking Rural Poverty* (Johns Hopkins, Baltimore, 1974). See also G. A. MacPherson, *First Steps in Village Mechanization* (Tanzania Publishing House, Dar-es-Salaam, 1973).

UNIDO's proposals for rural workshops are described in the papers of the International Forum on Appropriate Industrial Technology, New Delhi, November 1978 (ID/WG/282/39). Description of Sri Lanka's rural industry programme is based on H. A. de S. Gunasekera and H. M. A. Codipilly, 'Employment

Creation through Regional Development', in *International Labour Review*, Vol. 116, No. 1, p. 39.

India's handloom plans are outlined in Development Commissioner for Handlooms, *Handlooms: A New Look* (Government of India, New Delhi, 1978). The problem of introducing man-made fibres into hand spinning and weaving is discussed in *Man-Made Fibres for Khadi* (Khadi and Village Industries Commission, Bombay, 1978). For India's long experience with village industries, see *Khadi and Village Industries: A Review* (KVIC, Bombay, 1976).

The thorny problem of subsidies for *khadi* is reviewed in the *Report of the Khadi and Village Industries Committee* (Ministry of Commerce, Government of India, 1968), and is still apparent in figures given in Khadi and Village Industries Commission, *Annual Report 1976–77* (Government of India, Bombay, 1978), which also gives figures for other village industries. Prospects for individual village industries are outlined in a series of leaflets for each industry published by the Khadi and Village Industries Commission.

Chapter 8: Condoms, carrots and sticks

Excellent overall surveys of the dimensions and implications of the population problem are to be found in two publications from the United Nations Department of Economic and Social Affairs, *The Population Debate* (2 vols.), (United Nations, New York, 1975), and *The Determination and Consequences of Population Growth*, Vol. I (United Nations, New York, 1973). An ongoing survey and commentary on the whole population scene is to be found in the pages of *People*, the quarterly magazine of the International Planned Parenthood Federation, from which many of the programmes cited in this chapter are drawn. On community distribution, see the special issue *People*, Vol. 2, No. 4, and on household distribution, *People*, Vol. 4, No. 1. Other surveys of programmes in this field are Roberto Cuca and Catherine S. Pierce, *Experiments in Family Planning* (Johns Hopkins, Baltimore, 1977), and *Population Reports*, Series J,

No. 19, March 1978. On India's sterilization programme see Joseph Hanlon and Anil Aggarwal, 'Mass Sterilization at Gunpoint', in *New Scientist*, 5 May 1977. For the Singapore Solution, see United Nations Fund for Population Activities, *Singapore*, Population Profiles No. 1 (New York, 1976). Robert McNamara's views on the importance of more egalitarian development for population restraint are contained in his speech to the Massachusetts Institute of Technology, 28 April 1977. The International Planned Parenthood Federation's surveys of family planning are IPPF, *Unmet Needs in Family Planning* (IPPF, London, 1973), and *Unmet Needs in Family Planning 1971–76* (IPPF, London, 1977). On new methods of fertility control, see *Population Reports*, Series A, B, C, D, F, G, H and K, *passim* (Washington and Baltimore, 1973–   ).

Chapter 9: Feeding the five thousand

Data on the malnutrition problem in Indonesia is taken from United Nations Children Fund, *Statistical Profile of Children and Mothers in Indonesia* (UNICEF, Jakarta, 1976). Figures on the world distribution of food are from Food and Agriculture Organization, *Fourth World Food Survey* (FAO, Rome, 1978). An excellent general overview of nutrition problems and programmes is G. H. Beaton and J. M. Bengoa, *Nutrition in Preventive Medicine* (World Health Organization, Geneva, 1976). Material on the World Food Programme is digested from *World Food Programme News, seriatim* (FAO, Rome). On the problem of food storage, see *Ceres*, No. 60, November–December 1977, and two articles by Jim McDowell in *UNICEF News*: 'The Month When the Children Wait for Food', Issue 85, 1975, and 'Sunshine or Darkness', Issue 90, 1976. On Upper Volta's programme, the Kasa project in India and other programmes, see *Assignment Children*, No. 35, July–September 1976. For national level programmes, see Alan Berg *et al.*, eds., *Nutrition, National Development and Planning* (Massachusetts Institute of Technology Press, 1973).

Chapter 10: Heal thyself

For traditional medicine, see Una MacLean, *Magical Medicine*, (Allen Lane, 1971), and essays by McKimm Marriott on India and Oscar Lewis on Mexico in B. Paul, ed., *Health, Culture and Community* (Russell Sage Foundation, New York, 1955). See also the special issue of *World Health*, November 1977. India's attempts to utilize the Ayurvedic system in her medical services are described in K. N. Udupa, 'The Ayurvedic System of Medicine in India', in K. Newell, ed., *Health by the People* (World Health Organization, Geneva, 1975). Halfdan Mahler's statements on health care policy are culled from the pages of *WHO Chronicle* and *World Health, seriatim*. The new system of health care is outlined in V. Djukanovic and E. P. Mach, *Alternative Approaches to Meeting Basic Health Needs in Developing Countries* (World Health Organization, Geneva, 1975), and in *Primary Health Care* (World Health Organization, Geneva, 1978). Case studies of individual programmes exemplifying aspects of the new approaches are given in K. Newell, *op. cit.*, and in the special issues of *World Health*, May 1978, and in *Assignment Children*, No. 33, January–March 1976, and No. 42, April–June 1978. On China's barefoot doctor programme, see Peter Wilenski, *The Delivery of Health Services in the People's Republic of China* (International Development Research Centre, Ottawa, 1976).

For water supply, see World Bank, *Village Water Supply*, a World Bank Paper (Washington, 1976); R. J. Saunders and J. J. Warford, *Village Water Supply* (Johns Hopkins, Baltimore, 1976); and *Assignment Children*, No. 34, April–June 1976. For examples of the integration of traditional healers into modern medicine, see John Loftus, 'Medicine Man', in *World Health*, October 1976, and Mangay-Angara, 'New Status for the Hilot', in *World Health*, November 1977. On health education, see the special issue of *World Health*, April 1977, and on biomedical research see issue of June 1976. For the financing of health services, see Brian Abel-Smith and Alcira Leiserson, *Poverty, Development and Health Policy*, Public Health Papers, No. 69 (WHO, Geneva, 1978). On riverblindness, see World Health

Bibliographical note and recommended reading

Organization, *Onchocerciasis Control in the Volta River Basin Area*, Report of the Preparatory Assistance Mission (OCP/73.1) (WHO, Geneva, 1973). On malaria progress and problems, see R. Kouznetsov, 'Malaria Control', in *WHO Chronicle*, 31, 1977, and *WHO Expert Committee on Malaria, Sixteenth Report*, Technical Report Series 549 (WHO, Geneva, 1974). For a narrative of the smallpox eradication programme, see *World Health*, February–March 1975.

Chapter 11: Learning to develop

For general views on the development of education, see Edgar Faure *et al.*, *Learning to Be* (United Nations Educational, Scientific and Cultural Organization, Paris, 1972), and the companion volume of studies, Ontario Institute for Studies in Education, *Education on the Move* (UNESCO, Paris, 1975). On the concepts of basic education and minimum learning needs, see Kenneth King, 'Minimum Learning Needs', in *Prospects*, Vol. 6, No. 1, 1976, and Philip Coombs, 'L'Éducation périscolaire', in *Assignment Children*, No. 25, January–March 1974. On non-formal education, see Philip Coombs and Manzoor Ahmed, *Attacking Rural Poverty: How Non-Formal Education Can Help* (John Hopkins, Baltimore, 1974), which covers agricultural extension, artisan training, adult education, etc. Freire's method of literacy training is outlined in Paulo Freire, *Education: The Practise of Freedom* (Writers and Readers Publishing Cooperative, 1976). The World Literacy Programme is described and assessed in UNESCO, *The Experimental World Literacy Programme: a Critical Assessment* (UNESCO, Paris, 1976). Examples of community participation in education are described in *Assignment Children*, No. 44, UNICEF, Paris, 1978. For the Chinese educational reforms, see Peter Mauger *et al.*, *Education in China* (Anglo-Chinese Educational Institute, London, 1974), and Chapter 4 of David Milton *et al.*, eds., *People's China* (Penguin, 1977).

Other educational experiments mentioned here are described in the series Experiments and Innovations in Education, International Bureau of Education, UNESCO, Paris, including:

The Case of Cameroon (No. 8); *Innovation in Upper Volta* (No. 21) and *Basic Services for Children*, Parts I & II (Nos. 36 and 37). Accounts of People's School, Bangladesh, nursery schools in Peru, TV education in the Ivory Coast, radio school in Colombia and young farmers' education in Upper Volta are all based on personal visits and official documents. More radio projects are detailed in Peter Spain *et al.*, *Radio for Education and Development* (2 vols., World Bank Staff Working Paper No. 266, Washington, 1977).

Chapter 12: Reform will not be a Sunday school tea-party

On the need for redistribution as well as growth if basic needs are to be met, see International Labour Office, *Employment, Growth and Basic Needs* (ILO, Geneva, 1976); and papers by M. Hopkins and J. J. Stern in ILO Tripartite World Conference on Employment, Income Distribution and Social Progress, *Background Papers*, Vol. 1 (ILO, Geneva, 1976). The best summary of the kind of policies needed for redistribution is Chenery *et al.*, *Redistribution with Growth* (Oxford University Press, 1974), which contains a useful rundown of policies in Tanzania, Sri Lanka, Taiwan and Korea. Other policies are outlined in the sector policy papers and working papers of the World Bank, especially *Education, Health, Rural Development, Small Enterprises, Rural Enterprise,* and *Housing* (Washington, various years 1974–8). Redistributive and employment-creating policies for individual countries are outlined in the reports of International Labour Office country employment missions: *Towards Full Employment* (Colombia), 1970: *Matching Employment Opportunities and Expectations* (Sri Lanka), 1971; *Employment, Incomes and Equality* (Kenya), 1972; *Sharing in Development* (Philippines), 1974; and *Growth, Employment and Equity* (Sudan), 1976 (all ILO, Geneva). The political difficulties of reform are outlined by C. L. G. Bell in Chenery *et al., op. cit.,* while ways of falling into the clutches of the military are sketched in S.E. Finer, *The Man on Horseback* (Pall Mall Press, 1962). Nyerere's views on the one-party state are to be found in Julius Nyerere, *Freedom and Unity* (Oxford University Press,

Bibliographical note and recommended reading

Dar-es-Salaam, 1969). Experience on rural organizations is summarized in International Labour Office, *Structure and Function of Rural Workers' Organizations* (ILO, Geneva, 1978). The particular experiences of Colombia are recounted in Pierre Gilhodes, 'Agrarian Struggles in Colombia', in Rodolfo Stavenhagen, ed., *Agrarian Problems and Peasant Movements in Latin America* (Doubleday, New York, 1970), and for the north-east of Brazil in Francisco Julião, *Cambão – The Yoke* (Penguin, 1972).

Chapter 13: Fair shares

The most useful summary of trade problems of developing countries that I have come across is Kathryn Morton and Peter Tulloch, *Trade and Developing Countries* (Croom Helm, 1977). On the new international division of labour, see H.F. Lydall, *Trade and Employment* (ILO, Geneva, 1975); Bohuslav Herman, *The Optimal International Division of Labour* (ILO, Geneva, 1975). Figures on the effects on the West of increased imports of manufactures from the Third World are given in U. Hiemenz and K.W. Schatz, *Trade in Place of Migration* (ILO, Geneva, 1978); International Labour Office, Tripartite World Conference on Employment, Income Distribution and Social Progress, *Background Papers* (ILO, Geneva, 1976) Vol. II, *passim*; Vincent Cable, 'British Protectionism and LDC Imports', in *Overseas Development Institute Review*, No. 2, 1977.

Keith Marsden's calculations of the global benefits of cooperation are summarized in Keith Marsden, 'Global Development Strategies and the Poor', in *International Labour Review*, Vol. 117, No. 6, p. 675. The outline of the new protectionism is based mainly on Bela Balassa, *World Trade and the International Economy*, World Bank Staff Paper No. 282, 1978. Figures on north–south trade balances in manufactures are from *Economist*, 9 September 1978 (p. 87) and 25 November 1978 (p. 81), the projection of market shares from Robert McNamara, *Address to the Board of Governors* (World Bank, Washington, 1978), and the direction of Third World exports from *World Bank Annual Report 1978*. Figures on aid levels are from *Development Cooperation 1979 Review* (Organization for Economic Cooperation and Development, Paris, 1979). The forecast of future aid levels is given in McNamara, *op. cit.*

Chapter 14: Self-help economics

On commodity cartels, see Philip Connelly and Robert Pearlman, *The Politics of Scarcity* (Oxford University Press, 1976), and Kathryn Morton and Peter Tulloch, *op. cit.* Material on bauxite is taken from *Development Issue Paper 12* (United Nations Development Programme, New York, 1976), and on bananas from *Development Issue Paper 1*, Rev. 1 (UNDP, New York, 1977). Morton and Tulloch, *op. cit.*, give a rundown on regional markets, while a complete listing is given in IMF *Survey*, 4 July 1977, pp 211–13. For technical cooperation among developing countries, see the papers of the UN conference on TCDC, Buenos Aires, September 1978, especially the *Draft Plan of Action* (A/CONF/79/5). The close-your-borders school of thought is summarized and sensibly criticized in Paul Streeten, 'Changing Perspectives of Development', in *Finance and Development*, September 1977, Vol. 14, No. 3, p. 14.

Index

Index

Index

Index

Index

Index

FOR THE BEST IN PAPERBACKS, LOOK FOR THE🐧

In every corner of the world, on every subject under the sun, Penguin represents quality and variety – the very best in publishing today.

For complete information about books available from Penguin – including Pelicans, Puffins, Peregrines and Penguin Classics – and how to order them, write to us at the appropriate address below. Please note that for copyright reasons the selection of books varies from country to country.

In the United Kingdom: Please write to *Dept E.P., Penguin Books Ltd, Harmondsworth, Middlesex, UB7 0DA*

In the United States: Please write to *Dept BA, Penguin, 299 Murray Hill Parkway, East Rutherford, New Jersey 07073*

In Canada: Please write to *Penguin Books Canada Ltd, 2801 John Street, Markham, Ontario L3R 1B4*

In Australia: Please write to the *Marketing Department, Penguin Books Australia Ltd, P.O. Box 257, Ringwood, Victoria 3134*

In New Zealand: Please write to the *Marketing Department, Penguin Books (NZ) Ltd, Private Bag, Takapuna, Auckland 9*

In India: Please write to *Penguin Overseas Ltd, 706 Eros Apartments, 56 Nehru Place, New Delhi, 110019*

In Holland: Please write to *Penguin Books Nederland B.V., Postbus 195, NL–1380AD Weesp, Netherlands*

In Germany: Please write to *Penguin Books Ltd, Friedrichstrasse 10–12, D–6000 Frankfurt Main 1, Federal Republic of Germany*

In Spain: Please write to *Longman Penguin España, Calle San Nicolas 15, E–28013 Madrid, Spain*

In France: Please write to *Penguin Books Ltd, 39 Rue de Montmorency, F-75003, Paris, France*

In Japan: Please write to *Longman Penguin Japan Co Ltd, Yamaguchi Building, 2–12–9 Kanda Jimbocho, Chiyoda-Ku, Tokyo 101, Japan*